Mysteries of MONADNOCK

Eric Stanway

EMU BOOKS

Other books by Eric Stanway
History on a Plate
Another Course
The Old Rindge House
Vintage Blood Volume 1
Vintage Blood Volume 2
Madame Sherri
The Blood Is The Life
Mad Ghosts and Englishmen
Yuletide Spirits

"The Blake House" originally appeared
in the Nashua Telegraph in 2010, in
a slightly different form.

*For my mother, Vi Stanway,
in recognition of all her support.*

Published by Emu Books
Fitzwilliam, New Hampshire

MEMENTO MORI

Table of Contents

Mount Monadnock, as
seen in a 19th century
stereopticon photograph.

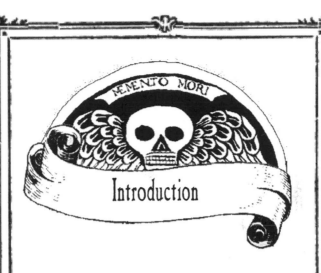

Introduction

Of all the places in the United States, New England seems to have the most legendary qualities. The great gothic writer H.P. Lovecraft recognized this in the last century, as he set his weird stories in various mythical villages in Massachusetts.

The towns that surround Mount Monadnock have their own strange atmospheres; hidden beneath the picturesque Commons and Town Halls, there are odd tales of murder, ghosts and betrayal. Talking to any of the old timers in these parts will reveal curious legends of days long past.

What I have gathered here is a sampling

of some of the tales that abound in these tiny communities. There are unsolved murders, fugitive ministers, ghost chairs, haunted houses, and a smorgasbord of things that Go Bump In The Night. Some of these stories might be familiar to readers; the 1918 unsolved murder of Dr. William Dean has already been the subject of several books. I have included the story here, however, as it would be unseemly to omit the tale.

Of course, there are others who have contributed to this work. Tim Derr, Linda Bussiere, Ken and Amy Raymond, and Karla Macleod, of the Rindge Historical Society, provided a great deal of background material on the haunting of the Freeborn Stearns House, and Richard Boutwell, of the Jaffrey Historical Society, graciously showed me the evidence in the murder of Dr. Dean. Additionally, Robert Deschenes, current owner of the Dean farm, took the time to show me around the property. Keene author Jack Coey, who has written two books on the Dean murder himself, was more than generous in providing me with numerous astonishing revelations about the case. The Fitzwilliam Historical Society also allowed me to photograph the interior of the Blake House, and provided me with considerable information on the hauntings there. Last, but certainly not least, Bobby Elgee, of the group Sights Unseen Paranormal, regaled me with tales of his experiences at Shipman's Tavern in Winchester.

I fully realize that I have barely scratched the surface of the strange and curious events that abound in this region; other books will certainly follow, as more stories come to light. Consequently, I encourage any readers who might have a strange tale to contact me at Eric.Stanway@yahoo.com, and let me know of any odd tale that might merit investigation.

Some of these tales are ghost stories; others involve murders that were once infamous, and are now largely forgotten. What they all have in common, however, is a sense of mystery -- a compelling feeling of ancient discovery that rings true in every stone and tree in this region.

Eric Stanway
October 31, 2012

Haunted Houses

By
Henry Wadsworth Longfellow

All houses wherein men have lived and died
Are haunted houses. Through the open doors
The harmless phantoms on their errands glide,
With feet that make no sound upon the floors.

We meet them at the door-way, on the stair,
Along the passages they come and go,
Impalpable impressions on the air,
A sense of something moving to and fro.

There are more guests at table, than the hosts
Invited; the illuminated hall
Is thronged with quiet, inoffensive ghosts,
As silent as the pictures on the wall.
The stranger at my fireside cannot see
The forms I see, nor hear the sounds I hear;
He but perceives what is ; while unto me
All that has been is visible and clear.

We have no title-deeds to house or lands;
Owners and occupants of earlier dates
From graves forgotten stretch their dusty hands,
And hold in mortmain still their old estates.

The spirit-world around this world of sense
Floats like an atmosphere, and everywhere
Wafts through these earthly mists and vapors dense
A vital breath of more ethereal air.

Our little lives are kept in equipoise
By opposite attractions and desires ;
The struggle of the instinct that enjoys,
And the more noble instinct that aspires.

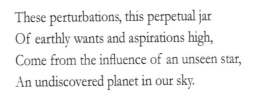

These perturbations, this perpetual jar
Of earthly wants and aspirations high,
Come from the influence of an unseen star,
An undiscovered planet in our sky.

And as the moon from some dark gate of cloud
Throws o'er the sea a floating bridge of light,
Across whose trembling planks our fancies crowd
Into the realm of mystery and night, -

So from the world of spirits there descends
A bridge of light, connecting it with this,
O'er whose unsteady floor, that sways and bends,
Wander our thoughts above the dark abyss.

-From The Courtship of Miles Standish, and Other Poems,
1858.

Photograph by the author

The Ghost Chair, in the Phillips-
Heil Cemetery, in Jaffrey.

MEMENTO MORI

The Ghost Chair

JAFFREY

Traversing the border between the towns of Fitzwilliam and Jaffrey is the Jaffrey Road, which crosses Route 119 and heads into Jaffrey, where it intersects Mountain View Road, in full view of Mount Monadnock. About halfway down this thoroughfare on the left, you'll see a small sign pointing out the dirt path that takes you to the Phillips-Heil cemetery, an ancient burying ground nestled deep in the woods. There, you'll find a peculiar sight; a

Photograph by the author
The gravestone of Persis
Welch, daughter of Jonas
Ross, who died in 1839.

group of gravestones, gathered around what appears to be a huge stone table, with a massive chair, carved out of a single piece of granite, and the inscription "J. Ross 1871" cut into the front.

This is actually the family plot of the Ross family, three generations of which were prominent in this area. Jonas Ross, the patriarch of the family, was born in 1784. On January 5, 1814, he purchased 100 acres of land on Cobleigh Hill, on the south end of the old Fitzwilliam Road. There, he raised five children and remained in residence for the next four decades, before selling the property in 1853 to one Nathan Stone.

The family was, by some accounts, a very tight-knit one, presided over by the stern and commanding hand of Jonas. None of the children lived to be very old; the first son, Martin, died on September 11, 1825 at the age of 17; Persis expired on October 11, 1839, aged 30; Abigail died on December 7, 1839, aged 29; Jonas, who lived less than a year, died on April 14, 1812; his brother Jonas, also aged less than a year, died on March 20, 1816.

The old man's death in 1861 didn't really

Photograph by the author

The gravestone of the infant
Jonas Ross, who died in 1812,
aged less than one year.

change the grip he had on the family. Ten years after his demise, his descendant, Eliza Jane Fay, erected the huge stone chair on the family plot. The History of Jaffrey describes the area in somewhat florid language:

"A striking memorial is that to the north end of the yard, looking across to Gap Mountain. It is a great stone chair, fit to be the throne of a monarch of the hills. It is a memorial of the Ross family, three generations of whom lived hereabouts. It is said that, according to the belief of a descendent, spirits often return to the scenes of their earthly existence, and so, with filial respect, she placed for them the chair, facing the sunset, where in seemly fashion they may sit at ease when they return to muse upon the scene of their earthly existence.

"For most of those who are resting here the final journey was brief as their temporal homes were near-by, and often they had looked with composure across the unobstructed fields to this pleasant hillside, where they counted on a peaceful sleep and glorious awakening. Upon their gravestones are the old sentiments

Photograph by the author

The Ross family plot, in the Phillips-
Heil Cemetery, with the Ghost Chair
at the head.

of sorrow and loss, sustained and soothed by an unfaltering trust in a better hereafter. Their epitaphs and inscriptions are our introduction to those who have come the way of the earth before us. They are the means by which they have sought to communicate to us, as in duty bound, the lessons they had learned from the brevity and life and certainty of death."

It certainly is a spooky place – and the idea that there might be spirits about, taking their ease in a great stone chair, considering the truths of life and death, only adds to the atmosphere.

Photograph by the author

The Blake House, in Fitzwilliam, as
it looks today. It presently houses
the Fitzwilliam Historical Society.

The Blake House

FITZWILLIAM

The picture-perfect town of Fitzwilliam seems an unlikely place for the supernatural. It comes as something of a surprise, therefore, to discover that the center of this little hamlet is home to not one, but two haunted houses. I'll cover the Fitzwilliam Inn in the next volume in this series – right now, I'm going to concentrate on the Amos J. Blake House, a stately old building which seems to have excited the attention of the spirits to an unusual degree.

Photograph by the author

Amos J. Blake's office, in the Blake House. This area is reportedly extremely haunted, with various objects moving of their own accord.

The Amos J. Blake House was built in 1837 as a commercial building by one Levi Haskell. There was a separate door at each corner for two stores and a door in the center, for Haskell and his bride to reach their living accommodations on the second floor.

By the way, the name of Levi Haskell will show up later in this book, in the chapter, "Bones in the Barn." In that tale, Levi was said to have killed one Seth Lucus, back in 1804. I can only conclude that this Levi was the son of the first.

By all accounts, the Haskell family didn't reside there very long, and a succession of owners ensued. By the time of the Civil War, it had become the residence and law office of Amos J. Blake, community leader, town official and state legislator. Amos lived in the house until his death in 1925, and his son Leroy continued to occupy the site until his own death nearly 40 years later. At that point, Leroy's cousin, Ida Mae Northrup, donated the building to the newly-formed Fitzwilliam Historical Society, with the stipulation that the Blake name continue to be associated with the house.

"The house was completely full of his

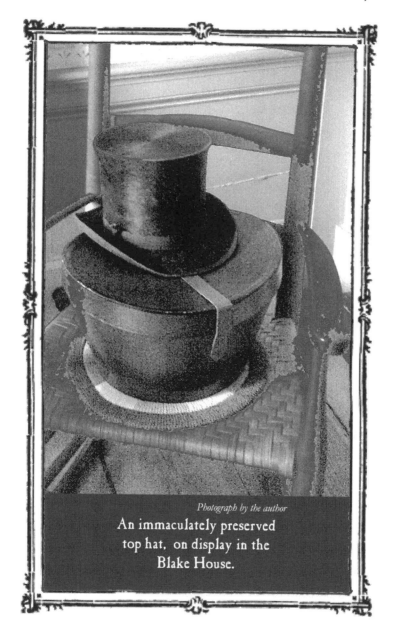

Photograph by the author

An immaculately preserved
top hat, on display in the
Blake House.

belongings," said Karen James, a volunteer with the Fitzwilliam Historical Society. "He didn't really even live here. After Leroy died, all of the furniture was taken over to the Fitzwilliam Inn across the road, for auction. The society bought a lot of the furniture, and moved it right back here."

It wasn't long before the volunteers began to experience strange occurrences in the house. "I was upstairs one night, heading from the children's room into the next room, and trying to find the light switch," said James, noting that there are three different kinds of lights in the house – old-fashioned button switches, chains, and modern switches. "I was getting very frustrated in trying to turn the lights on, when I heard a man behind me in the doorway, laughing. I was pretty angry, and yelled 'what?' and turned around. There was nobody there."

The odd events continued. In Amos' old lawyer's office, situated at the front of the house on the first floor, there is an old music box and a small case for donations. "I was looking at the donation box, and the money started to move around of its

Photograph by the author

An old piano, on display in the Blake House.

own accord," said James. "I mentioned it to the other person in the room; she turned around, and it just stopped."

Upon leaving the room, the two could hear the music box suddenly turn itself on. "The box has a lid that has to be lifted, in order for it to work," said James. "It just turned itself on. This happened a couple of times over the course of the night."

Then there's the cat, which has been witnessed by a number of volunteers. "One of my friends was clearing up underneath the sofa, when she heard something," said James. "She looked up, and there was a cat standing there, staring at her. She blinked, and it was gone."

All of these spooky shenanigans soon attracted the attention of the TAPS society, the team behind the SyFy channel show "Ghost Hunters." In the summer of 2009, they decided to make an investigation of the property, bringing with them all of their high-tech paranormal detection equipment.

"There's a length of chain hanging from a wall in the central room downstairs," said James. "The crew put a video

Photograph by the author

A display of old school desks, which were rescued on their way to the dump. Strange markings have been reported on the blackboards in this room.

camera in there, and it caught that chain being pulled away from the wall and then dropped back again." A member of the team also encountered the cat – but this time, down in the cellar, where he could feel it brushing up against his leg.

There are, of course, the requisite unexplained footsteps, heard in other rooms and sometimes upstairs. "Some people say there are a man and a woman in the attic, as well," said James.

Other workers at the site have observed toys being left about the floor in the morning, as spectral children leave their belongings scattered about.

One of the upstairs rooms contains a quantity of old school furniture, rescued on its way to the local dump. There are blackboards in this room, which sometimes will manifest strange marks in chalk. "When I first came here, I brought my dog with me," said James. "He usually follows me everywhere. Well, this time, I headed downstairs, and noticed he wasn't there. I went back into the schoolroom, and he was just sat there in the corner, whining a little and not moving."

Photograph by the author
An example of some of the
ornamentation on display in
the Blake House.

The opinion of the dog notwithstanding, the volunteers at the Blake House find nothing malignant in the activities of the dozen or so spirits that haunt the place. As a matter of fact, the atmosphere seems to exude a sense of peace and quietude. "I generally suffer from chronic pain," said James. "But the moment I came in here, all that just subsided. From the man and woman who are said to be in the attic, the small boy who runs from room to room, and the cat that seems to have the freedom of the place, it's an active but happy haunt."

Photograph by the author

Shipman's Tavern, in Winchester, as it looks today. The house, which has had extended periods of vacancy, has been neglected over the years.

WINCHESTER

The tiny town of Winchester is notable for one particularly haunted house – the old Shipman's Tavern on Main Street.

Once a fashionable stopping-off point for tourists heading for the White Mountains, the house is now in a state of deplorable disrepair. It's a massive structure, with over 30 rooms and a huge barn in the back. Its once-impressive façade is draped in cracked and peeling paint, and the numerous windows are broken, revealing empty rooms.

Image Courtesy The Boston Globe

A piece from the January 30, 1930 edition of the Boston Globe, marking the end of the "Uncle Tom's Cabin" road shows.

According to some accounts, over 150 people have perished within these walls in the last century and a half. Some of them are still in residence.

This tavern was once run by one James W. Shipman, a retired circus entrepreneur. Shipman had been a tireless self-promoter throughout his career. Born on August 5, 1865 in Williamsville, Vermont, he worked for eight years with Sig Sawtelle's circus, before striking out on his own. For three years, he managed a stage show based on Harriett Beecher Stowe's "Uncle Tom's Cabin," with his wife, Ada, playing the character of "Topsy."

Shipman was the owner of a large farm on a mountain midway between Winchester and Vermont, from which he managed his troupe. Traditionally, circuses were a summer recreation; Shipman, however, determined to extend the season by taking his show on the road throughout the winter. He opened the revue in Winchester, and played in various theaters, moving as far east as Livermore Falls, Maine. At that point, however, the entourage became snowbound, and Shipman barely made

A 1910 postcard, depicting Shipman's Tavern. Note that the third story has yet to be added.

it back to Winchester. Chastened by the experience, he determined never to take the show on the road again.

Eschewing show business entirely, he began to make ends meet by driving a stagecoach between Keene and Brattleboro, Vermont.

In 1907, Shipman purchased the Winchester House on Main Street, and renamed it Shipman's Tavern. The house had originally been the home of Elisha Rich, a Justice of the Peace for the town. The property was taken up by the Jennings family in 1882, before selling it to Shipman.

The business was a huge success, as various show folk, especially drummers, began to patronize the establishment. It hosted various guests of note, including Major League baseball players Ty Cobb and Tris Speaker.

So well-regarded was this establishment that it gained mention in the 1909 edition of "The Town Register: Hinsdale, Walpole, Westmoreland, Winchester, Chesterfield:"

"The Winchester House is a pleasant home for travelers kept by Mr. J. W. Shipman, is heated by steam and has an

WIDOWS LAY CLAIM TO CIRCUS MAN'S ESTATE

EACH PRESENTS A WILL FOR PROBATE FOLLOWING SHOW MANAGER'S DEATH

Brattleboro, April 6.—Two women, each of whom claims to be the lawful widow of James W. Shipman, former circus man and proprietor of the South Vernon Hotel, whose death occurred on March 10, have appeared to lay claim to the small estate left by him. Judge A. F. Schwenk, of the probate court, has had the claims of one of the women presented to him. The other will present her claims on April 17.

A clipping from a 1915 edition of the Watertown, New York, Daily Times, reporting on the dispute over James W. Shipman's estate.

excellent livery attached. To know Winchester you must also see Ashuelot village as it is today one of the most attractive in Cheshire County."

As the business grew, Shipman had a third story built onto the building. He also purchased a second hotel in South Vernon, Vermont, and operated both businesses until his death in 1915.

Successful as he was in business, Shipman was somewhat more messy in his domestic affairs. A dispute over his will erupted immediately after his demise, and two widows showed up at the same time to seek his inheritance. The Watertown, New York, Daily Times published a report of the dispute in 1915.

"WIDOWS LAY CLAIM TO CIRCUS MAN'S ESTATE," ran the headline. "Each presents a will for probate following showmanager's death," elaborated the subhead. The account is as follows:

"Brattleboro, April 6 – Two women, each of whom claims to be the lawful widow of James W. Shipman, former circus man and proprietor of the South Vernon Hotel, whose death occurred on March

Shipman's Tavern, in its
more prosperous days.

10, have appeared to lay claim to the small estate lefty by him. Judge A. F. Schwenk, of the probate court, has had the claims of one of the women presented to him. The other will present her claims on April 27.

"A woman, claiming to be Ervine Shipman, of Syracuse, N.Y., who is represented by Gibson & Daley, of Brattleboro, claims to be the lawful widow of Mr. Shipman. She says they were married in Syracuse about 25 years ago when Mr. Shipman conducted the Seneca hotel and livery in that city. She told of the cause for their separation. In support of her story Ezra O. Shipman, of Brattleboro, a brother of the late J. W. Shipman, testified to having lived with his brother and having known the claimant as his brother's wife.

"The other claimant is a woman known as Mrs. Ada S. T. Shipman, whose home is in Winchester, N.H. where Mr. Shipman some years ago conducted a hotel known as Shipman's Tavern. She has offered through her attorneys, Phillip D. Faulkner of Keene, N.H., and Harold E. Whitney of Brattleboro, a will for probate, purporting to be the last will and testament of James

Photograph courtesy Bobby Elgee

Photograph taken by paranormal
investigator Bobby Elgee on
February 9, 2003, of the front
room on the ground floor of
Shipman's Tavern. Note the dust
"orb" to the left of the window.

W. Shipman. In this, he leaves all his property to her.

"Mrs. Ervine Shipman has waived all provisions of his will, as permitted by law, and claims the estate, which is estimated to be worth about $2,000, as her property.

"Mrs. Shipman was a native of Williamsville, and after leaving Syracuse, N.Y. was a business manager for Sig Sawtelle's circus for several years, was connected with Frank A. Robbins' shows in the same capacity and at one time was proprietor of an Uncle Tom's Cabin show that traveled in wagons. He died following an operation for acute appendicitis."

It is known that Ada Shipman carried on managing the tavern throughout the 1930s. She outlived two more husbands, and expired at the age of 85.

After World War II, the town of Winchester fell into economic decline, and the fortunes of Shipman's Tavern similarly suffered. From 1949 to 1965, the house became a nursing home, under the proprietorship of Mable and George Brown. Following that, there was a stint of five years, when a building supply company ran

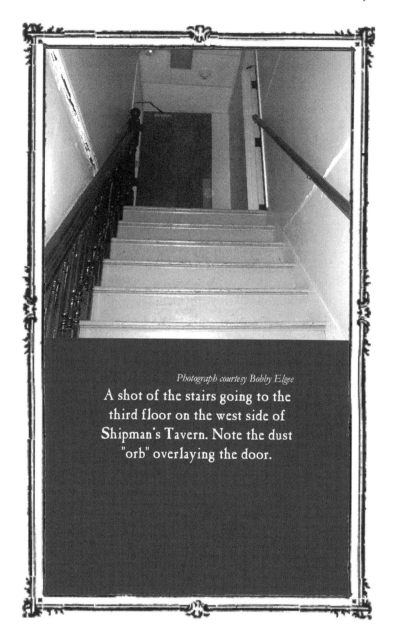

Photograph courtesy Bobby Elgee

A shot of the stairs going to the third floor on the west side of Shipman's Tavern. Note the dust "orb" overlaying the door.

a store out of the barn. In 1970, Velma and William Sawyer bought the property, and ran it as a boardinghouse, a tradition continued by Josie Marsh, under whose ownership the home became locally known as "Josie's House."

In 2004, the house became vacant, and has only been tenanted sporadically since. At one point in 2008, the building was considered as a possible home for a performing arts center, but nothing ever came of it.

Perhaps due to the vast number of elderly residents that passed away within these walls, the house has developed a significant reputation as being haunted. Paranormal investigator Bobby Elgee, of the group Sights Unseen Paranormal, recalled his own investigation of the tavern, on the evening of February 9, 2003.

"In this specific instance, I happened to live right down the road from the house," he said. "My roommate knew the owners who were selling it, and we got permission to go in there. At the same time, another friend of mine, who is a really competent historical researcher, went through the town records and was able to confirm over

Photograph courtesy Bobby Elgee

Shot of a room on the second floor of Shipman's Tavern. Note the "orb," which seems to be rising out of the floor.

150 deaths in the building over the years."

Elgee said that, before the investigation could commence, the police had to come in and clear out the homeless people who were living there. The investigation itself took place from 8:00 p.m., finishing at 11:00 p.m., with investigators on each of the floors.

"The first thing I noticed was a smell of Old Spice cologne," Elgee said. "It wasn't like a regular smell, though – it was something that you just sensed for a second. As soon as it was there, it was gone."

Other manifestations soon became apparent, including photographic evidence and electronic voice phenomena (EVPs).

"I captured an image of a white fog on a staircase," said Elgee. "It's a strange light thing, without any tendrils on it. I also managed to record an EVP of something that sounds like an elderly lady saying 'we died here.' It wasn't very clear, though.

"I was a little green and inexperienced at the time we did this investigation, so a lot of stuff creeped me out. I started hearing these scratching noises in a room down the hall where there were a couple of mat-

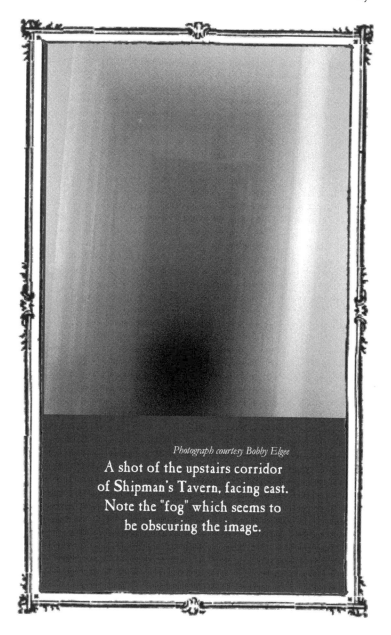

Photograph courtesy Bobby Elgee

A shot of the upstairs corridor
of Shipman's Tavern, facing east.
Note the "fog" which seems to
be obscuring the image.

tresses. I kept sticking my head around the door frame, but I was just too scared. At the time, I thought it might be a giant raccoon."

One of the most startling events took place when Elgee decided to investigate the attic of the house.

"This was one of the few investigations I've been on where I've encountered a real cold spot," he said. "That's when something comes up and touches you, and you can feel the temperature drop something like 15 degrees.

"When I went up into the attic, I could feel the air getting kind of heavy. Then, all of a sudden, I sensed this cold spot on my right shoulder, close to my neck. It sat there for 15 or 20 seconds, so I moved, and it went away. Then it came right back, and touched me again. I would say the phenomenon lasted a total of 30 or 40 seconds. I reached out to touch my shoulder, and my clothes felt really cold in that spot, like someone had put an ice pack there."

Investigators on the other floors reported a feeling of being constantly watched by a large number of entities, and one group observed a shadow, moving

Photograph courtesy Bobby Elgee

The stairway leading to the attic. It was here that paranormal investigator Bobby Elgee reported encountering a cold spot.

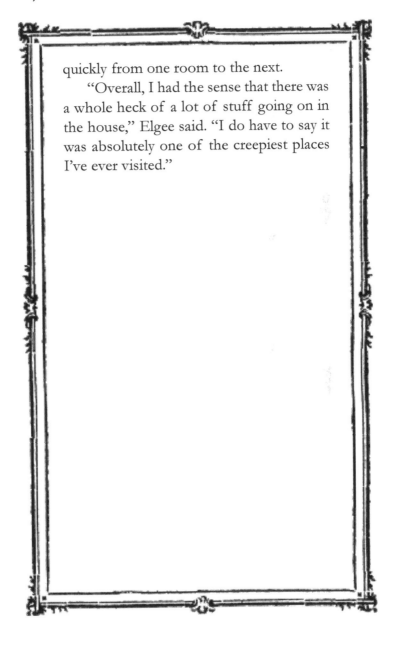

quickly from one room to the next.

"Overall, I had the sense that there was a whole heck of a lot of stuff going on in the house," Elgee said. "I do have to say it was absolutely one of the creepiest places I've ever visited."

Photograph courtesy Rindge Historicaal Society

Simeon Mayo's house, in Rindge, photographed
circa 1960. This was the home where the Rev.
Ephraim K. Avery was run to ground by
private investigator Harvey Harnden.
The building was demolished by Franklin
Pierce University in 2007 to make way for
Petrocelli Hall.

RINDGE

As you head west down Route 119 in Rindge, you'll see University Drive, just before you hit Pearly Pond, on your right hand side. This is the entrance to Franklin Pierce University, which has been serving the student community since 1962. A little way down the road, you come across Petrocelli Hall, a university building dating only back to 2008. At one time, however, this was the site of the Simeon Mayo house, the epicenter of one of the most spectacular criminal cases of the

Sarah M. Cornell meets with Rev. Ephraim K. Avery on the night of her murder, from "The Terrible Hay-Stack Murder" (1878)

Victorian age.

This house was once the home of Captain Simeon Mayo, an upstanding and respected citizen of the town. On one night in 1833, however, he was accused of harboring a desperate fugitive, a primary suspect in the murder of a young woman.

The suspect in question was one Rev. Ephraim K. Avery, a Methodist minister from the town of Fall River, Massachusetts. His alleged victim was Sarah M. Cornell, a worker in the local mills.

Our story opens on December 21, 1832, when the body of a young woman was found hanging from a haystack on the farm of John Durfee in the village of Tiverton, Rhode Island. Durfee sent for the coroner, and news of the discovery traveled quickly into neighboring towns. When word reached Fall River, a group of potential witnesses arrived at the farm to identify the body, including the Reverend Ira Bidwell and John Smith, overseer at the weaving room at the Fall River Manufactory. There was no doubt; the victim was Sarah M. Cornell. Sarah's doctor, Thomas Wilbur, weighed in and said that the girl was pregnant when she

"The unsuspecting girl was strangled by the scoundrel ere she became aware of his cruel intention," from "The Terrible Hay-Stack Murder" (1878)

died, and he presumed she had killed herself in despair. Dr. Wilbur stated that Sarah had confided her condition to him in recent weeks, and had named Reverend Avery as the putative father.

The discovery of the body is outlined in lurid detail in Catherine Read Williams' "Fall River: An Authentic Narrative" (1834):

"It was on a cold frosty morning, the 21st December that the doctor observed some people running up the street, apparently in great haste; he stood at the window watching when they should return, to know what the matter was; but no body came back, while another and another party followed close upon the heels of the former. The women appeared to be horror struck as they collected in groups at the doors or in the streets, and many leaving their families just as they were, (it was about breakfast time) and hastily throwing something over them pushed on in the direction of Durfee's farm. Presently someone came running into the doctor's saying a young woman had just hung herself up at Durfee's. The doctor stopped to ask no more, but catching his hat, ran up to

Farmer John Durfee discovers the body of
Sarah M. Cornell hanging from a haystack.

the farm without however having the least suspicion who it was. Upon gaining a stack yard some fifty rods south of the house, he perceived a female lying on the ground, for they had taken her down. She lay with her cloak, gloves and calash on, and her arms drawn under her cloak.

"'Does any one know her?' asked one. 'She is well dressed,' said another, 'I think she must be somebody respectable.' 'Yes I know her,' said the Methodist minister who had arrived on the ground a little previous to the doctor — 'she is a respectable young woman, and a member of my church.'

"Just then the physician reached the yard, and hastily lifting the profusion of dark locks that had fallen entirely over her face, he discovered with grief and astonishment the countenance of his late interesting patient. Horror struck, he endeavored to loosen the cord from her neck; it was nearly half an inch imbedded in the flesh. But alas! there was nothing in the usual remedies to produce resuscitation that would have availed anything here, for the young woman appeared to have been there all night and was frozen stiff.

Frontspiece for "A Brief and Impartial Narrative of the Life of Sarah Maria Cornell," written anonymously in response to her murder.

And is this the end of the sorrows, poor unfortunate, thought the kind physician, as bending over the helpless victim of unhallowed passion. He gazed upon that altered countenance — altered it was indeed — it was livid pale, — her tongue protruded through her teeth — pushed out her under lip, that was very much swollen as though it had received some hard blow, or been severely bit in anguish, gave a dreadful expression of agony, while a deep indentation on the cheek looked as though that too must have been pressed by some hard substance; but whatever he thought at that time respecting the means by which she came to her death, he wisely forbore to utter it, and the jury of inquest was summoned in immediately. In the meantime the respectable farmer on whose premises the deceased was found, after having her carefully conveyed to the house, inquired of the Methodist minister if she had any friends in the place, and if not whether the society of which he said she was a respectable member would not see to the expense of her funeral. That person replied that he did not exactly know their rules in such

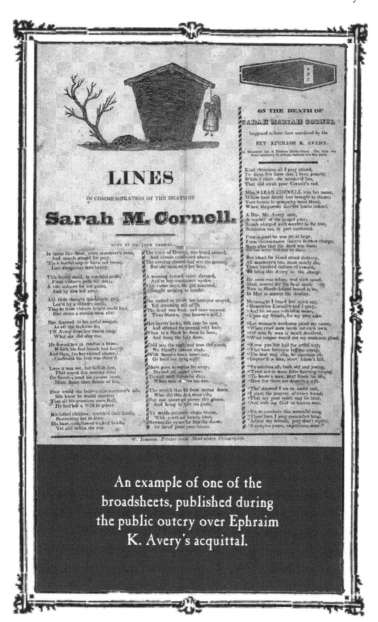

An example of one of the
broadsheets, published during
the public outcry over Ephraim
K. Avery's acquittal.

cases, but he would go and consult them and return soon and inform them. Meanwhile the truth struggled hard in the breast of the doctor. He had felt himself bound to secrecy in case the girl had lived, respecting the name of her betrayer, but her death and the awful manner of it impelled him to reveal what he believed to be the cause. He felt that death had taken off the injunction of secrecy; and stepping after the clergyman, he related the confession of the unhappy girl to him, and what she hid said respecting his brother Avery."

The whole situation was dire; the accusations against a member of the cloth were not to be tolerated, and Sarah was buried on Saturday. The next day, however, a note came to light, in her bandbox. It read as follows:

"If I should be missing enquire of the Rev Mr. Avery of Bristol he will know where I am Dec 20th S M Cornell."

The evidence began to accumulate against Avery. A letter was discovered in Sarah's trunk, speaking of a secret assignation. Furthermore, it was discovered that the cord around her neck was tied with a clove hitch, which left out the possibility

An 1833 print, entitled "A Very Bad
Man," responding to the acquittal
of Ephraim K. Avery. While he is
strangling Cornell, a group of demons
are seen hovering over the haystack,
commenting on the event: "Do you see
what is going on here?" "I never sleep
on such occasions." "How will this be
managed if it should go to a jury." "A
Jury ye young fools is nothing. what's
to be done with Public Opinion."

of suicide. Sarah's body was exhumed, and bruises were found on her abdomen, indicating a possible attempt at abortion.

Things were reaching a head. On Sunday, the coroner declared that Sarah had been murdered, and a warrant was issued for Avery's arrest, but the authorities in Bristol would not release the prisoner.

A hearing was held on Christmas Day, 1832, presided over by Justices John Howe and Levi Haile. The prosecution was apparently hogtied from the outset – the testimony of Sarah's sister, brother-in-law, or even Dr. Wilbur, were barred from the court, and the defense had the luxury of bringing forward witnesses attesting to the Reverend's character. Avery was accordingly acquitted on January 7th.

To say there was a public outcry over this verdict would be an understatement. Cartoons and songs soon proliferated, depicting the hideous murder and even showing Avery being hounded to hell by a legion of demons. A mob mentality was quickly taking hold. John Durfee, on whose farm Cornell's body had been found, was particularly upset over the outcome, and

NARRATIVE

OF THE

APPREHENSION

IN RINDGE, N. H.

OF

THE REV. E. K. AVERY,

CHARGED WITH

THE MURDER

OF

SARAH M. CORNELL,

TOGETHER WITH THE PROCEEDINGS OF THE

INHABITANTS

OF FALL RIVER.

BY HARVEY HARNDEN.

PROVIDENCE:
W. MARSHALL & CO. PRINTERS
1833.

Frontspiece of "The Narrative of the Apprehension in Rindge, N.H. of The Rev. E. K. Avery, Charged With the Murder of Sarah M. Cornell," published by Harvey Harnden in 1833.

formed a Committee of Vigilance, through which he swore out a complaint with a magistrate in Newport.

Well, Avery wasn't hanging around. He immediately hightailed it to Lowell, and then to Dedham. But the public were not to be deterred. They hired an investigator, one Harvey Harnden, to pursue the fugitive, and he doggedly followed the Reverend's tracks, eventually tracking him down to the home of Captain Simeon Mayo, in Rindge, New Hampshire.

Harnden published a pamphlet in 1833, entitled "Narrative of the Apprehension in Rindge, N.H., of the Rev. E.K. Avery," in which he described in detail his arrest of the suspect at the Rindge farm:

"I however concluded from all the circumstances that there might be a strong presumption raised that we should find Avery at that place; and that, at any rate, it would be impossible much longer of keeping the object of my being in that part of the country a secret. I then asked Mr. ----- if he would accompany us to the house of Mayo. He said he knew no good reason why he should refuse; that if he under-

Detail from "A Minister Extraordinary Taking Passage & Bound for a Foreign Mission to The Court of His Satanic Majesty." (1833), showing Avery being forced off a cliff by two demons.

stood the object for Avery was wanted,
there could be no objection to it, as it was
only for the purpose of investigating the
subject. He then said he would call on his
neighbor, and if he would consent to go,
he would also. He called the man, and they
finally both agreed to go with us. They, in
addition to the men before me, increased
the number to six besides myself. Being
now all together, it was proposed that, if I
would undertake to manage, they would do
as I might direct. To this I consented, and
we started for the house of Capt. Mayo.
When in sight of the house, and seeing
a light therein, I directed that the outside
doors of the house should be properly
guarded – that I wished all to remain outside of the house, except Mr. Foster, the
deputy in that county – that I wished him
to go into the house with me, and when I
was once in legally, as I should be with him,
I would do all the talking and fighting if
any should be necessary. (I had previously
discovered that some of the men who were
with me entertained fears that there might
be some personal danger in apprehending
Mr. Avery; which, when it is considered

REV. EPHRAIM K. AVERY.

Ephraim K. Avery, as he
appeared at his trial.

that they were in pursuit of a man, to them a stranger, who was accused of murder and had fled from his family and friends, seems not at all unreasonable.) When the deputy and myself had approached near the door, we concluded to omit the usual ceremony of knocking. The deputy opened the door and entered with me into the room in which the family live, the outside door opening into the room. (I will here remark, that this room was in a porch built on the end of the house instead of the back, as is usual; and that the front of the porch was parallel with the front of the main building, although thrown back perhaps six or eight feet, so as to give a window in the end of the main building into a front room.) When I was in the room I inquired of Capt. Mayo was at home. A sort and rather stocky man arose from the corner with a pipe somewhat shortened in its dimensions, first in hand then and then in mouth, and said his name was Mayo. I then said, I am here after Ephraim K. Avery. 'Ephraim K. Avery!' said Mayo. Yes sir. 'Ephraim K. Avery!' he says again. Yes sir, you speak his name right. By this time a gentleman who sat in

The grave of Sarah Maria Cornell,
in Fall River, Massachusetts.

the room, and who I afterwards heard was a minister who had preached in the same room that evening, spoke and said, 'Avery, Avery, there was a man by that name who preached at Lowell, though I never saw him or knew his Christian name; is that the man?' Yes sir. 'Ephraim K. Avery,' Mayo says again – 'I never knew such a man as Ephraim K. Avery.' The minister again said, 'there has been a great deal about a murder in Rhode-Island, and a Mr. Avery accused, is that the man?' Yes sir. 'Ephraim K. Avery!' said Mayo again, 'I don't know such a man.' Then I said to Capt. Mayo, I know such a man; I have come a great way after him – I came on purpose after him and must have him; and Capt. Mayo, the better way is for you to go to the room where Mr. Avery is, and tell him a Mr. Harnden is here and wishes to see him, and let him come forward; for he is in your house, and if he comes not forward I shall search your house, for I must have him. At this instant a lady who sat in the room, and who I found out was Mrs. Mayo, got up, went into another room without a light, and closed the door after her, while

REPORT

OF THE

TRIAL

OF THE

REV. EPHRAIM K. AVERY,

METHODIST MINISTER,

FOR THE

MURDER

OF

SARAH MARIA CORNELL,

AT TIVERTON,

IN THE

COUNTY OF NEWPORT, RHODE ISLAND,

BEFORE THE SUPREME JUDICIAL COURT OF THAT STATE,

MAY 6th, 1833.

Containing the evidence of the numerous witnesses unabridged, and the speeches of General Albert C. Greene, Attorney General; the Hon. D. Pearce, and William R. Staples, Esq., Counsel for the Prosecution; and those of the Hon. J. Mason, Richard R. Randolph, Esq., and other Counsel for the Prisoner; together with the charge of

HIS HONOR CHIEF JUSTICE EDDY,

IN FULL, AS TAKEN IN SHORT HAND, BY

A LAW REPORTER OF NEW-YORK.

—————" Murder,
"Though it hath no tongue, will speak
"As with a most miraculous organ."

New=York,

PUBLISHED BY WILLIAM STODART, 6 CORTLANDT-ST.

Frontspiece for the "Report of the Trial of the Rev. Ephraim K. Avery, Methodist Minister, for the Murder of Sarah Maria Cornell, at Tiverton in the County of Newport, Rhode Island" (1833).

her husband continued to smoke, and pronounce the name of Ephraim K. Avery, and disclaim knowledge of any man by that name.

"Very soon I heard the rap of fingers on the window of the room in which I was, and near the door where I had entered. I stepped to the door, and was told by Mr. Edwards the deputy from New Ipswich, 'that while standing near the front door of the house, he had heard some person go up stairs and rap on something and call 'Mr. Avery.' I informed Mr. Edwards that I had told the people there that I was after Mr. Avery, and of course if he was there they would call him, and at the same time requested Mr. Edwards to see that the doors were well guarded – I very soon took the only light there was in the room, and through I would endeavor to learn what had become of Mrs. Mayo. I then went through the same door she had passed through – I found myself in a small room back of a front room, with a door that opened into said front room. I entered and went through the front room into the front entry, and from thence up stairs. On

A map showing Tiverton
and Fall River, from the
transcript of the trial,
published in 1833.

arriving at the head of the stairs, I discovered a door, opening into the chamber over
the front room opposite to the one I have
named, to be open. On looking in, I saw
that there was a low fire on the hearth,
a light stand before it, with a candle on
it from which the blaze had been extin-
guished, though there was fire still remaining on the wick. I entered that room, and
saw no person in it. I there saw a bed which
had been tumbled, and found by intruding
my hand into it that it had been recently
dislodged by someone. I then went into a
bedroom which was back of the chamber
and there found no one. I then returned
into the front entry chamber, and there
saw Mrs. Mayo standing in the other front
chamber. I then went into that, while she
passed me into the entry chamber. While I
was searching the chamber in which I then
was, Mrs. Mayo remarked, that I was a persecutor, and I was after innocent blood. I
replied (without discontinuing my search
however) that I was not after innocent
blood, but that I was after Mr. Avery, that
if he was innocent he had nothing to fear;
and that being the case instead of my being

"A Minister Extraordinary Taking Passage &
Bound for a Foreign Mission to The Court of
His Satanic Majesty." (1833).

a persecutor, I certainly was endeavoring
to do him a favor, as, if I found him, it
was only to put him in a situation to prove
himself so – after searching the chamber
and two small room, I returned to the front
entry chamber, and from thence up the
garret stairs, which led from it. On entering upon the stairs, I found there was as
trap door over them at the garret floor, and
turning up that door I was informed, by a
very intelligent cat that was on some rub-
bish very near the door, that no one had
passed that way, (the cat gave me to understand this, by gently raising herself from her
couch, and rounding up her back, is if to
stretch herself; meaning, all the time, I had
no doubt, to say, 'Mr. Avery has not been
up here, sir, but, as I am a member of the
family, it will not do for me to speak out.')
I was certainly obliged to the well meaning
animal for the hint she had given me, as I
have no doubt it saved me the trouble of
overhauling many old flour barrels, boxes,
bins, warping bars, looms & c. with which a
country garret twenty-eight by forty is usually furnished – I then returned to the entry
chamber, and from thence into the cham-

Detail from "A Minister Extraordinary Taking Passage & Bound for a Foreign Mission to The Court of His Satanic Majesty," (1833), showing Cornell hanging from the haystack while letters lie at her feet.

ber in which I first made search. I then
thought to look behind the door, where I
ought to have looked in the first instance,
and should if the object of my search had
been as large around the breast as some
men I know of; however the case was otherwise, and I must give the gentleman the
credit of having put himself in a position,
to require less room than I thought it possible for any man to do – I however found
him not there, on my second visit t the
room, for the very good reason that while
I had been in the garret, observing the very
natural, and to me satisfactory conduct of
a cat, I had given him a chance to leave his
room, and go downstairs, which he had
improved, and attempted to escape at the
front door, as I afterwards learnt from a
man stationed thereat on the outside, who,
as the door opened and Mr. Avery shew
himself, endeavored to fix his hand upon
him. Mr. Avery, not liking thus rudely to
be treated, closed the door so quick that
it endangered the hand which had been
extended to receive him. Mr. Avery then
turned into the front room directly under
his chamber, and had not time to shut and

LINES

Written on the death of

Sarah M. Cornell.

In times like these, when murderers roam,
And search around for prey,
'Tis a fearful step to leave our home,
Lest dangerous men betray.

This lovely girl in youthful pride,
From virtue's path did stray,
A vile seducer for her guide,
And by him led away.

O little thought the simple girl,
Lured by a villian's smile,
That he from virtue's height could hurl
Her down a stream most vile.

She listened to his artful tongue,
And thought his words were true,
Till Avery from her bosom wrung
What she did after rue.

He forced her to confess a flame
And then to her eternal shame,
Confessed his love was sham.

Love it was not, but hellish lust,
That urged this monster dire,
On Sarah's head his passion burst
More fierce than flames of fire.

How could she believe this murderous tale,
She knew he would deceive:
That all his promises were frail,
He left a wife to grieve.

His infant children stretched their hands,
Beseeching her to shun
His base unhallowed wicked hands,
Yet still to him she run.

The voice of Heaven was heard around,
The clouds departed from above,
The evening showers had wet the ground,
But she must meet her love.

The wretch has fled from mortal's doom,
Who done this deed most vile,
But one above can pierce the gloom,
And bring to light his guile.

Ye girls all sound in virgin bloom,
With youth and beauty blest,
Beware the crime for fear the doom,
Of Sarah Maria pierce your breast.

SECOND PART.

Kind Christians all I pray attend,
To these few lines which I have penned,
While I relate the murderous fate
That did await poor Cornell's end.

Miss Sarah Cornell was her name,
Who by deceit was brought to shame.
Your hearts in sympathy must bleed,
When Shepherds murder lambs indeed.

A Reverend Mr. Avery, sure,
A preacher of the gospel pure,
Stands charged with murder to the test,—
Seduction too, in part confessed.

First inquest he was set at large,
By circumstance from further charge:
Soon after that the deed was done,
He ran away the law to shun:

But blood for blood aloud doth cry,
All murderers surely ought to die.
Five hundred dollars of reward
To bring this Avery to the charge.

He soon was taken and with speed,
Was brought to answer for this dead,
Now in Rhode Island bound was he,
In May to receive his destiny.

Methought I heard a spirit say,
"Remember Cornell's end I pray,"
And let no one reflections make,
Upon my friends for my poor sake.

A poem, published in response to
Avery's acquittal.

latch the door, when I again returned into the front entry below.

"On arriving there, I discovered that the door into the front room last named was not entirely closed, though I distinctly recollected that when I passed up, it was shut. I then placed my hand against the door, and found there was a gentle pressure upon the other side, that in withholding my hand the door would return gently to its former position. I then concluded that I had got within an inch of the person I had long been looking for. I therefore opened the door with one hand, holding the candle in the other, and behind the door I discovered Mr. Avery, who stood as motionless as any piece of furniture in the room. He had on, either a surtout or peajacket; he held in his hand a cap, which I have no recollection of seeing afterwards. He had, since I had last seen him, which was then two weeks, left his beard to grow except on the front part of his face, which, as his beard is black, and having left it unshaven on the back parts of his cheeks, and so round under, and out to the point of this chin, it had very materially altered

THE

CORRECT, FULL AND IMPARTIAL

REPORT OF THE TRIAL

OF

REV. EPHRAIM K. AVERY,

BEFORE THE

R. I. SUPREME JUDICIAL COURT

OF THE

STATE OF RHODE-ISLAND,

AT NEWPORT, MAY 6, 1833, FOR THE

MURDER

OF

SARAH M. CORNELL.

PROVIDENCE:

MARSHALL AND BROWN.

The frontspiece of Avery's own
description of his trial, published in
an attempt to vindicate himself.
It didn't work.

his looks; so much so that the gentlemen
who were with me, remarked that from
the description I had given of him, they
should not have thought him to be the
man described, as I had told them he wore
no whiskers. I presented my hand and said,
Mr. Avery, how do you do? He attempted
to speak, but utterance failed him. (As I
had been informed by a sheriff who had
arrested him on another occasion that Mr.
Avery fainted, and from his appearance at
this time, fearing that might now be the
case,) I took Mr. Avery by the hand and
said, 'do endeavor to overcome this agita-
tion; you need fear no personal violence;
you shall be kindly treated;' and requested
him to step into the entry where there was
more air. He walked into the entry with me
and very soon spoke, (it being the first time
I ever heard him speak,) and said, 'I suppose you cannot legally take me from this
state, without a warrant from the Governor; have you such a warrant?' I replied I
had not, but that I supposed I had a warrant sufficient for that purpose which I had
obtained from a justice."

Harnden had come well prepared,

Ephraim K. Avery,
photographed in
1865, after he had
moved to Ohio and
become a farmer.

and immediately extradited his prisoner to Newport, Rhode Island, where he was placed in a small, unheated cell. He remained imprisoned for the next five months, awaiting trial.

The trial opened on May 6, 1833, attracting a huge amount of attention from the media. The lawyers for the prosecution were Rhode Island Attorney General Albert C. Greene and former attorney general Dutee Jerauld Pearce. The defense was made up of six lawyers, hired by the Methodist Church, led by former United States Senator and New Hampshire Attorney General Jeremiah Mason -- who, incidentally, was also a law partner with Daniel Webster.

The stakes were certainly high, and many parties had a lot to lose, should the verdict not go their way. The Methodists were just becoming accepted in New England, but the powerful Protestant establishment still held them in deep suspicion. On the other hand, the mill owners relied on young women for their work force, and the assertion that they would not be safe in an industrial environment put their business in peril.

Consequently, the trial was long on

Ephraim K. Avery's wife,
Sophia, photographed in
1865.

character assassination and short on actual forensic analysis. Cornell was portrayed as a wanton character of loose morals, and Avery an unjustly maligned man of the cloth.

In all, the trial proceeded for 27 days. Avery was not permitted to speak in his own defense, but both the prosecution and the defense brought in a large number of witnesses; 68 for the prosecution, 128 for the defense.

The jury reached its conclusion on June 2, after deliberating for 16 hours. Avery was found not guilty, freed, and resumed his position in the Methodist religion. Even now, though, public opinion was against him; effigies were burned in public and Avery himself was almost lynched in Boston. Avery attempted to clear his name by going on a speaking tour, but this turned out to be fruitless. In 1836, he gave up, left the Methodist ministry, and moved out, settling in New York State. In 1851, he moved to Pittsfield Ohio, with his wife, Sophia, and his sister, Nabby, where he raised six children, two of which died in infancy. Reluctantly, he took up the profession of farming, and also held the post of coroner.

Ephraim K. Avery's grave, in
South Pittsfield Cemetery,
Lorain County, Ohio.

While in Ohio, he wrote a pamphlet, entitled, "The Correct, Full and Impartial Report of the Trial of Rev. Ephraim K. Avery." It did little to vindicate him, and he died on October 23, 1869, at the age of 70, and was interred at South Pittsfield Cemetery, Lorain County, Ohio.

As infamous as this crime was, it was eclipsed, some 50 years later, by the case of Lizzie Borden, who was also accused of murder in Fall River. Everyone remembers Lizzie now, but Avery has been all but lost in the mists of history. Even the students of Franklin Pierce College seem to know little about the dramatic events that once took place on the campus where they study every day, when a dogged pursuer ran a fugitive to ground on that long-ago night.

Photograph courtesy Jack Coey

Dr. William Dean in his
library, circa 1908.

MEMENTO MORI

The Death of Dr. Dean

JAFFREY

The story of the Dean murder is well documented; several excellent books have already been written on the subject, and it has excited considerable interest over the years. Consequently, I thought long and hard about whether or not to include it in this volume. Given its historical significance, however, I decided it would be remiss of me if I didn't give it some notice. So, here goes.

The quiet town of Jaffrey woke up to an ugly surprise on the morning of August

Photograph courtesy Rindge Historicaal Society
The Dean farm, as it looked
in 1918.

14, 1918. Dr. William Kendrick Dean, a highly respected member of the community, had suddenly disappeared, seemingly without a trace.

Dr. Dean lived on a picturesque hill on the outskirts of town, a physician who had abandoned the medical profession due to pulmonary disease, and had settled on the former Elijah Smith Farm in 1899. Born in Wilmington, Delaware, in 1855, he attained a degree at Hamilton College and married his cousin, Mary. It was said that, in his younger days, he had been quite the ladies' man, and his wife entertained jealous thoughts about her husband that lingered well into old age.

Dr. Dean was, apparently, something of a night owl. He milked his cow at midnight, and would gaze up at the peaks of Mount Monadnock and Temple Mountain for hours at length. It was during these nocturnal ruminations that he began to notice odd lights, appearing at the tops of both peaks. As the First World War was, at that time, reaching fruition, he harbored suspicious thoughts about what might be transpiring.

He had good reason to be concerned;

The German ambassador Johann
Heinrich Graf von Bernstorff, who
was expelled from the United States in
1917, amid accusations of espionage.

in the last year alone, the Germany embassy in Washington had come under fire from Woodrow Wilson's administration, accused of fomenting sabotage and espionage. The ambassador, Johann Heinrich Graf von Bernstorff, and his two assistants, Captain Franz von Papen and Captain Karl Boy-Ed, a naval attaché, had been expelled from the country following various attacks, including the 1916 "Black Tom" explosion in Jersey City, New Jersey, where a large quantity of ammunition intended for use by the allies was destroyed.

Dr. Dean had built a large house on the property, which many of his neighbors considered somewhat ostentatious. As lean times transpired, however, he found the home to be somewhat too large for his wife and himself. Consequently, he decided to retire to a cottage at the bottom of the drive, and let out the large house to tenants. The couple that moved in, Mr. and Mrs. Laurence Colfelt, Jr., seemed, at first, to be an ideal fit; that, however, would soon change.

Colfelt was a quiet, secretive man, of unknown means. Some 20 years after these events, the writer Alice Lehtinen described

Image courtesy the Jaffrey Historical Society

Bert Ford, a reporter for The Boston
American, who covered the inquest of the
Dean murder in 1918.

him in her 1937 "History of Jaffrey:"

"The writer recalls Colfelt as a courteous man who was frequently seen on horse back on Old Peterborough Road, and sometimes assisted her mother in turning her horse and buggy around at a point beyond the Dean farm road, after taking her children part way to school. But he appeared to be a man of few words and rather mysterious. Shortly afterward Dr. Dean had asked the Colfelts to leave and they moved to Greenville, New Hampshire."

In retrospect, the chain of events appears ominously clear. According to author Jack Coey, von Bernstorff made a couple of visits to neighboring Dublin in 1916. Even more troubling is the revelation that the Department of Justice had information indicating that Colfelt was, in fact, von Bernstorff's illegitimate son.

Bert Ford, a reporter for the Boston American, covered the case at length during 1918, and offers considerable background information on the case. In his article, "Strange Night Riders Figure in Dr. Dean Tragedy," published on Friday, October 26, 1918, he describes the interest the Federal

Photograph by the author
The view of Mount Monadnock,
from the back of the Dean farm.
It was from here that the doctor
began to notice the strange lights.

authorities had in the case:

"If the German military lords overseas included the international bridge at Vanceboro in their war plotting, it is reasonable to deduct that a system of military signal lights from mountains in New England, visible to U-boats that could prowl at will in the darkness, with little fear of detection, was also part of their military machinations in this country.

"Monadnock Mountain is famous among mariners approaching the New England coast because it is the first land visible under the glass. Monadnock is also within easy vision to the naked eye of Wachusett Mountain in Massachusetts, from which flares and dot and dash lights attached to captive balloons could be handily relayed. Some of the lights used in the New Hampshire mountains that range around the Dean home were so powerful and vivid that the country folks first took them for heat lightning, but later discovered what they really were.

"Such lights as these flashed from mountain peak to mountain peak, and, when occasion demanded, relayed to

Image courtesy Jack Coey
Dr. Dean playing with his dogs, from a photograph in the Boston American.

points along Cape Cod on the south and Maine to the north, were easily visible to the German sea wolves lurking off shore under the convenient mantle of night.

"The Federal records show that suspicious lights were sighted at various points along Cape Cod and the New Hampshire and Maine coasts. The signals in the vicinity of East Jaffrey and Dublin, N.H., where many persons of German blood and pro-German sympathies reside, were complained of so persistently that squads of soldiers and plain clothes men hunted for them night after night without making a capture.

"But those who took part in these nocturnal hunts were satisfied beyond any doubt that the signals were operated for the benefit of the enemy. Another significant fact is that the Department of Justice agents were sent to that region on the strength of very plausible complaints many months before Dr. Dean was killed.

"Miss Mary Lee Ware of the Back Bay, with a Summer home at East Jaffrey, was so concerned about these lights that she spent much of her time and money investigating them with the aid of private detectives.

Image courtesy the Rindge Historical Society
Dr. Dean, riding in his sleigh,
about the time of the murder.

Her lawyer wrote a lengthy report concerning them. Mrs. Morison, another wealthy woman of Boston, also devoted much time to ferreting out German activities in that section, prompted like Miss Ware and Dr. Dean and all other loyal Americans solely by a spirit of patriotism to protect the lives of our troops in transports."

Throughout that summer, Dr. Dean noted the frequency of the lights had increased, and confided his suspicions to a few neighbors in cryptic terms. This, in itself, may have been somewhat unwise, as it apparently attracted the attention of the saboteurs. In June, he received a threatening letter in his rural mail delivery box, unsigned. This unnerved him to such a degree that he sought out help from the local police.

"About July 13, I met Dr. Dean in front of the post office," testified Officer Walter A. Lindsey at a deposition before Justice of the Peace Walter E. Merson. "He noticed my police badge and asked if I was still on the force, and I told him 'yes.' Then he said, 'I have lived on the farm for twenty-eight years and I have never been molested in any way, shape or manner, but

Photograph by the author

The Dean farm, as it
appears today.

if I should want police protection where would I telephone to?' And I said, 'Either to the police station, Duncan's (drug store) or Fred Stratton's Livery Stable.'"

As time drew on, Dr. Dean began to become more and more certain that his life was in danger. On the Sunday prior to his disappearance, he visited the home of Professor Benjamin L. Robinson, an instructor of botany at Harvard. During his visit, he started to tell about the signals, and fell suddenly quiet. "I must not burden you with my troubles," he simply stated, and fell quiet.

It was at this time that the Parmelee House, in Peterborough, was being converted into a hospital, and various fundraising events were being set up to help pay for the new facility. Mrs. Horace Morison volunteered to help with a sale, and set about the neighborhood, seeking donations. She ended up at the Dean farm, and began a somewhat troubling conversation with the doctor.

Dr. Dean confided in Mrs. Morison at length, implying that there was trouble coming. Her testimony, taken from newspaper accounts, was as follows:

DEAN BUNGALOW AT EAST JAFFREY, N. H., AND SCENE OF THE CRIME

It was in this bungalow on the hillside at East Jaffrey in which William K. Dean was living at the time he discovered the mysterious signals. The other picture shows the mouth of the cistern in which Dean's battered remains were found. The picture was taken shortly after the murder.

Image courtesy the Jaffrey Historical Society

A clipping from The Boston American, depicting the bungalow in which Mr. and Mrs. Dean resided, and the investigators on the scene on the morning after the murder.

"Dr. Dean said, 'could you show me where you saw them?' I said, 'yes, I can show you.' We walked to a large stone and stood there for a time. Dr. Dean turned and said, 'What do you know of the Colfelts? Have you met them?

"I said 'Yes, at the Golf Club last July, but I think, Dr. Dean, you know more about them than I do. Why did he leave to go to Greenville?' Dr. Dean said, 'I gave them 24 hours to get out. I am too good an American to have them in my place.'

"I said, 'What do you mean by that, Dr. Dean?' Dr. Dean said, 'Well, in the first place, (hesitating) a man like Colfelt, young and strong, who will not do useful work at this time is not the man I want on my place. I offered him my land to use for agricultural purposes. The rent I need. When are you going to Boston, Mrs. Morison?' He asked me this after we had walked a few steps.

"I said, 'Tomorrow, Dr. Dean. Tomorrow morning."

"He said, 'Will you go in and ask them to send the best men they have as soon as possible?'

"I said, 'I will, Dr. Dean.'

BARN WHERE MURDER OF DEAN OCCURRED

View of building in which Dr. William Kendrick Dean of East Jaffrey, N. H., met his death at the hands of a gang. The photo was taken from the cistern in which the body was found, showing distance it was carried by slayers.

MAY BORE INTO INTERIOR OF

Twenty Navy Women Urged for Jobs by Chaplain

DORCHESTER BOY BREAKS BONES STEALING RIDE

Image courtesy the Jaffrey Historical Society

A clipping from The Boston American, depicting the barn in which Dr. Dean was killed.

"Dr. Dean then said, 'I will come out to this stone at 12 tonight and if I see anything I will ring you up.' It was agreed to use a code message about turkeys. I said to Dr. Dean, 'Can't you tell me now, as it will save time?'

"Dr. Dean turned quietly and said, 'Mrs. Morison, you are a woman. What I know would be too dangerous for a woman to know.'

"I said, 'Why did you not take it to the authorities if you knew this?' He said, 'Well, in the first place, I can't leave my wife, and, in the second place, I want to make sure that I am right, and I am ready now.'

"We parted then, Dr. Dean having given me some books and a bronze statuette and a basket to raise funds for my sale to raise funds for the hospital. I left the next day (on the 8:30 a.m. train) for Boston where I placed the request before Mr. Giffort at the headquarters of the Department of Justice at No. 45 Milk Street."

Actually, Mrs. Morison was fully conversant with the entire situation. In April of that year, three Department of Justice agents, Nathaniel Nash, Harry Marshall and Martin Hare, arrived in Peterborough

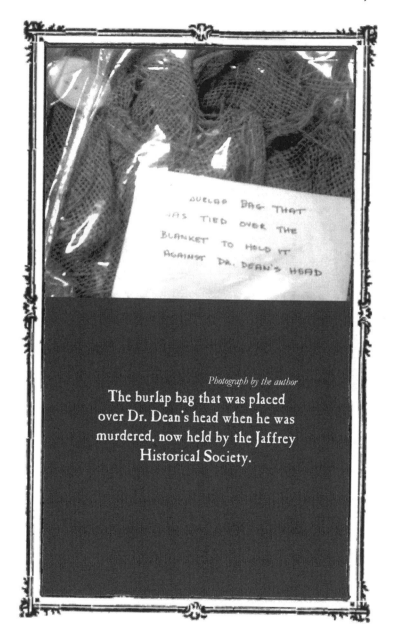

Photograph by the author

The burlap bag that was placed
over Dr. Dean's head when he was
murdered, now held by the Jaffrey
Historical Society.

to check out the goings-on. They decided to stay at the Tavern in that town, and started to look for the lights. One night, after a fruitless sentinel on Moore's Field, they met up with Mrs. Morison. Harry Marshall recounts the event in his report of April 26:

"On the way back we noted that Mrs. Morison had arrived at her farm, and as Agent Nash said that if we did not let her know our whereabouts, she might arouse suspicion by trying to locate us at the Tavern. We stopped and talked to her for a few minutes. She claims that this being the full moon and also the end of the week, the lights are almost certain to 'work,' during the next two or three nights. She was very anxious for one of us to stay at her house, and as her house is an excellent point of observation, for any lights that might appear on Pack Monadnock Mountain, it was arranged that Agent Marshall would spend the weekend at her farm."

The night before she was to leave for Boston, Mrs. Morison stood outside, and watched for the lights. She waited for Dr. Dean to call, but in vain. She was not to

E NIGHT RIDERS FIGU

This is the house which crowns the high hill at East Jaffrey and which Dr. Dean let to a named Kollets, said to be Germans. The doctor ordered them to leave the premises shor fore he was murdered, because, he is quoted, he "was too much an American to have t his house."

Image courtesy the Jaffrey Historical Society

A clipping from The Boston American, showing the Dean house as it looked in 1918.

find out what had become of him until the next morning.

Even as Dr. Dean was communicating his suspicions to the authorities, cryptically complaining that "two-legged foxes" had stolen the turkeys in his barn, the spy ring that was already at work was aware of his intentions, determined that he would never divulge what he knew.

Mary Dean was, by this point, allegedly suffering from some form of dementia, and was excessively frail. Consequently, Dr. Dean was intent on shielding her from the unfolding situation. On the night of August 13, he visited his neighbors, Mr. and Mrs. Charles L. Rich, returning about 9:30 p.m., and went out to milk his cow at about 11 p.m. What happened then is a matter of public record. It would appear that a car drove up the road adjacent to the Dean farm road somewhere prior to 11 p.m., and a group of people made their way through the woods, accosting Dr. Dean outside his barn. Bert Ford takes up the tale:

"Dr. Dean was struck in the left temple by an implement which left three marks, triangular in shape. It is thought that before

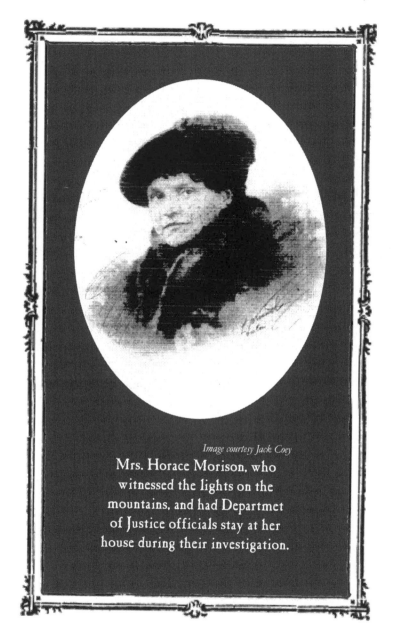

Image courtesy Jack Coey

Mrs. Horace Morison, who
witnessed the lights on the
mountains, and had Departmet
of Justice officials stay at her
house during their investigation.

the blow was struck he may have had time to attempt to defend himself, because he had sufficient spirit and agility. It is thought that he struck one of the assailants with his fist.

"The blow from the weapon used, however, while not sufficiently powerful to cause instant death, was powerful enough to render the victim insensible. The murderers next looped a convenient halter rope around his neck twice and someone from behind drew the loose end so tightly that Dr. Dean strangled to death. The rope was drawn so powerfully that it cut into the flesh of the neck and snapped the vertebrae.

"The man who did the garroting did not find it necessary to tie the ends of the halter which was left around the neck. A light-weight horse blanket was bound around the bleeding head and fastened with a lighter rope which resembled window cord. A rock which was later found to weigh 27½ pounds was placed over the blanket and then the bran sack was drawn over the rock and turbaned head.

"All this took time and strength and many fingers.

"Dr. Dean's hands were clenched when

Photograph by the author

The bloodstained floorboards
from the barn, now held by the
Jaffrey Historical Society.

he died. They were tied behind his back. Rope was bound around his knees and ankles. He resembled a hapless mummy when they dumped him into the twelve-foot cistern which was half-filled with water.

"It took at least two men to carry the body. The shrouding and weighting might have been done beside the cistern, but it isn't logical to think so with the light of a lantern and the seclusion of the barn handy and plenty of strong hands to do the carrying."

By all accounts, the investigation was a complete botch. Numerous people were permitted to wander about the yard, obliterating any footprints that might have indicated how the murder was committed, and the body disposed. At the time, there was some speculation that Mary may have killed her husband; that, however, was quickly dispelled, as she weighed under 100 pounds, and there was no way she could have carried the body from the barn to the cistern. Again, from Mr. Ford:

"Dr. Dean used the side or porch side door and everything indicates that he was attacked inside that entrance. It was an

Photograph courtesy The Jaffrey Historical Society

Charles L. Rich, the Jaffrey banker who
was initially suspected in the murder of
Dr. Dean.

oppressively hot night and the moon had been bright until about 11. The only person to consider on the premises, and the light in the bungalow, where she awaited the return of her husband shone, a safe distance of 150 or 200 feet away.

"While they obviously did not dread interference from Mrs. Dean, they were cautious enough not to drop the body in the large well next to the bungalow. Carried further, that degree of caution would have induced them to bundle up the victim under the light of his own lantern in the barn. A light in the field might be seen by Mrs. Dean.

"Hence it is fair to deduct that the killing took place just inside the door where the blood marks were found. Nimble use of the horse blanket and burlap bag prevented much of a blood trail. But there were marks and spatters on the barn floor and door and blood daubs on the door knob which were almost obliterated before finger prints were taken. This was a serious oversight.

"It was also wrong of the authorities to permit R. B. Henchman, the town postmaster, to clean up the barn that day. Henchman

Photograph by the author

Robert Deschenes, the current owner of
the Dean farm.

is the brother of Miss Susan Henchman, assistant cashier of the local bank of which Charles L. Rich is the cashier.

"The cleaning of the barn incensed the selectmen and the majority of the citizens of East Jaffrey. Robert Hamil, who has a garage and blacksmith shop near the railroad station, says the Federal authorities found a footprint of blood on the barn floor which he sawed out for them as an exhibit later on. Government agents used Hamil's automobiles a great deal.

"There were small bloodstains on the porch and larger stains in the grass, indicating that the shrouded body may have been placed on the grass a brief time, the murders probably feeling that the dripping would be absorbed by the soil and be less likely to show. But there was not a great amount of blood anywhere."

The interference of the crime scene by Mr. Henchman undoubtedly irked the Federal authorities, and suspicion fell upon Charles L. Rich, cashier of the Monadnock National Bank. He showed up at work the morning after the murder with a black eye and a laceration on his cheek, injuries he

Photograph by the author
The calendar from the Dean farm. Dr.
Dean's wife, Mary, has circled the 13th,
and notated it with the words, "Billie die."

attributed to being kicked in the face by his horse the night before.

Dr. Dean had been visiting the Rich family on the night of his murder, and the banker was the last man to see him alive. Evidence produced after the autopsy also indicated that the currant buns Dr. Dean had eaten at lunch were not completely digested, complicating the timeline of Rich's alibi. This from Bert Ford:

"If Dr. Dean had lived until midnight he would have returned to his bungalow to telephone Mrs. Morison as planned. He went to the barn at 11 o'clock, according to Mrs. Dean's statements to all who arrived on the premises on the morning after the tragedy, and these statements by the widow, in the excitement of that day, for one with an impaired mind, are convincingly consistent.

"It is difficult to fix the time by the condition of the stomach contents, but it would appear that Dr. Dean was killed about 11:15, and that he returned earlier than Mr. and Mrs. Rich claimed he left their home, possibly in the vicinity of 10 o'clock or soon after, as Mrs. Dean claimed. She insisted that he came home about 9:30

Photograph by the author
Dr. Dean's sleigh and coat, preserved at the
Rindge Historical Society.

while living with Pastor Enslin after the tragedy for a year before her death."

Lines of loyalty were quickly drawn throughout the tiny community, and the people of Jaffrey were split over their opinions on the case. According to Jack Coey, the Masons may have been involved in the murder and its subsequent cover-up, as a secret meeting was held on March 22, 1919, between County Solicitor Roy Pickard of Keene and the Masons of East Jaffrey. As a result of this meeting, John Bartlett, the Governor of New Hampshire, ordered a Grand Jury investigation, which was held from April 11 to April 22 of that year. He also throws doubt on Rich's alibi, stating that the whereabouts of Rich's horse may be in question. Apparently, a night watchman saw the horse at about 9:00 that night, meaning he wasn't in the barn in time to kick his owner in the face.

The Dean farm still stands in East Jaffrey, though changed significantly from the palatial structure seen in old photos. The porch and veranda have been removed, and the mountains, which would have been clearly visible from the house, have been

Image courtesy Jack Coey

Mary Dean, photographed about
the time of her husband's murder,
in a photograph published by the
Boston American.

all but obscured by new tree growth. The barn where Dr. Dean was murdered has also been demolished, and all that remains is a cellar hole, bordered by huge boulders.

Robert Deschenes, the current owner of the property, was all too happy to show the author around the farm, and point out just where the tragic events took place.

"If there was something to be investigated, it just wasn't or it was investigated in the wrong way," said Deschenes. "There was a torrential rain the day after the murder, and it washed away a lot of the evidence. Furthermore, the first people here were the selectmen and the postman, and they were tampering with the site. On top of that, a tool believed to be the murder weapon disappeared in Boston, before the trial."

The cistern where the body was found is now concealed by a concrete slab, but Deschenes said that, at the time, it was covered with a wooden lid. He explained that the vessel, some 12 feet deep, ballooned out toward the bottom, allowing ample room to hide the body.

Mrs. Dean had been the only person on the property at the time of the murder, but,

Photograph by the author
The bloody doorknob
from the barn, where Dr.
Dean was murdered.

as a witness, she was pretty much useless.

"She had some sort of dementia," Deschenes explained. "She just kept on saying, 'my Billie's in the water. My Billie's in the water.' She had a fear of water herself, and probably thought he'd fallen into the swamp behind the house. It's sort of ironic, the way it turned out."

The repercussions in the community were devastating. The town split along socioeconomic lines, with the largely Catholic working-class people suspecting their rich – and primarily Protestant – employers of being involved in the cover-up. Charles Rich, in particular, was singled out as being one of the possible perpetrators.

"My father remembered that, when he was a boy, there was a lot of distrust around Rich," said Deschenes. "He said that they just wouldn't walk on the same side of the street as him, and when they saw him coming, they would cross the road. It was amazing that there was so much fear in the town at that time."

The rift in the community would not be healed for over a generation. The verdict in the murder was that it was commit-

Photograph by the author
The cover of the cistern
in which Dr. Dean's body
was discovered.

ted by a person or persons unknown. Dr. Dean's sleigh and fur coat were acquired by Mary Ware, who in turn donated them to the Rindge Historical Society. The items are still there, in a shed adjoining the building. The evidence of the case still sits in a box in the Jaffrey Historical Society – the rope that bound the doctor, the burlap bag that was put over his head, portions of the bloodstained barn floor. These are grim reminders of a crime that tore apart a small town, nearly a century ago.

Photograph by the author

Haunted Lake, in Francestown.

MEMENTO MORI

Haunted Lake

FRANCESTOWN

The small village of Francestown is the epitome of New England charm. Founded in the early 18th century, its stately homes bespeak centuries of genteel living. The center of the village has the ubiquitous white church and meeting house, and the general store has been serving the community for the last 200 years or so.

All is not what it seems, however. Like many of these Yankee towns, Francestown has a dark side – an ominous body of water known as Haunted Lake.

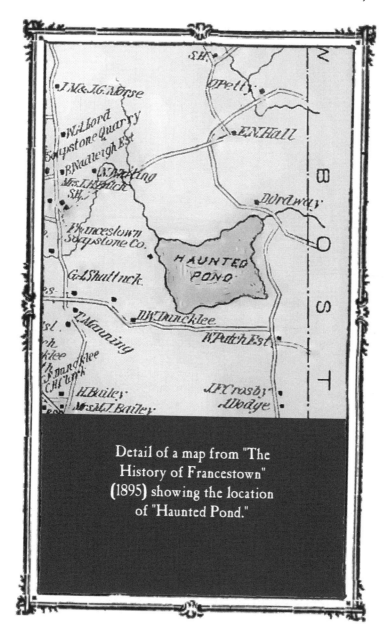

Detail of a map from "The
History of Francestown"
(1895) showing the location
of "Haunted Pond."

As lakes go, it's not particularly large — just shy of a mile in length, and five-sixths of a mile in width. Reportedly, it's also quite shallow. That doesn't mean, however, that it doesn't have a nasty reputation, and a number of people have met their premature ends in its waters.

The history of how the lake got its sobriquet is a little clouded, and several tales have come up that would account for it. Apparently, it has always been known as "Haunted Pond" or "Haunted Lake" right back when the village was originally founded. One explanation is that there was once a fire that raged on its shores that was so fierce that everything along the perimeter was consumed. All that was left was a black, twisted mess of branches and trees, the skeletal remains of the forest that once thrived there. It left such an impression on the early surveyors that they attributed supernatural ramifications to the area.

The lake is fed by a number of small streams, among them Whiting Brook. For an in-depth explanation of the topography of the area, we turn to "The History of Francestown, N.H. From Its Earliest

Photograph by the author
Part of the remaining dam of the Scoby
Mill, on the shore of Haunted Lake.

Settlement April 1758 to 1891," by Warren Robert Coltrain and George K. Wood:

"Whiting Brook, which empties into Scoby Pond, or 'Haunted Lake,' on the north, rises near Weare line, is about three miles long, flows nearly south, has at one place a broken fall, somewhat remarkable, of 15 feet, has broad pools of clear water, like the White Mountain streams, and, after having crossed the New Boston road and received the Pettee Brook, it really becomes quite a pretentious stream, cutting a wide channel through the meadows. For a quarter of a mile before entering the Lake, it is deep, dark, sluggish, over-hung with banks, and resembles a small Florida creek, alligators and cypress excepted. And for this distance the fisherman rows his boat up the stream, and counts it a favorite place to drop the line. There are no mills on this stream, and it has been noted for suckers in spring and trout in summer."

The lake itself appears to be a remnant of the ice age, an indentation left by retreating glaciers. Coltrain and Wood make specific notes as to its geography:

"Haunted Lake has been described as

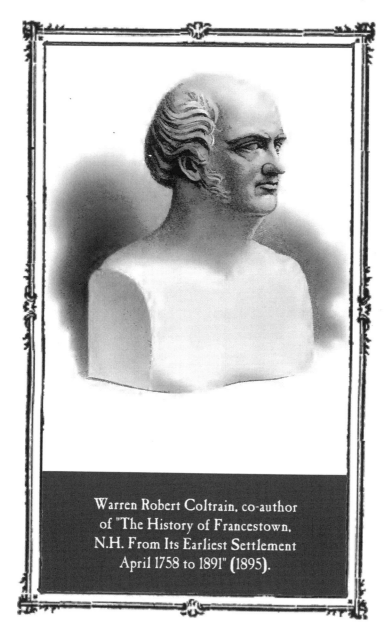

Warren Robert Coltrain, co-author
of "The History of Francestown,
N.H. From Its Earliest Settlement
April 1758 to 1891" (1895).

'circular in form,' but recent surveys have made its map outline look more like a parallelogram. It is nearly a mile in length (east and west), and nearly five-sixths of a mile in width. It is spoken of as 'rather shallow.' No doubt in distant years the water was much deeper than now, and higher water then for ages may account for certain peculiarities of its banks as they appear now. The high dike-like deposit on the west side has been called 'a lateral Moraine of the glacier period.' On the north side there is a portion of what appears like the same moraine which has been described as a dike or 'bar 20 rods long, six feet high, and three or four feet thick,' and also parts of the same appear on the east bank. To many of us this 'moraine' explanation is open to doubt, as is any other yet advanced. This is not the place to discuss the matter ; but the student of nature may find many things remarkable and suggestive in the environments of Haunted Lake."

Two early legends associated with the lake illustrate the fear that it held for local residents. In about 1741, two young men arrived at Francestown from Hillsborough,

Photograph by the author

View from the shore of Haunted Lake.

intending to buy land around the lake. Although they had left separately, they met with each other in the forest, and decided to travel together, having the same destination.

Somewhere along the way, however, the relationship between the men seemed to have soured, and an altercation erupted. One of the men ended up killing the other, and deposited him in a shallow grave covered with tree branches. The story is that the man's spirit never rested, and can be heard crying and moaning as he desperately tries to make his way out of the forest.

Another tale of violence concerns two hunters from Dunstable, Massachusetts, who determined to try their luck around the lake. Setting up camp west of the Great Meadows in New Boston, they settled into a routine of setting their traps each morning, which they located around the bank of the lake and headed up to the south branch of the Piscataquog River. They would take the rounds in turn, meeting up at camp about noon. Coltrain and Wood take up the story:

"One day one of them did not return, and after waiting till satisfied there was trou-

The grave of the Hon. Matthew Patten,
in the Old Bedford Cemetery. Patten was
the first man to survey Haunted Lake, and
personally encountered its spirits.

ble, the other started on his companion's route, and near this water was startled by the growl of a wild beast, and saw only a few feet ahead a huge catamount standing over the dead and torn body of his comrade. He loaded his gun and shot the savage beast, and then buried his friend as well as he could, and returned to camp. Knowing these savage animals roamed the forest in pairs, and as they were dreaded by all hunters, he returned the next day to Dunstable."

In 1753, the Hon. Matthew Patten, of Bedford, proceeded to make a complete survey of the pond. This project would take several days, and his group was obliged to camp on the shore of the lake. They got more than they bargained for, as the supernatural manifestations for which the area is known began to assert themselves. This from Coltrain and Wood:

"At the time of this incident, whether in 1753 or a little earlier, Patten and his two chainmen, with their assistants, encamped for the night near the outlet of the Pond. Soon after darkness set in, there commenced groanings and shrieks as of a human being in distress, and these contin-

Photograph by the author
The remains of the Scoby Mill,
on the shore of Haunted Lake.

ued, most plaintive and affecting, till nearly morning. These chainmen were hardy fellows not accustomed to fear the face of man, but they had some superstition, and some alarm at 'signs' and 'bad omens,' and they could not be persuaded to continue their work, even for an hour. They started at once, in the morning, for their home in Bedford. This event, of course, confirmed previous rumors that the place was 'haunted.' and established the name, 'Haunted Pond.' For more than a generation it was known by no other name."

The lake's reputation didn't deter David Scoby, an immigrant from Belfast, Ireland, from setting up a sawmill on the banks of the river, in 1780. While digging the foundation of the mill, the workmen were horrified to discover the skeleton of a young man, buried in a shallow grave. This event cemented the lake's legend in the minds of the local population, but Scoby went ahead and built the mill anyway. He operated the business on the site until his death in 1834, upon which it fell to one Daniel Fuller, who ran the business until 1860, whereupon the site was abandoned.

Photograph by the author

Some of the dense underbrush that
surrounds the shore of Haunted Lake.

Along the way, the lake continued to take in more victims. The first was a 12-year-old boy named Jacob Langdell, who was drowned on July 11, 1813. When the body was discovered, a bunch of lilies were found to be clasped in his hand.

Over the years, more bodies were dredged from the lake. A boy by the name of Samuel Allen perished in its waters in 1816; Ichabod Gay followed him to a watery grave on June 20, 1824; and one Nathaniel Aiken shared his fate in 1830.

Francestown is a quiet place, and the young people of the community were understandably desperate for diversion. Accordingly, in the early 19th century, Scoby's sons took note of the reputation of haunted lake, and decided to use it for their own amusements. As any haunted area is likely to have its share of amateur ghost hunters, the Scoby boys were determined that they would not go away disappointed. Again, Coltrain and Wood take up the tale:

"Another tradition is that the 'Scoby Boys' were given to frightening certain 'liquor-laden loafers,' who, having imbibed enough to put the mind into a very medita-

HISTORY

······OF······

FRANCESTOWN, N. H.

From its Earliest Settlement April, 1758
to January 1, 1891.

WITH A BRIEF

GENEALOGICAL RECORD

OF ALL THE FRANCESTOWN FAMILIES.

By REV. W. R. COCHRANE, D. D.
OF ANTRIM, N. H.

——AND——

GEORGE K. WOOD, Esq.
OF FRANCESTOWN.

PUBLISHED BY THE TOWN.

NASHUA, N. H.:
JAMES H. BARKER: PRINTER.
1895.

Title page of "The History of Francestown, N.H.
From Its Earliest Settlement April 1758 to 1891,"
by Warren Robert Coltrain and George K. Wood.

tive and susceptible state, were accustomed to pass by the 'dark shades and weird waste of bog-land and water' adjacent, in the 'wee sma' hours,' and were 'helped' to see various 'ghosts' and 'visions' that were both real and 'unco wild.' And no doubt this also had a basis of fact, the state of mind of these belated travelers, and the cunning of the 'Boys,' combining to set afloat various 'dreadful representations of dreadful things,' so that timid people became half-afraid to pass that way even in clear sunlight. Many people fully believed the whole vicinity to be 'haunted.' But this tradition, after all, does not account for the name, since this was known as 'Haunted Pond' long before there were any 'Scoby Boys' in this vicinity. They only took advantage of the well-known name to help them carry out their 'dreadful' jokes!"

A recent expedition to Haunted Lake revealed that the ruins of the Scoby Mill still stand on the lake's shore. I had decided to make this trip on a particularly wet and dreary October day, and discovered how treacherous the shoreline can be, filled with fallen trees and wet leaves. The channel lead-

Photograph by the author

The dam that marks the spot of David Scoby's sawmill, on the shore of Haunted Lake.

ing upstream from the mill is almost dry, a huge beaver dam having cut off the outflow stream. Consequently, the water level is very high, breaching the banks in several places.

Haunted Lake certainly lives up to its name; desolate, dark and foreboding, one can almost hear the cries and moans of its many victims, as they cry for release from their earthly bonds.

Photograph by the author

The Freeborn Stearns House, in
Rindge, as it looks today. It is
presently the headquarters of the
Rindge Historical Society.

MEMENTO MORI

The Freeborn Stearns House

RINDGE

Just off the center of Rindge, on School Street, there stands an inconspicuous-looking house, with asbestos siding slowly deteriorating on its exterior. It's the kind of house that you wouldn't look at twice – unless you knew its history.

This is the Freeborn Stearns House, which dates back to about 1815. Since 1994, it has been the home of The Rindge Historical Society. Although the house is a Colonial, it was extensively renovated

Photograph courtesy The Rindge Historical Society
The Freeborn Stearns House, as it
looked at the turn of the 19th century.

in the mid-19th century, and most of the original aspects have been covered over.

According to the people who work there, however, some of the older residents may still be present – albeit in spirit form.

Captain Joel Raymond bought this land from Benjamin Bancroft in 1779. Raymond came to Rindge early in his life, marrying Mary Ball, of Holden, Massachusetts. He quickly became notable as a farmer, merchant, and proprietor of extensive tracts of land.

Although he built the house himself, he did not tarry long; in 1810 he sold the entire property to Captain Freeborn Stearns, a blacksmith, farmer and sexton of the town. A love for the ironwork seemed to run in the family; four of his sons, as well as one grandson, took up the trade.

The Stearns family held onto the property for the next century, before selling it to the Hoyt family.

The house was again sold in the 1940s, to Frank "Pop" Allen and his wife, Hazel. By all accounts, "Pop" was an extremely extroverted individual, serving as Selectman in the late 1960s, later becoming

Photograph by the author

Linda Bussiere, curator of the Rindge
Historical Society Museum, in one of the
more active rooms in the house.

Town Moderator. In 1975, he suffered a fatal heart attack while in the house, and his ashes were reportedly scattered in the back yard. His wife inherited the property, eventually selling it to the historical society.

"It was the pipe smoke that we noticed first," said Linda Bussiere, curator for the historical society museum. "My son was doing some work here when we first moved in, and he said, 'mom, I can't work up there. The smell of pipe tobacco is just too strong.' Now, it's said that 'Pop' was a constant pipe smoker, so I had an idea that was him. I said this to a few people, and they just told me that I couldn't wish for a nicer ghost."

It seems like "Pop" was just checking out the house, as items were being brought in to furnish the museum. After a while, Bussiere said, Allen's spirit seemed to just fade away. Something else, however, had come to take its place. Something not quite as friendly.

"I've heard that sometimes spirits can become attached to particular objects," Bussiere said. "So I guess it's possible that we brought something into the house with

Photograph by the author

One of the upstairs rooms in the Freeborn Stearns House. The chandelier in this photograph has been known to move of its own accord.

one of the artifacts."

Almost immediately, weird things began to happen. Staff members started hearing footsteps and voices coming from the upstairs rooms, and the neighbors reported seeing shadows moving behind the windows.

"I was in a room adjacent to the downstairs hallway, and I could hear someone calling 'Nora' or 'Dora,' clear as a bell," said Bussiere. "We originally had our office in the downstairs kitchen, and the door kept opening and closing – 'bang, bang, bang – well, I was just terrified, and ran out of there."

These events scared Bussiere to the point where she refused to come in after nightfall. As time went on, the paranormal events began to escalate.

"We had some old dresses, neatly folded and stacked on top of the showcases," said Bussiere. "I came in one day, and the whole lot had been taken off, and thrown violently around the floor. Now, I know that none of the volunteers here would have done that."

Tim Derr, president of the historical

Photograph by the author

A rocking chair in the upstairs of the
Freeborn Stearns House, which has
been seen to rock by itself.

society and a member of the East Coast Transcommunication Organization, has also experienced more than his share of psychic phenomena at the house, particularly in the upstairs area. Remote cameras recorded light switches turning on and off by themselves, and "Pop" Allen's pipe smoke permeated the building.

"We got a lot of strong energy in the room with the ladies' clothing," he said. "I was using my dowsing rods in there, when, suddenly, the chandelier started to rock back and forth. It wasn't just a little rocking – that thing was really moving. At the same time, my dowsing rod started spinning around in circles. I could feel the energy moving up through my arms and my shoulders, and it got so strong that I just had to leave the room."

This bizarre behavior doesn't restrict itself to the chandelier, however; in adjoining rooms, a rocking chair and a cradle have also been seen to move of their own volition.

Other investigators have shown an interest in the house and its lively ghosts, according to Bussiere.

"It's very strong in the corridor adja-

Photograph courtesy The Rindge Historical Society

The office of the Rindge Historical
Society, in the upstairs of the Freeborn
Stearns House. Note the mist which
seems to emanate from the left side of
the photograph.

cent to the office," she said. I always get the creeps up there. The first investigators we had were two ladies and a young man, who were interested in the place. They didn't have any sophisticated equipment – just a regular camera.

"Anyway, they started taking photos in the corridor, and, when the photos were developed, a mist showed up at the door at the end of the corridor. It moved through the room and formed into the shape of a person before disappearing."

Derr also experienced some odd events in this area of the house during his four-hour investigation.

"The air in that corridor was very heavy," he said. "There was kind of a mist in there, which made it very difficult to breathe.

"That was when we entered the office, which was very muggy and still. The temperature in there must have been in the eighties. I started pendulum dowsing in the room, and contacted the spirit of Hazel Allen, and began asking her questions. Suddenly, the temperature dropped about 20 degrees, and two of the investigators could feel a sensation of something brush-

Photograph by the author

A crib in the upstairs of the Freeborn
Stearns House, which has been known
to move of its own volition.

ing across their faces."

The team began to make their way out of the room, but the ghosts weren't quite finished with them yet.

"As we started to go downstairs, I was walking down the corridor, and three or four heavy books literally launched themselves out of the second shelf of the bookcase and flew across the room," Derr said.

According to witnesses, most of the events take place on the second floor of the building. There are, however, the odd events on the first story as well.

"I went into the house to investigate water problems we were having in the building," Derr said, "and I could clearly hear children singing and playing in an adjoining room. When I went in there, however, the sound just stopped."

According to Bussiere and Derr, the house continues to be an active hotspot of ghostly activity, even attracting the attention of the neighbors.

"The lady across the road said she can see the lights going on and off in the house, when there's nobody in there," Bussiere said. "Occasionally, shadows will flicker

Photograph by the author

An upstairs corridor of the Freeborn Stearns
House. A number of strange events have occurred
in this area, including unexplained mists, and
books flying off the shelves.

across the windows, as though someone is walking from room to room."

This part of Rindge has been no stranger to odd events over the years. In the 19th century, there was a tavern adjacent to the Freeborn Stearns House, at which a particularly intoxicated customer showed up for a drink. As the bartender refused to serve him, he went back to his carriage, and grabbed his horsewhip. Returning to the taproom, he proceeded to beat the bartender to death with it.

There was another strange occurence in 1861, when the Sixth New Hampshire Volunteer Infantry was being mustered to see action in the Civil War. As they prepared to leave on December 14th, a ceremony was being held at the Meeting House just a stone's throw from the farm. Presiding was Stephen B. Sherwin, a highly respected member of the community. As a ceremonial sword was being presented to Captain Ebenezer Converse, Sherwin suffered a fatal heart attack, and died on the spot.

Despite all of these phantasmagorical events, the Rindge Historical Society has no intention of giving up their home.

Photograph by the author

The barn on the Freeborn
Stearns House. According to
reports, the door has been seen
moving back and forth.

Indeed, over the years, they seem to have taken all of it in stride.

"When I was talking to the spirit of Hazel Allen, she was telling me of positive experiences she had in the house," Derr said. "We generally have the impression that ghosts are related to tragedies, but that isn't always so. I think the people who lived there liked it so much that they just didn't want to leave. So, in a way, the house itself is a conduit for this kind of energy."

For her part, however, Bussiere still makes sure that she isn't alone in the house after dark.

Photograph by the author
The site of Levi Haskell's farm,
as it looks today. The large
porch in the front of the building
marks the spot where the barn
once stood.

MEMENTO MORI

Bones in the Barn

TROY

I t is a frequent truth that many folk stories and legends have at least some grain of truth in them. Tales that have been passed down throughout the years might suddenly gain credibility, as new evidence comes to light. In this instance, I'm thinking of the story of the haunted barn in Troy, which had excited the attention of the locals ever since a stranger had disappeared in that vicinity in 1804, and foul play was suspected.

The grave of Dr. Abiel Moore
Caverly, in Pittsford, Vermont.

At this time, Troy had yet to be established as a town. The village, which straddled the border of Marlborough and Fitzwilliam, had grown considerably at the close of the 18th century, and most business dealings were being conducted within its immediate vicinity. Additionally, the area being quite hilly, the occupants found it difficult to deal with municipal affairs in the centers of the two towns. Plans for a new meeting house had been in the works since at least 1794, but it wasn't until 1815 that the new town was actually incorporated.

The barn in question had once belonged to one Levi Haskell, who had lived on the property for many years. There was a common notion among the people of the town that the barn was the residence of a ghost, some murder having been done there in the past. So pronounced were these beliefs that they were taken note of by Dr. Abiel Moore Caverly in his "An Historical Sketch of Troy and her inhabitants, from the first settlement of the town in 1764, to 1855" (1859), where he says, "it appears that the opinion had long prevailed, to some extent, that human blood

AN

HISTORICAL SKETCH

OF

TROY,

AND HER INHABITANTS,

FROM

THE FIRST SETTLEMENT OF THE TOWN.

IN

1764, TO 1855.

BY A. M. CAVERLY, M. D.

" Vado, age, et ingentem factis for ad æthera Trojam."   VIRG.

KEENE:
PRINTED AT THE N. H. SENTINEL OFFICE.
1859.

The frontspiece of ""An Historical Sketch of Troy and her inhabitants, from the first settlement of the town in 1764, to 1855" (1859) by Dr. Abiel Moore Caverly

had been shed upon those premises; and it had been currently reported that there had been seen, in and about the barn, many marvellous phenomena which were considered indicative of the commission of a horrid crime. Many of these phenomena were substantiated by men whose veracity we should hardly dare question; but we have a very imperfect idea of the various phantoms to which the imagination under certain circumstances will give birth."

A series of curious events in the winter of 1818 brought these stories into sharp focus, and lay bare the site of a horrendous crime. At that point, a fellow by the name of Aaron Holt was in residence at the farm, and his son had taken ill. Deacon Samuel Griffin rode up to the farm from Fitzwilliam, with intention of looking after the sick boy. When he arrived, Holt's other son, Joel, came out of the house with a lantern, so they could put up the Deacon's horse in the barn. Well, somebody got a little careless with the lantern, and, in no time flat, the whole barn was fully engulfed in flames.

When the fire died down, and the site

TOWN HALL, TROY

Troy Town Hall, from "An Historical Sketch of Troy and her inhabitants, from the first settlement of the town in 1764, to 1855" (1859) by Dr. Abiel Moore Caverly

was inspected, onlookers discovered a small mound of earth, under the floor of the haymow. This was dug out, and a number of bones were discovered within. At first, nobody was sure if the bones were human or animal, as they were largely incinerated in the fire. Many members of the community had their own ideas, however, as they recalled the story of a man who had disappeared in the area some 14 years earlier. Accusations began to fly in the small community, and the Selectmen were obliged to issue a public statement, in order to keep the general peace. It ran as follows:

"A SUPPOSED MURDER.

"We the undersigned Selectmen of the town of Troy, county of Cheshire, State of New-Hampshire, hereby certify, that on the 3d of January 1818, a barn in this town was accidentally burnt;—that a few days after there was discovered the evident appearance of the remains of a full grown human body, laying on a board, slightly covered with sand, under the place of the floor of the hay mow. This appearance was examined, and bones found,

Photograph by the author

The Village Cemetery in Troy, just
down the road from wherre Levi
Haskell's farm once stood.

which were, by those present, judged to
be human; though they were so affected
by time, and the intense heat of the fire,
that their original form was not entire, nor
were they capable of being arranged in due
order by the anatomist. It is the current
opinion of people in this town and vicinity,
that these are the remains of a man, whose
death was occasioned by unlawful means,
and whose body was concealed in that
place; and many circumstances are called
to mind, which go far towards strengthen-
ing this opinion. About fourteen years ago,
it is very generally recollected that inquiry
was made after a stranger of whom it was
said, that the last which was seen or heard
of him was in this town; but his name
and place of residence, and those of his
friends, who were in search of him, are not
recollected. The undersigned request that
printers of newspapers, throughout the
United States would be so good as to pub-
lish this, as soon as convenient; and also
that any people who can give any information respecting a person, who was missing,
or supposed to be murdered, in or near this
town, previous to the time said barn was

Image courtesy Troy Historical Society
A painting of the center
of Troy, as it appeared
in 1895.

burnt, would, without delay, forward to us such information, that all possible means to detect, and bring to justice the perpetrators of the supposed horrid deed may be speedily employed. (Signed) SYLVESTER P. FLINT, DANIEL W. FARRAR, GEORGE FARRAR."

The notice had the desired effect, and, about one year later, a man by the name of Joseph Nimblet, of Woodstock, Vermont, appeared in town and testified that his brother-in-law, Seth Lucus, had left Provincetown, Massachusetts, heading for Woodstock, with the object of buying a farm.

According to Nimblet, Lucus had a large quantity of money on his person intended for this purpose, and was an easy target for would-be thieves. The last anybody ever heard of him was when he arrived in Marlborough, and stayed at a hotel owned by Christopher Harris. At this point, it appeared, he took up company with two local men, Levi Haskell and Jonathan Lawrence, Jr. Haskell apparently told Lucus that his own farm was up for sale, and suggested that they go and look over the property. Lucus agreed, and accompa-

An aerial shot of Troy, as depicted in a 19th century postcard.

nied them out of the hotel. That was the last time anybody saw Lucus alive.

Haskell and Lawrence were promptly arrested on this evidence, and, on January 11, 1819, they were questioned at the Town House by Elijah Dunbar, of Keene. The prosecuting attorney was James Willson, while Joel Parker represented the prisoners. It was noted at this inquest that, following Lucus' disappearance, Haskell was suddenly in possession of a large quantity of cash for which he could not readily account.

As a result of this examination, Haskell was imprisoned, while Lawrence was ordered to appear at the next Supreme Court, where he would testify on behalf of the state.

Haskell remained in prison for the next five months before his trial in front of the grand jury, in Charlestown. Upon examination of the evidence, however, the Attorney General decided that there wasn't enough evidence to hold the man, and he was subsequently released.

And that, apparently, was that. Although the townspeople were determined that Haskell and Lawrence were the culprits,

Photograph by the author

**The Village Cemetery, in
Troy, looking in the direction
of Levi Haskell's farm.**

they had been exonerated in a court of law. This cloud of suspicion hung over Haskell for the rest of his life, hounding him to his death, which came on November 22, 1830. The crime remains unsolved to this day, and the murderer of Seth Lucus has never been brought to light.

Made in the USA
Columbia, SC
01 December 2018

WHAT WOULD HAVE HAPPENED IN THE PAST TWENTY-ODD YEARS—

If someone had been there to stop Lee Harvey Oswald from getting his shots off from the roof of the Texas School Book Depository in Dallas?

If John F. Kennedy had had a chance to live and continue on as President of the United States?

If the course of history in America and the entire world had not been so suddenly and savagely altered on that unforgettable and unforgivable 1963 November day?

This is your chance to find out . . . if you have the nerve. . . .

A TIME TO REMEMBER

"Elegantly suspenseful, gracefully written . . . a breezily entertaining tale of time travel gone amok."   —*The Philadelphia Inquirer*

(For more memorable reviews, please turn page . . .)

A TIME TO REMEMBER

STANLEY SHAPIRO

A SIGNET BOOK

NEW AMERICAN LIBRARY

SIGNET TRADEMARK REG. U.S. PAT. OFF. AND FOREIGN COUNTRIES
REGISTERED TRADEMARK—MARCA REGISTRADA
HECHO EN CHICAGO, U.S.A.

SIGNET, SIGNET CLASSIC, MENTOR, ONYX, PLUME, MERIDIAN
and NAL BOOKS are published by NAL PENGUIN INC.,
1633 Broadway, New York, New York 10019

First Signet Printing, August, 1988

1 2 3 4 5 6 7 8 9

PRINTED IN THE UNITED STATES OF AMERICA

to
my dear parents
Esther and Samuel Shapiro
(a guiding light)

and to
Paul Henning
(who symbolizes all
that is good about
America)

A TIME TO
REMEMBER

CHAPTER 1

I T ALL BEGINS WITH LAURA. ONE MO-
ment I am an indifferent guest at a social
gathering—the next moment she has entered
the room, changing my life forever. Usually at
ease with women, I stand rooted to the floor. I
feel heavy-legged and fear that if I try to cross
to her, she will notice that I am having trouble
lifting my feet off the carpet.

Without even knowing her name, I would
marry her on the spot. If a man looks at a
woman for the first time and cannot picture
himself having sex with her, nothing good can
come of that relationship. Looks come before
character, desire before dialogue, sex before
companionship.

I watch her as she moves around the room.
How easily she fits in with each group, entering

1

their lives with a smile, a handshake, or a kiss on the cheek. She brightens faces, creates laughter, and when she walks on they look after her with a sense of loss.

Frantically, I think of a myriad of subjects I might talk to her about. I cannot afford to have her find me ordinary and walk away. I have waited too long for this woman, too long for this feeling, to lose her before getting a chance to know her.

Turning, she steps toward me, offering her hand and a smile. "I'm Laura Watkins."

I remember the tremor, the soft jolt of electricity that passes through my body as I take her hand. "I'm David Russell, and I am desperately trying to think of something to say that will make you find me the most interesting of men."

"Then tell me you're not married, not engaged, and not involved with anyone," is her encouraging reply.

I stare into her eyes—into what are called the soul of a person—and I see my reflection housed there, home at last.

In those first months together, I see nothing else, and seek nothing else, but the fantasy wonderland lovers find in each other's bodies.

It is not that the passing of time has lessened my desire for her, but rather that time passed together has made me aware of the superior person who lives in that desired body.

With a master's degree in communications,

she has mastered the art of holding down multiple jobs on a single salary. She is the host of a television talk show, the station's program manager, and her own girl Friday, all at the same time.

KDAL is an independent educational channel that survives on dollars painfully extracted from private donations. Occasionally it even receives funds from the network affiliates—for, with its sole function being to improve the human mind, it is no threat to them.

Laura's weekly taped show, *Intellectually Speaking,* is on opposite shows like *Knight Rider, Falcon Crest,* and *Miami Vice,* which means that she can go anywhere in Dallas, secure that no one will recognize her.

It does not seem to distress or depress her that KDAL walks almost unseen and unheard among the network Goliaths. Like a minister tending to her flock, she sees each viewer as a precious being rescued from that vast wasteland.

Is there a single incident that shows a person's character? Late one night we were walking down a street, arms around each other's waists. On the corner, selling newspapers, stood a crippled, horribly misshapen little man, kept upright by crutches. As we approached him she took our arms from each other's waists so that we passed as friends, not lovers. I knew why she had done it. This man—who would never know a lover's arms around him, who would never

3

hear a woman say "I love you"—needed no further reminder of his emasculation.

Above all, she understands the depth of my feelings about Christopher and encourages me to talk about him. I will love you forever, Laura, for you have seen and you have understood. You've heard and you've cared. You have given dignity to my grief. I love you today, and I will love you tomorrow, because you have never tried to get me to forget yesterday.

CHAPTER 2

I T WAS CHRISTOPHER WHO OPENED MY
eyes and ears to a world and to thoughts
outside of Linnett, New Mexico. Otherwise I
might have grown into manhood clinging to my
childhood teachings that the Presbyterians and
the Republicans were the linchpins that held
the American dream together.

To understand my parents you must understand the conservative nature of those who farm
the isolated areas of our country. A man who
works the earth and watches nature faithfully
repeat herself year after year is not a man who
will accept sudden and unexpected change.

I have never been able to connect this cautious couple I call "Mother and Father" with
the free spirit they created in my brother.

What Kennedy was to my brother, Christopher was to me—the ultimate hero.

5

I was seven when Kennedy was elected. Too young to understand the politics and the passions of those times, I could only follow the faith of an older brother and be swept along with him and his peers by the Kennedy mystique. Suddenly the youth of a nation could relate to a man in the White House. It was no longer a building filled with the sound of old men's voices. A young President and his lady now slept in the master bedroom—laughing children rode tricycles down its halls—poets, philosophers, and artists graced its dining tables. There were movie stars, athletic stars, opera stars, and scientists who spoke of reaching the stars.

It was Christopher who gave up a scholarship at Rice University and joined the Peace Corps for two years. It was Christopher who again sacrificed his education as a new President began *his* education by sacrificing his soldiers in an undeclared war. It was Christopher whom the Army returned to us in 1965 for burial.

All that life, all that potential, all that noble spirit wasted. The wife he would have wed, the children he might have bred, all of it lowered into a grave because it pleased a group of round-eyed old men to keep a slant-eyed old man from unifying his country.

And all of it, all of it, could have been avoided. Just three weeks before President Kennedy left for Dallas, at a meeting of the National Security Council, he had issued instructions that the withdrawal of American military advisers from South Vietnam should begin immediately—and that he wanted *all* American military personnel out of South Vietnam by 1965. Two weeks later, just eight days before he died, he announced that the first one thousand men there were packing and would be on their way home by Christmas.

With the passing of the years, the shadows of Christopher and Kennedy have blended into one reflection, their two lives into one, their two deaths into one. I have become convinced that if one had lived, the other, too, would still be alive.

Christopher knew the conflict was wrong before it became a full-blown war. He told me so the last time I saw him alive. It was April of 1965.

The sky was of a blueness and a texture where one felt one could reach through it and touch hidden mysteries beyond. The plane, like a silver phaeton, split the eastern sky and delivered Christopher on his last furlough. In eleven-year-old adoration, I raced toward him and leaped into his arms. He caught me in mid-leap and swung me up high above his head, as he always had. For that split second I was eternal, floating high above my mortality, impregnable, invulnerable.

Upon entering the Army he had immediately been selected for officer training. That is the one faculty the Army has—the ability to spot a leader and put him at the head of a charging platoon.

Those last few peaceful days we spent together as a family. My father, forgetting his farmer's nature, left the fields to their fate. My mother abandoned all household chores that did not relate to Christopher's well-being. Every meal she prepared was dedicated to him. Her iron pressed a mother's love into his uniform. She would run a gentle hand over his hair and kiss his cheek. She would reach over and touch him as though that touch covered him with a protective wall.

Christopher and I hiked into the solitude of the Zuni Mountains. We stood on a ridge that had once been a meditation point for Zuni Pueblo chiefs. Indian legend had it that only until one stood in the silence of the wilderness was one able to hear his own thoughts. It was here, mere specks in this vast landscape, that I heard my thoughts and spoke my fears. "I don't see why you have to go to Vietnam, Chris."

"Well, pal, I'd sure appreciate your writing the Army and telling them that."

"Does President Johnson want to go to war?"

"He only wants to do what's good for the country."

"Is war good for us?"

"War is never good."

"Then why are they sending you to Vietnam? Do you know what Poppa said?"

"What did he say?"

"He said President Johnson was either as right

as rain on the desert, or as wrong as a pig in a henhouse."

"Poppa has a way with words."

"I wish President Kennedy was still alive."

Christopher just nodded his head. Even though almost two years had passed, he rarely spoke about Kennedy. It was a time of trauma for a mourning generation. They could not accept the initial transfer of power from JFK to LBJ.

"Won't a lot of soldiers get killed?"

He took my trembling hand in his. "Look at me, David."

My hands clutching his, my eyes beginning to fill with tears, I looked up at him, trying to memorize, for all time, every feature of his face. I will never forget you, Christopher. I will remember you forever. If I didn't tell you that I loved you often enough, it's because little boys feel love without saying it.

He tried to comfort me. "Nothing's going to happen to me, David." But an eleven-year-old whose world was falling apart could only cry out in anguish, "I don't want you to die, Chris," and begin to weep.

He took me in his arms and held me until the flood of tears became scattered drops of brotherly love. "I'm not going to die, David. You have my word."

I nodded. Having his word helped, for he had never made a promise to me he had not kept. Nevertheless, there might be some enemy soldier over there who didn't know Christopher had made that promise, so I continued to grasp at lifesaving straws. "I heard Mr. Berger tell Poppa that you didn't have to go to the Army—that you could get a college deferment."

"But then someone else would have to go in my place, and that wouldn't be fair, would it?"

"I don't care. Let someone go who likes war."

"If we do only the things we like, *you'd* have to find someone to go to school for you."

I tried to hide my pleasure at the thought. As he wiped the tears from my cheeks he said, "Remember when Poppa would tell me to clean out the barn? I'd have given anything not to. It sure would have been more fun to say, 'Not me. Let David do it.' "

He had me smiling now. "I'd have said no too."

He had explained it to me in simple terms, and it all made sense.

"Promise me again, Chris, that you'll come back."

"I promise. Hey, I still have to teach you how to throw a curve ball."

"And you said you'd help me with algebra when I got to it."

"Right. And don't forget that ski trip we have to take."

"And you'll take me to see the Beatles when they come back to America." Each obligation forged another link in a promissory umbilical cord that would stretch across an ocean. A man couldn't die when he had so many commitments to honor.

As we walked through the air terminal I clung to his hand. Then, one last embrace, one last good-bye, and he was gone. The plane soon became a shining dot against a blue curtain. Christopher was within that dot. How could someone so much larger than life be contained within a speck in the sky?

☆

I would sit in his room for hours, protectively surrounded by his books, clothing, trophies, and photographs. I prayed to God to protect him. I prayed to anyone who might have access to God's ear. There was an autographed picture of Kennedy that was Christopher's favorite. I asked this slain President to put in a good word for a man who had loved him.

The camera's eye and the writer's pen began to send back word of this Asian holocaust . . . of mortars, grenades, mines, and napalm bombs . . . of snipers, sappers, ratholes, and sinkholes . . . of body bags and body count . . . of death in the rice paddy, the elephant grass, the mountaintop and the river bottom . . . of villagers buried . . . of deflowered virgins and defoliated virgin land ... of groups like VC, PF, MACF, NVA, and ARVN. You couldn't tell who was friend and who was enemy without a government informer.

Christopher wrote of a race of people he felt a great affection for. Caught between the worlds of Buffalo Power and Nuclear Power, they endured. Caught between communism and capitalism, they accepted both and believed in neither. He described a countryside of tiny hamlets and green valleys—a land of bicycles and Buddhist shrines. We knew he became a captain, but he never told us why—for heroics and medals suggest danger, and he spared us that. Only in his last letter to me, perhaps reacting to some instinctive foreboding, did he even begin to relate the fate of that sad land and of the people sent to fight there.

... We have lost no battles, and yet I do not see us winning the war, for the enemy is not here—he is a thousand miles away. Vietnam is simply a safe place to take out our frustrations about each other.

Why are we fighting communism in the streets of Saigon and Hanoi, and not on the streets of Warsaw and Prague? Is it because Europeans mean total war and Asians only limited action? Is one group a safety valve and the other a grand finale?

I know these are troubled statements, but

one cannot see friends die and not ask, "Has his death made our country more secure?"

I keep asking myself what I'm doing here. Why am I so far away from home and the people I love? You and I should now be fishing at Eagle Nest Lake. . . .

I started to cry the moment I saw the government car with the soldiers in it. The Army doesn't send its people out to deliver good news.

I only remember becoming hysterical, breaking free of my father's grasp, and starting to run. I ran as fast and as far as I could, hoping that if I went fast enough and far enough I could outrun the words I had just heard. Christopher, this most beloved of all brothers, was dead. I remember shouting "No" over and over again. I ran toward Cooper's Bluff. It had always been Christopher's favorite spot. He would be there waiting for me, and he would say "Hey, pal, you can't believe everything the Army tells you." I remember screaming "I love you, Chris," and then falling to my knees and crying out "Take me with you. Take me with you."

In shock, sedated, inconsolable, I did not go to the funeral. I know I could never have survived seeing his coffin taken off the plane.

We gave the country Christopher. They gave us back a folded flag.

☆

My parents went about their lives outwardly stoic but inwardly broken people. There is the silence of people at peace with themselves. Theirs was the silence of people with nothing left to say. They have quietly marched forward into a dark future, having to believe that someday a Presbyterian God will explain why He did what He did. For my parents' sake, I hope there is no God to meet on Judgment Day. It would be too painful for them to face a God who was at a loss for words.

☆

With no heavenly fate to rely on, I reconciled myself to an earthly fate which changed with every street corner I came to. As the years passed, every street corner I crossed took me closer to Dallas, Texas ... the college years in Houston ... my first teaching job in Austin ... then my transfer to the Dallas school system. The city had become an emotional magnet. I would again drive the route of the Kennedy motorcade. I would slow down as I passed beneath the Texas School Book Depository Building and imagine myself to be the President with only seconds to live. If he had just turned his head a few inches either way, or leaned forward to wave at someone ... if the motorcade had suddenly slowed down or speeded up ... if some Secret Service agent or police officer had only glanced up toward the sixth-story window and seen the rifle's barrel. There were a hundred ways he could have been saved and only one way he could have been killed.

I would look up toward the death window and I could swear I saw Oswald aiming, firing. If I could still see him over twenty years later, why couldn't someone have seen him in 1963?

I have taken Laura to Linnett to visit Christopher's grave. I wanted him to meet the woman I loved. I wanted him to say to his kid brother, "You did all right, pal."

"Beloved Son. Beloved Brother" are the words chiseled into the headstone. The dates below tell the years of his life, 1942–1965. Was it really possible that this man I had spent my youth worshiping was only twenty-three when he died? ... Laura's hand, holding mine, gave me the strength to cry.

My parents' grief is always painfully evident there. In the spring and summer carefully tended flowers protect Christopher. In the winter the fallen snow is cleared away. The headstone looks as new as the day it arrived on its melancholy journey from the quarry. I once saw my mother, on her knees, cloth in hand, wiping it and gently talking to the son beneath it. I could not hear what she said, but I knew she was speaking words of love, of comfort. Only a mother knows what to say at a time like that.

Later, at my parents' house, I took Laura up to Christopher's room—the first person I have shared that pilgrimage with.

After dinner she sat next to my mother as my mother showed her faded photographs in an old album. She, too, wanted to share Christopher with Laura, for she knew that Laura loved her living son and cared for her dead son.

In the early evening, as we looked out the living-room window, we saw my father standing by the far fence gazing into the distance. Laura quietly said, "He sees Christopher coming down the road."

If it was not for Laura, I would never have known the passion, the joy, the fulfillment of loving a woman. If it was not for Laura, I would never have met Dr. Hendrik Koopman.

CHAPTER 3

LAURA AND I RETURNED TO DALLAS just hours ahead of the heat wave. We wisely spent most of that steamy September afternoon in an air-conditioned bedroom making love.

Afterward, showered, with a towel around her as she selects her clothes, she says, "Don't forget to watch the show. I have a really interesting guest, Dr. Hendrik Koopman."

"Who's Dr. Koopman?" I idly reply as I more than idly watch her move around the room. There is almost no moment more satisfying than observing a person you have just made love to—viewing from a distance the graceful movements of a body that has just given you such

17

pleasure—listening to that most pleasant voice gently talking to you where but moments before it was passionately crying out the sounds of love.

"He won the Nobel Prize in time/space physics, and he is the dearest little man in the world. I just love him."

"You are dedicated, even to be admired," I admit, "but very much misled, young lady, trying to find an audience for time/space physics on a Saturday night."

"A journey starts with a single step, and an audience starts with a single viewer," she insists.

"And I'm that viewer," I conclude.

"You're that viewer," she declares as she removes the towel and begins to dress. I am too interested in what I am now viewing to argue the point.

☆

Dr. Koopman is a cherub-faced, pudgy man with a headful and beardful of uncombed gray hair. His Ben Franklin eyeglasses sit atop a bulbous nose like two mountain-climbers stranded on a rocky protrusion. A wrinkled suit looks as though it has just been taken out of a washing machine. A polka-dot tie not only clashes with a striped shirt but seems to be winning the battle. His voice is mellow, his accent Dutch, his smile part of his nature. He looks like a battered Santa Claus who has been mugged somewhere over Central Park.

Secure behind a Nobel Prize and an army of lesser awards, he triumphantly enters the few homes that have tuned him in. He looses a barrage of scientific facts upon Laura and the unseen audience, speaking to all concerned as though they were tenured professors.

I instinctively feel that he doesn't mean to intimidate but merely to inform, like when we speak complex sentences to our pet dogs and cats, assuming they understand what we are telling them.

Dutch is his native language, English his adopted language, and science the language of his mind. He speaks of time/space physics in terms of de Broglie waves, quantum mechanics, canonical variables, spatiotemporal and orthogonal turns, hyperspace, superluminal velocity, electrostatic scales potential waves, and not of four dimensions but eleven.

It is as if a gifted pianist is playing an intricate concerto and one can occasionally recognize a note here and there. "All action is energy times time, or mass times momentum. Every mass is continually emitting and absorbing photons. The photon is the basic quantum of action.

"The de Broglie wave, for which Louis de Broglie won the Nobel Prize, is a 'matter wave,' which always travels faster than light. Every object makes one when it moves. Its matter waves are everywhere in the universe. You pulse the entire universe when you scratch your nose." Then, with a smile, he says to Laura, "Do you understand what I am saying?"

"Not really," she admits.

"You are a nice lady, so I will tell you what I am saying." I get the feeling that if he did not think Laura was a nice lady, he would never tell her. "If we could take an object and break it into energy patterns—then into individual scaler waves—then beam them through space or time— then reinterfere to recover their energy pattern and then intensify the pattern and condense it into matter again—the object will condense in the future or in the past. It is theoretically possible for an object to travel forward or backward in time."

The message, though only partially understood, is staggering, electrifying, overpowering. They are not the words of some streetwise psychic or cunning cultist. They are not drug-induced hallucinations that give life to bizarre illusions. It is the concept and belief of a respected scientist. To go forward or back in time . . . back in time.

☆

Almost bursting with the energy Dr. Koopman's words have aroused in me, for the first time in our relationship I am temporarily unwilling to share my thoughts with Laura, I simply admit that Dr. Koopman is indeed a most remarkable man and it has been a most interesting show. That satisfies her.

I am unable to sleep that night. . . . To go back in time . . . I leave our bed and step to the window. Somewhere in that vast darkness, sitting in the center of those tiny lights, is the city of Dallas. They say that in the dark all cats look alike. So do all cities. So do all years. There is no way, by gazing out that window, that one could tell 1985 from 1963. Eternity has no meaning at night. It is only when we can see our surroundings that we identify with them. We see children born, people getting old, flowers bloom, rivers flood, the sun rise and set. We measure time with our eyes.

To a microscopic creature those city lights might be what the stars are to us—distant worlds too far to reach. And yet I could lift that tiny life form up and deliver it across those vast distances in a matter of minutes. Knowledge and reality are often a matter of proper transportation.

Is Dr. Koopman right? Can the past and the future be reached by the proper transportation?

21

Can we disassemble matter, the basic blocks of existence, and propel it backward faster than the speed of light, creating a negative time flow? And when we reach the desired period can the matter then be reassembled again in that new time frame?

I am unable to control the emotional forces within me. I am almost feverish with the imagined possibility. Am I simply playing mind games? Can I really go back to 1963 to stop the unspeakable crime, to unstitch historical fabric and resew the past? Can Dr. Knopman do it?

CHAPTER 4

ALTHOUGH I DO NOT REALLY EXPECT Dr. Koopman to be there on a Saturday, I am nevertheless drawn to his laboratory. It is similar to walking to the pool's edge and putting a toe in the water to test the temperature, preparing for the eventual immersion. I once had a friend who made a dry-run drive from Dallas to Las Vegas to familiarize himself with the route he would take on his elopement.

Grants from private foundations have built a complex for Dr. Koopman adjacent to Southern Methodist University. Foundations are generally the last earthly wish of men who have run up billions in profits and deficits in goodwill. As they prepare to depart, they try to make peace with those who will remain behind to talk about them. Soon all power will be in the hands of those they have ruled over. Lowly animals could urinate on them if they wished to do so. Vengeful employees could dig up their graves and do nasty things with their bones. The foundation seeks to correct the damage the donor has done during his life. It also enables the departed to face God with, if not clean hands, certainly generous hands.

I am surprised how easy it is to enter the building. I simply walk in, go past an unoccupied desk, then down an empty hall. I somehow feel that scientists don't quite rate up there with other groups worthy of protection. They are as recognizable as the unknown soldier. Any teenager can rattle off the names of twenty rock stars—but can he name two Nobel laureates?

"Can I help you, young man?" are the words I hear as I pass an open door. Although the voice is gentle, I am momentarily startled. It is Dr. Koopman. He is seated behind a desk that is cluttered with papers of all kinds, magazines, two drinking glasses filled with pens and pencils, a three-foot wood ruler, a green shoehorn, a small stuffed animal, a silk fan, and an ancient-looking inkwell. There are other objects there, but those are the ones I recognize at first glance.

"Come in. Come in." He urges me. It is easy to respond to that friendly invitation.

He is wearing the same worn suit, the same

warm smile. He is everyone's favorite uncle. My
heart, already beating beyond its need, has further demands put on it, for hanging on the wall
is a photograph of Dr. Koopman and John Kennedy, arms around each other's shoulders.

The moment I tell him that I am Laura's fiancé,
my credentials are in order, my credibility established. "The television lady," he says with
remembered fondness. "Such a pretty lady," he
reminds me—then, touching his forehead with
two fingers, adds another positive factor: "And
such a smart lady too. When you both get older,
smart also becomes important," he counsels.

Laura has opened the door for me. I squeeze
the rest of myself through the opening she has
established. "We stayed up half the night talking about you, sir." I can tell that pleases him.
"It was fascinating, sir—that talk you gave about
the possibility of time travel."

He nods his head and in that melodious Dutch
voice says, "Years ago I would include slides
with all my talks, but I am getting older and I
don't slide so good anymore."

He is most pleased with the joke he has just
told. He sets his lips together and his cheeks
puff out as he tries to hold back the laughter
within them. Unable to do so, he lets his inner
joy out in short bursts of breath, and then repeats the punch line—"I am getting old and I
don't slide so good anymore." Still pleased with
himself, he squeezes his eyes shut as he savors

the humor of the statement. It produces a tear from his eye, which rolls down his cheek and falls to a watery death on his shirt below.

He puts a handkerchief to his eyes, then assures me that time travel is not part of the joke. "To travel in time," he says, as solemnly as possible, "that will be the next big step for science, either forward or backward."

I cannot tiptoe around the subject. "Is it really possible, sir? I mean, it can be spoken of theoretically, but can it actually be done?"

He is not annoyed but amused. "If I said so, then I think so. Why would I lie?"

I mentally kick my butt. "I didn't mean that you would lie, sir. It's just that it seems like such an impossible thing to do."

"What it seems is not necessarily what it is," he cautions me with a mysterious smile. "Remember, at one time the thought of an electric light seemed like a miracle."

"That's true," I concede, "but to travel in time—"

"Will one day be no more difficult than it is to travel by plane today," he assures me.

"Then it *can* be done," I reply, almost trembling.

As he studies me for a brief moment I sense that behind his constant cheerfulness there is a more than casual interest in why I have come to see him. "If I say, 'Yes, it can be done,' what will that mean to you?" he asks.

I take a deep breath, and then begin to stumble over simple words. Like a schoolboy on his first date, I know what I want—I just don't know how to go about getting it. Finally, almost in desperation, I blurt out what is in my heart. "Dr. Koopman, I know that what I'm going to tell you may sound mad, but you're the only one who can help me." I point to Kennedy's photograph on the wall behind him. Somehow that gesture gives me a bit more courage. "I know you must have liked President Kennedy, because you're not the sort of man who would pose for a picture with a man you didn't like." Then, after another fateful breath, I plunge in. "It's not too late to save him, sir. You can change the world. I can help you." I am filled with a fanatic's fervor to finish what I came to do, no matter what the consequences. I tell him everything as quickly as possible, omitting nothing pertinent, adding nothing superfluous—just the truth and the hope as I see it.

Pudgy fingers gently intertwined, resting on an ample belly, he studies me as I stand by his desk, drained of my energy and my story. It is hard to tell what a man is really thinking when he is always pleasant. Those innocent blue eyes reveal nothing. Though innocence may be erotic in a woman, it can be erratic in a man. Does he take me seriously or is he trying to figure out how this nut got into his office?

"So, young man, you want me to send you back to 1963 to save President Kennedy?"

"Yes, sir."

"And if President Kennedy lives, then there will be no big Vietnam War, and your brother will also be alive." He nods his head, pondering the possibility. "It is a noble thought, to save a President *and* a brother."

I say nothing. Why press a man who already thinks my dream noble?

"I had an older brother once. Did you know that?"

"No, sir, I didn't."

"Willem was his name. He also died."

I leap at this opportunity. "Wouldn't *you* go back to save him if you could?"

His response is immediate. "No. Willem was not a very nice man. He made my mother cry." Leaning forward, he confides, "Whiskey, gambling, not-nice women. If I brought him back, he would only start all that hanky-panky again."

Frantic, stalled at this bad-brother roadblock, I search for the right words. Dr. Koopman provides them for me. "Your brother—this Christopher—he was not like Willem?"

"No, sir," I quickly assure him. "He never gave my mother a day of grief."

He nods in approval, satisfied. That answer seems to carry much weight with him. "Have you spoken of this to your friend, the television lady?"

I must be careful with my answer. Just as my betrothal to Laura has caused him to accept me, a seeming betrayal of her might cause him to reject me. "Yes, sir. She said it would all depend on whether you said it could be done. She has an enormous amount of faith in you."

"Such a nice lady," he says, and again touching his forehead, reminds me, "And a smart lady too." He turns, glances at Kennedy's picture, then turns back to me. "To send a person back in time is not as simple as sending an animal back."

A startling statement—is it also an admission? "Did you send an animal back?"

He doesn't respond to that, but instead points out another obstacle. "To send someone back outside the laboratory, that is a risky situation."

Again I hear the distant pealing of bells of hope. "Did you send someone back *inside* the laboratory?"

Ignoring that question too, he says, "And once sent back in time, can I be sure that I can bring them back to today?"

The more he speaks of the problems, the more certain I am that he knows the answers.

"To change what has already happened. Don't you think I haven't thought of that a hundred times? But is it wise?"

"Not wise?" I protest. "I don't understand."

For a portly man, he pushes himself lightly to his feet, comes around the desk, takes my arm in his, and as he starts to lead me out of the office he says, "John Kennedy was my friend.

29

He was a friend of science, a friend of new thoughts. Don't you think that his still being alive wouldn't fill me with great joy?"

"Yes, of course."

He guides me down the hall. "And don't you think that I haven't thought about all the good things a man could do if he went back in time? But there is also the possibility of the bad things he could do."

"That depends on how much you trust the man you send back," I counter. I must not let myself be easily dissuaded.

We are approaching what looks like a heavy metal door. "People who are alive today might no longer exist," he warns.

"More who are dead might still be alive," I reply. I feel I am holding up my end of the argument.

"The question, young man, is, should it be done?"

"The question, Dr. Koopman, is, can it *really* be done?"

He stops and just stares at me in wide-eyed sincerity. I feel I am being judged. I must not lower my eyes or step back or smile a foolish smile. I must look into his heart as he is trying to look into mine. And just as a man can look at a woman and in an instant know he will fall in love with her, so can a man meet another man and immediately know they will be friends.

I have passed the test. He tightens his grip on

my arm to emphasize his next statement. "You have asked a fair question that deserves an honest answer." The metal door opens slightly and easily.

To me even a high school laboratory is a magical realm of sorcerer's equipment. I stand in awe of simple test tubes, flasks, and Bunsen burners. Here I am rooted to the floor by what I see. It is the Valhalla of high technology, an electronic jungle of the future. Banks of humming, blinking computers line the walls, with what seems like miles of cables and wires running from their silicon hearts. There are dozens of monitor screens and control panels filled with buttons, switches, lights, and dials. There are square machines, squat machines, and cylindrical machines that rise from floor to ceiling like surrealistic trees. Enormous silver coils dominate a section of the laboratory and seem to disappear into a cavernous hole in the floor. I later learn this is an accelerator, and that its metal coils run for miles under the city of Dallas. Its job is to smash atoms and their constituent parts into even smaller pieces, and to then propel this disassembled matter at faster-than-light speeds. It is the engine that will drive nature's pieces forward or backward in time.

One can't just walk through the laboratory, but must bob, weave, duck, and step over the crisscrossing cables and wires that litter the floor.

Dr. Koopman picks up a small tweezerlike

31

instrument from the floor and carefully places it in a glass jar. It is as if someone were to replace a coat hanger after a twister had demolished the house.

"To travel in time, young man, is merely a matter of unlocking nature's secrets. What we do when we get there involves man's secret nature—and that is the real danger each scientific discovery faces."

"But you know why I want to go back," I protest, defending my secret nature.

I watch, fascinated, as he flicks a dozen switches on one of the control panels and a half dozen or so previously silent machines start to voice the life within them. Strange clicking sounds come from them, like a bunch of old ladies knitting.

"To go back in time with today's knowledge of events. What man can resist the temptation to enrich himself in some way?" As he presses more buttons he nods knowingly. "Can *you* resist temptation? It is like the Ten Commandments. We all agree they are noble and wise laws. Is that not true?"

"Yes, of course."

"Yet how many of those commandments have you broken, young man?"

I have no answer, for outside of "Thou shalt not murder" and a few others, I've broken the rest in one way or another.

He doesn't press me for a guilty answer. "And if you break God's commandments, can I expect you to honor the rules *I* set down?" He steps up to a thick, circular window, about ten inches in diameter, set in the far wall. He looks through it, then motions for me to do the same.

I gaze into a small chamber whose walls are filled from floor to ceiling with coiled pipes. The ceiling itself is covered with hundreds of tube-like structures that resemble fluorescent lights. There is something majestic, yet frightening about that enclosure—beautiful, yet ominous. On the floor, in the center of the chamber, is a small cage, and sitting in the cage is a white miniature poodle.

As Dr. Koopman turns dials and presses buttons on a control panel, he says, "It is basically a matter of taking apart what we are made of—accelerating the pieces beyond the speed of light, backward or forward, and then, at a designated time, putting the pieces back together again."

Are all such monumental concepts so simple to state? Did Einstein, Newton, Moray, Tesla, and the other pioneers in science walk such a simple word path?

As I inwardly tremble at the possibilities, I say, "Have you actually done it?"

His serene smile almost leaves me unprepared for the wondrous answer. "In actuality, yes."

I stare at him, momentarily unable to speak, my face flushed, my breaths coming faster as my body and mind absorb the incredible news.

He quickly modifies his miraculous statement, but it remains miraculous nevertheless. "I have actually done it, but I do not yet have the proof." Pointing to the poodle inside the chamber, he says, "That is Schatzie. I have sent her back in time, but when I bring her back to today, she cannot tell me about it."

As Dr. Koopman adjusts other machinery a beatific calm seems to envelop him. He is on his home turf, playing the game in which he is a superstar. "As important as sending someone back in time is also figuring out a precise place they should be sent back to—an exact location where they should reappear. That, too, I have done."

Reduced to a state of open-mouthed awe, I am a worshiper at the feet of this earthbound, but not time-bound, God. As he flips a row of tiny, glowing switches he says, "It is urgent that when I send the subject back in time, I can determine the spot on the earth it comes back to. Don't you agree, young man?"

I just nod my head. I would agree with him if he told me he could prove the earth was flat.

Indicating the cage inside the chamber, and the poodle inside the cage, he says, "To prove a point, do you think I can send Schatzie from where she is now to someplace else? Do you think I can send her from here to my office?"

He doesn't wait for my answer. The tubings that look so much like fluorescent lights start to descend from the ceiling toward the floor, much like venetian blinds being lowered. They encircle the cage and the poodle inside it. The laboratory is filled with deep, full, powerful sounds that roll, rumble, and reverberate throughout the room and against my eardrums. Panel lights flash on and off. Electronic numbers in the computers go wild as digits change at speeds too fast to follow. Coils and rods almost sizzle as they gather and dispense units of energy.

The tubings that surround the cage emit a brilliant silver glow as they try to contain the forces surging within them. They must be the very substances that hold the universe together.

Suddenly all sounds cease, blazing colors are gone, computers stop chewing up numbers, panel lights go out, dials go back to zero. The lowered tubes rise toward the chamber's ceiling—and cage and poodle are both gone.

He's done it. He's taken a dog's bone and flesh—a cage's steel—taken all their atoms and made them disappear. I feel him tugging at my arm. In a daze, I awkwardly follow him as he leads me out of the laboratory and down the hall. My heart leaps as I hear a dog's bark coming from his office.

On the floor, next to his desk, is the cage and the poodle inside it.

I am again aware of him pulling on my arm. "Come, my friend, we'll talk."

He takes me across the street to a Baskin-

Robbins ice-cream parlor, where he orders a Matterhorn sundae. It is a mountain built out of seven scoops of ice cream, cherries, nuts, and a whipped-cream topping. Anxious, expectant, I order a single scoop of vanilla.

It's obvious he is worried by the trouble a human can cause. "To send a dog back is one thing," he counsels me. "What harm can a dog do?"

"What good can it do?" I remind him.

He stares at me with those large, unblinking blue eyes. I have scored a point. I must press the advantage. I must convince him that I would indeed change things for the better. How can he doubt it? "You said President Kennedy was your friend. Isn't the thought of his leaving Dallas alive worth any risk?"

"Yes, of course," he agrees. "But *to send a man back*." He is voicing a concern he never had to show for an animal. "And where would I send you back to?" he poses the challenge. "Where is there a place in 1963 that is exactly the same as it is now?"

He's right. It would not be comfortable to reappear in 1963 in the middle of a concrete column. But while Dr. Koopman looks for roadblocks, I look for open highways. There are dozens of landmark places in Dallas that haven't changed in more than twenty years. Suddenly I connect the landmark with the assassin. "The roof of the Texas School Book Depository Building," I cry out, beginning to flush with excitement. "It's the same now as it was then." And it is. Emptied of its books, it was bought by the county of Dallas in 1977, and in 1981 it became known as the Dallas County Administration Building. Its first two floors have been opened as the commissioner's court. The rest of its floors have been sealed off. They are the same in 1985 as they were in 1963. Only a Hertz sign has been removed from the roof and a fire escape taken down from the backside of the building. It is the perfect point of return.

"Send me back there," I plead. "Just ten or fifteen minutes before Kennedy's motorcade passes. That's all I'll need. Oswald will be on the sixth floor, by himself." How well I knew where Oswald was every minute of that fateful day. How often I have retraced his steps on the pages of a dozen books that have also followed him the days and hours before his final madness. While other workers on the sixth floor had left to go to lunch, or to go down to see the President pass by, he remained, alone, assembling his rifle, waiting.

"Just a few minutes. That's all I'll need," I promise him. "I'll stop him. I give you my word. Then I'll return to the roof, and you can bring me back. That's all I'll do—stop him—and then come back. Nothing else."

Dr. Koopman stares at the Matterhorn, now reduced to a modest hill. "*Can I* send you there?

Can I bring you back?" he asks. I have made progress, for he is now questioning his ability, not the advisability. "I don't know," he sighs, "I just don't know."

It is difficult to keep the frustration out of my voice. "Even if you never tell anyone about it— someday, somewhere, somehow, someone else will learn the secret. Hundreds of men will be sent back in time to do God knows what deeds. Other men will be sent after them to undo what has been redone. The same events will be changed over and over again. At least, this very first time, we can do something that we know is right, is honorable, is good for mankind."

He reaches over and takes a spoonful of my ice cream. He must feel some kind thoughts toward me. One doesn't eat the ice cream of an enemy.

"Let me think about it," he says. "I will think and I will call you. One way or the other, I will call you."

CHAPTER 5

SEPTEMBER 27, 1985

I T HAS BEEN A WEEK OF GREAT EXPEC-
tation—and greater disappointment. I have
not heard from Dr. Koopman. I do not call
him, for if he is on the fence I cannot risk push-
ing him off onto the wrong side.

At school I have been absentminded, less than
efficient, but I have kept the students contented
and controlled by giving no tests and assigning
no homework. In appreciation, they have faded
in and out of the classroom, hoping this way of
life will go on forever.

At home, not having told Laura anything, I
have gone out of my way to be agreeable as a
companion, attentive as a lover. With her arm
around me, her head against my chest, she sleeps

peacefully—the good sleep of a woman who is happy with herself, happy with the man who shares her bed.

It is all the quiet before the storm—the sleeping woman, the silent scientist, the suffering I endure as I wait.

☆

Twenty minutes after Laura leaves to do her Friday night show, Dr. Koopman phones. "Did I interrupt you?" he asks.

"No, no, not at all, Doctor," I hastily reply, not wanting him to even consider hanging up and calling at another time.

"Can you meet me at Lowry's so we can talk about the situation?"

Lowry's is a twenty-four-hour hamburger place that caters to the night people of Dallas, which generally means hookers, pimps, vice squaders, those without homes, and those who break into homes.

"Yes, I think I can," I say, spacing the sentence out. A hurried speech might show too much anxiety.

"Good. I'll meet you there in . . ." After a pause: "What time is it now? I have no watch."

Why should I have expected a man like this to carry a watch? A man who has conquered time is above having to look for it on his wrist. "It's about six-fifteen, sir."

"Get there as soon as you can" are the last words I hear before the line goes dead.

I arrive at Lowry's and quickly spot the car that must belong to Dr. Koopman. It is an unwashed, two-tone 1960 Buick, with a bumper sticker that reads, "Have You Hugged a Scientist Today?"

Dr. Koopman sits in a corner at one of those dreadful tables and chairs which the fast-food industry has made fashionable. They're made of hard plastic and are attached to the floor, as if some customer might want to walk out with them. Dr. Koopman has changed wardrobes to a sportier pair of baggy green pants and a yellow turtleneck sweater. He is halfway through Lowry's late-night special—a chiliburger with cheese, fries, beer, and apple pie. People who eat that have to expect to stay up late into the night.

I get a cup of coffee, avoiding eye contact with the hookers at the counter, who are getting ready to hit the streets. They are sullen, aggressive, as all athletes are before the game.

I barely push myself into the nailed-down chair when he nails me to my word. "If I agree to send you back, you will definitely go, yes?"

Before he can change his mind, I say, "Yes, absolutely, definitely, I promise." I want to hurl

41

as many affirmations at him as I can so there will be no doubt in his mind as to my availability.

He lays down the ground rules. "You will return for a few minutes . . . enough time to stop this Lee Harvey Oswald . . . then I will bring you back."

"That's all I want to do, sir—stop Oswald."

"You must promise to do nothing else."

"Nothing else. I promise. You have my word." I must pin him down to a definite departure time. "When do you think we can do it?"

"Two, maybe three weeks." He sees the disappointment in my face. "There is so much to be done." I then see a look which I can only guess is concern cross his face—for even when he is concerned he does not look worried, just less happy. "I cannot guarantee that nothing will go wrong."

"Yes, I understand."

"Everything must go just perfect."

"It will. I feel it," I try to assure him.

"But what if something *does* go wrong?" he insists. "How will we contact one another?"

I realize that within every adventure there is the seed of misadventure, but I haven't given any thought to that possibility, and I mustn't right now. Without waiting for the answer that I do not have, he asks, "How old are you, Mr. Russell?"

"Thirty-two."

"So, in 1963 you were—"

"Ten," I answer quickly, saving him the embarrassment of possibly making a mistake in simple arithmetic. "Why do you ask?"

His reply is also the postulation of the problem he is posing to himself. "When I send you back to 1963 you will arrive as you are now, thirty-two years old."

"Is that a problem?"

"Can the same life force exist in two different bodies at the same time, Mr. Russell? What will happen to the ten-year-old when you return?"

I have always thought of myself as I am at the moment. I remember the events of years gone by, but I never remember myself as a separate person. How can I think of myself as a thirty-two-year-old meeting myself as a ten-year-old and holding a conversation? I don't feel threatened by such a meeting, for it will never occur. I will be in Dallas, and the ten-year-old in Linnett, New Mexico. Yet Dr. Koopman is quite right. I will be existing in two different bodies at the same time. "What do you think will happen?" I ask.

"I don't know."

It's all mind-boggling, the future problems that might exist in the past, but I mustn't show any hesitation. I must give him no cause to reconsider. "It's a matter of risk against potential, sir, and it's no contest. *I'm* the risk, *a President and a brother* the potential."

I can tell that has an effect on him. I hold my hand out. "Is it a deal, Dr. Koopman?"

He puts his hand in mine. "It's a deal, Mr. Russell."

I go to get a refill of coffee. Out of the corner of my eye I see one of the hookers go up to Dr. Koopman. She says, "Hi. Would you like some head?" In all artlessness, he holds his half-empty glass of beer up and says, "Yes, thank you, I *would* like a top put on this."

CHAPTER 6

October 9, 1985

THE ANTICIPATION IS INTENSE. IT IS like a military operation. Dr. Koopman is the general planning this surprise attack into 1963. I am the time commando who will appear, do this work, and depart. The longer I stay, the more risk I run. The closer I am to Oswald, the surer the outcome.

Dr. Koopman will attempt to return me to the roof of the Texas School Book Depository Building at 12:15 P.M. on November 22, 1963. That will be fifteen minutes before Kennedy's twenty-car motorcade comes down Elm Street. I will go down the stairwell to the sixth floor, where Oswald has just finished his lunch and is assembling his weapon. At thirty-two I am at my physical peak. Oswald will never fire that rifle. After Kennedy has safely passed at 12:30 P.M., I will go back up to the roof, where Dr. Koopman will, at 12:45 P.M., return me to a better 1985 world.

We go to the Building and Safety Department at City Hall, where we secure the blueprints of the Texas School Book Depository Building. After photocopying them, we return to the laboratory. Dr. Koopman feeds the blueprints' equations into a computer, which delivers a holographic image of the building onto a monitor screen. Then, selecting a precise point on the roof to which he will return me, he feeds the mathematical coordinates into other computers. My point of arrival and departure are now locked in.

Outside of the clothes on my back, with all labels removed, I will take nothing else. No driver's license, no credit cards, no money. If the worst should happen, there must be no items that tie me into a date twenty-two years into their future.

Just as Christmas holiday decorations are seen earlier and earlier each year, so it is with the Kennedy legend. It is only October and already the tale is starting to be retold. Kennedy books, magazine memorials, and television specials start to appear. At KDAL, Laura has helped prepare a documentary called "The Last Year." She has tears in her eyes as she sees a youthful President walking with his son along a deserted beach— helping his daughter onto a spotted pony—sailing with his wife into the morning sun. While he tacks the boat toward the future another man sits in a boardinghouse, separated from his wife and his reason, planning the crime that cost us Camelot.

If all goes well, those children will know a father again—the woman her husband—and I my brother.

I have tried to prepare myself for every emergency, every contingency that might come up, but there is no way I can prepare myself for what happens when I get home that night and see Dr. Koopman coming out of my apartment building.

☆

He sees me and waits as I cross the street, come up to him, and say, "Well, hi," in a low voice—a voice that desperately seeks to give the mind behind it time to come up with satisfactory answers.

"I thought you told her," Dr. Koopman says, almost apologetically.

He has caught me in a lie—a small, white

lie—but can this man, with his almost childlike belief in good and bad, in right and wrong, see the difference between a well-intentioned lie and a premeditated, hurtful lie? Am I now no more to be relied on than his brother Willem?

"I meant to tell her," I say. "I was going to."

"I came here to tell her not to worry," he explains in innocent befuddlement. Then, shaking his head, almost not wanting to accept his next line of reasoning, he says, "If you do not tell me the truth in 1985, can I trust you in 1963?"

I must defend myself in the present and in the past. "What I didn't tell her has nothing to do with what I tell *you*. I mean, it hasn't been easy. How do you say to a woman, 'Don't worry, dear, I'll just be gone into 1963 for maybe a half hour or so?'"

Almost sadly, he says, "She was hurt that you didn't tell her."

"I told you, I *was going to*."

"Such a nice lady," he adds reflectively.

My God, will his feelings for Laura cause him to turn on the man who hurt her? "We're still going through with it?" I ask, trying to make it more of a statement than a question.

His answer is a deep, uncertain, indecisive breath.

"You can't back out now," I plead. "We've come too far." I mustn't let an old-world sense of chivalry keep me from the new world I envision. I mustn't let a lie trip up what lies ahead. "I'll talk to her. I'll straighten it out. Trust me."

That seems to only temporarily satisfy him. "I will not do it if it makes her unhappy."

☆

"Damn it, don't touch me," Laura says as I try to put my arms around her, attempting to reach familiar ground. Pulling away from me, she starts toward the kitchen, and I follow. All is not lost. An angry woman is one who can eventually be reasoned with. A silent woman who will not talk is an unknown, and dangerous, adversary.

"I am so freakin' mad at you, David," she says as she practically slams open the kitchen door.

"I was going to tell you. I swear it."

"When?" she replies sarcastically. "Were you going to phone me after you got there—or maybe write me a letter?" Reason, logic, and common sense, her strongest allies, are now her worst enemies—for they tell her that a man like Dr. Koopman doesn't deal in fantasy—that everything he told her is indeed possible.

As she starts to pull pots and pans out of a

cupboard she says, "Just let me alone, will you? Just let me cook dinner."

Her preparing dinner is a bad sign. She is nervous, insecure, worried, else she would never volunteer it. When things are going well she very rarely cooks—and when she does they are usually potluck meals, spontaneously thrown together. There are many mansions in Laura's happy kingdom, but none of them contain a kitchen.

However, if things are going wrong at work, or if we should be starting an argument, she will head for the kitchen and expunge her anger, her frustrations, or her guilt on speechless meats and vegetables, on passive pots and pans. Some people say they are sorry, some send flowers—Laura prepares large meals. In the incalescence of the stove's flames, she burns away her problems.

She fumbles with frozen meats and vegetables, with uncooperative knives and forks. This is one problem she will not be able to cook away. Finally, in exasperation, she throws a pan into the sink and turns to me, tears of frustration in her eyes. "I can't ask you *why*, David. I know why. . . . I can't say he's a mad scientist. He's not. . . . I can't say it's impossible. He said it wasn't. . . . I can't say I want you to go. I don't. . . . I can't believe I'm standing in a kitchen in 1985 trying to talk a man out of going back to 1963, but I am."

I reach out for her hand, and she lets me hold it. I must not rush her, but very carefuly lead her along. She has been hit with a mind-boggling situation. To her credit, where another woman might have been thrown into an irreversible catatonic state, Laura has only become flustered. I can handle confusion, but not a coma.

"If you don't want me to go, I won't. I mean that, Laura," I say, not really meaning it. She trusts Dr. Koopman. I must call him and have him arrange some demonstration that will convince her it can be done, and done safely. Observable facts often lead people to blind faith.

CHAPTER 7

D R. KOOPMAN GREETS LAURA WITH A hug, a kiss on the cheek, and the ultimate tribute: "Such a pretty lady. All my life I have wanted a daughter like you, but I never found a woman good enough to be your mother." His sentences don't always make sense, but the goodwill behind his words act as a bonding agent between clarity and intent. There is no way to look at, and listen to, this agreeable man and harbor any thought that he would be partner to a dark deed.

He knows that Laura is concerned, unsure, just as he once was. Over the weeks his attitude has changed from willingness to enthusiasm. My obsession has gained a foothold in his thought processes. It has been emotionally electrifying to speak of Kennedy in the present tense. There is not the air of the supernatural in our dialogue. We are not raising the dead but merely raising the chances of a man not being dead to begin with.

As he leads her into the laboratory, his arm linked through hers, he says, "That you almost don't dare to believe is natural. That you will believe is inevitable." It is an all-encompassing statement that precludes an argumentative answer.

Then, as he begins to turn dials, press buttons, flip switches, program computers, set gauges, and activate control panels, he talks to Laura. "You are worried about your young man. I understand. . . . Can we send him back in time? I think so. . . . Can we bring him back to the present? I think we can do that too."

It is not as positive a statement as I would have liked, but it will have to do.

With a confident smile, Dr. Koopman then says to Laura, "Just to make you feel better, we will have a trial run." Turning to me, he says, "Come, we will show the nice lady what we can do."

A trial run, with *me* involved? That catches me by surprise. I have been assuming he would do some other kind of demonstration, maybe one with the dog. I mean, I am quite prepared to go, but not at this particular moment. It is like a bridegroom thinking he is going to the wedding rehearsal and suddenly finding himself at the real wedding. There are things I want to settle first—a final moment with Laura—a phone call to my parents—things I would do if I were about to take an ordinary plane trip, much less a trip such as this.

Dr. Koopman modifies his intent. "I will not be ready to send him back in time until next week." His words act like a palliative. "But I am prepared to transport him to the building we have selected as the point of return."

I am relieved, but still uncertain. He intends to take me apart atom by atom in front of my fiancée and deposit me onto the roof of the Book Depository Building. I look into Laura's eyes. She will forever judge my beliefs, my sanity, and my determination by my response. If I am insecure, even a bit frightened, she must not see that.

"Good idea, Doctor," I say as calmly as possible. Then, for Laura's benefit, adopting a John Wayne type of bravado, I say, "I think the little lady's in for a surprise."

A panel door I hadn't noticed before slides open and an entranceway is created into the adjoining room, where I had last seen Schatzie, the poodle. Like a cold shower, the quicker one gets into it, the sooner the algid sting is absorbed. I give Laura one last movie-hero look, this time the Harrison Ford type of innocent and yet at the same time smirky boyish grin. That's been the one great legacy the film industry has given us—fictional heroes to emulate when we find ourselves in nonfictional tight spots.

Dr. Koopman and I have often talked of a test run, but without setting an actual time for it. To my question of what it would feel like, he has, with a smile, said, "Who knows? You may not feel anything unusual—but, then again, you might." It is not a very comforting explanation, but certainly to the point.

The panel door closes behind me, and where once I was the observer, I am now the observed. Dr. Koopman's voice comes over the intercom system: "Step into the circled area, please." I step and wait. "Now we will try to get you to the spot on the roof we have picked out, David." A slight tremor passes through my body at the word "try."

"When you get there just wait there for a moment, and I will try to bring you back." Another tremor at the second use of that inconclusive word "try." I am buffeted by two emotions, apprehension and expectation. I do not doubt that Dr. Koopman can disassemble a body in one location, then reassemble it in another. I've seen him do it with Schatzie. I am confident I will arrive on that roof in one piece—but what will that one piece look like? There is the inquietude of visualizing my appearing with all my body parts put back together the wrong way— with arms where legs should be, with a nose where once there was an ear—a creature only Picasso would love.

Will the machinery be as accurate with me as it was with a dog? Worse yet, has the machine's memory locked itself into the atomic structure of that dog, so that I will arrive on the roof in poodle form?

Despite these natural anxieties, there remains the inner exultation that this is the semifinal step before the big leap itself.

☆

As the overhead tubings are lowered, enveloping me in their incandescent brilliance, the energy sounds reach a pitch where I no longer hear them but only feel their pulsating pressures. There is no pain, only the sudden intake of breath as I seem to be hit with a soft but powerful punch to every part of my body. I feel like I am caving in on myself, and then it is all reversed and I am expanding outward beyond my body's normal parameters. Frightened, momentarily panicked, I instinctively try to keep myself from disassembling, but I have lost control of the elements I am made of. Even my fear and my instincts have broken into millions of minuscule parts, all of them leaving me at blazing speeds. My mind is being pulled out of me as I am "whooshed" off, much like the last few drops of soda through a straw.

Sight and sound and awareness return—the sky above, the traffic below, and my feet on the roof of the Texas School Book Depository Building. Trembling, I look at my hands and feet and feel my face. Then, an instinct returned to me, I reach for my genitals and breathe a sigh of relief. All is well there. The Dutchman has done it again. There is not a part out of place, not a hair misplaced, not a bone misaligned.

I am ecstatic as I look out onto the city—a city I am now certain I will soon see again twenty years in the past—1963 is in my future.

I stiffen protectively as I again feel the jolting thump to my body—like an experienced fighter, this time I try to go with the punch. Controlling natural alarm mechanisms which scream out that I am being taken apart cell by cell, I attempt to stay in contact with the millions of parts of me that are leaving. The last thing I remember is feeling myself being scattered into a dark void.

I am dimly aware of my parts returning from the endless abyss. Then I am fully aware I am again standing in the laboratory, and through the glass partition I see Dr. Koopman's smiling face. Over the intercom I hear him cheerfully declare, "You were on the roof, David. No?"

Overwhelmed, almost unable to speak, I nod my head and manage to say, "Yes."

"And it wasn't as bad as you were afraid it would be. Yes?"

I shake my head in agreement. "No."

A silent, stunned Laura steps up alongside Dr. Koopman and just stares at me. This is no time to say to her "I told you so." My words aren't needed. Her voicelessness admits it all.

She has just seen me disappear and then rematerialize, with every body particle collated. She has heard me admit that I was on the roof of the Book Depository Building. Her reasoning powers can no longer reasonably tell her that things like this can't happen. But what doors logic has opened, love may attempt to keep closed.

When we get home we both silently prepare for bed. Her silence is her most potent argument against my going. Mine is my loudest statement that nothing will stop me.

She finally breaks the silence. "I want to have a baby, David." That is how she announces her acceptance of my going, and what she thinks of my chances of coming back. As I reach over to embrace her she says, "Don't touch me."

"How do we have a baby without touching?"

"I mean, until I'm ready. I just want to think first." Nevertheless, she allows herself to be held, at first reluctantly, and then more easily as she eases herself into more comfortable and familiar positions. Let her think, for her thoughts will be my allies. She loves me, which means that when I am catapulted into the past she will not stand there screaming, "All right, go but I won't be here when you get back." She is a survivor, which is why she wants our child, for a child is the image we leave of ourselves. By being with my child, if I am lost in the past, she is ensuring part of me being found in the future.

☆   *OCTOBER 12, 1985*

The next day we solve the problem of communication in the event an emergency arises. If anything should happen when I am back in 1963 and I need to communicate, I will simply go to the Dallas *Morning News* and take an ad out in the personal column addressed to an Uncle Hendrik. I will spell out my situation. Whatever my needs, Dr. Koopman can deposit them for me in a location I suggest.

By computer, Dr. Koopman and Laura will be able to search through the back issues of the Dallas *Morning News* to find the ad I place.

In the Historical and Archives Division of the Dallas Public Library we buy full-page microfilm copies of the Dallas *Morning News* covering that Friday and the three days that followed. We then have photos made of the microfilmed pages. We then connect a video camera to a

MacVision computer, which in turn is connected to an Apple Macintosh. The camera photographs the newspaper's pages, then the MacVision system digitizes the picture and puts it into Mac-Paint. Two powerful technologies are linked up, video and the computer. Graphic photos can now be sent along with the word.

This MacVision system will also serve another need. The frontpage headline of the Dallas *Morning News* of November 22, 1963, reads "Kennedy Assassinated." In the lower right-hand corner of the front page is a photograph of Lee Harvey Oswald. It is a foolproof way for Laura and Dr. Koopman to know immediately what has happened. As soon as I stop Lee Harvey Oswald that headline will have to change.

Covering *all* contingencies, we have to plan for the possibility that, through unforeseen circumstances, I can neither be brought back nor can we contact one another. How would I survive? One coin solves the problem. It is a $20 Brasher Doubloon that was left to Laura by an uncle. Worth over $20,000 today, it was selling for almost $3,000 in 1963. With my knowledge of events to come, particularly in the stock market, that $3,000 would soon become an immense fortune. But it is an emergency I hope never to face, and a fortune I hope never to accumulate.

Although the sixth floor of the Book Depository Building has been closed to the public, it is open for special tours or to those who can give a better reason to see it than mere morbid curiosity. I feel I have a good reason. Through a friend of mine who works at the Dallas County Historical Commission, I receive a permit under the pretext that I am planning to film an educational documentary for my school.

That infamous sixth floor, sealed off, is like a tomb, holding not bodies but bitter memories. Unheated, the raw morning air has found refuge there, so that I must pull up my jacket collar to keep out the biting chill and what seem like hostile emanations.

The security guard, my guide on this visit, points to the window. "That's where he shot the President from." Then, reflectively, he says, "All it would have probably taken was for somebody to be here and he couldn't have done it."

I look around. Yesterday the shelves were stacked with books, the door between the stairwell and the sixth floor had not been locked. It is a short distance from the stairs I will come down to the window Oswald will be standing at—a few yards I can cross in seconds. The only danger I must guard against is overconfidence.

The security guard lets out a sigh and says, "What a shame. With a little luck, it might never have happened."

I cannot tell him that it might still not happen.

☆   *OCTOBER 14, 1985*
I have rented a wardrobe at Hennings Costume Rental Company—a circa 1960 Hart Schaffner & Marx three-piece suit, authentic in every detail down to shirt, tie, and shoes. I have removed all identification from my wallet. My watch and pen will also be left behind. If something should go wrong, the people in 1963 must not be confronted by a man from 1985.

I understand the reason for all these precautions, but the more one prepares for emergency procedures, the more one becomes aware that an emergency may occur—something I have really tried not to think about. However, watching Dr. Koopman standing there staring helplessly at a tangled mass of wires in a computer terminal he has just taken apart starts to unnerve me. "Is there a problem with that?" I ask timidly.

He shakes his head in despair. "The way they build things today." Then, pointing to the wires, he says, "Tell me, how can I depend on something like this tomorrow?"

Timidity is replaced by trepidation. Indicating the wires, I say, "*Are you* going to depend on them tomorrow?"

"Of course." Then, noting my rapidly paling features, he comforts me. "Stop worrying. You should see what I've done with equipment that was even worse than that."

Trepidation is superseded by alarm. "Are you sure you can bring me back?"

"One hundred percent sure," he replies as he starts to cut into the wires with some instrument. "But still, there is maybe a two or three percent chance I can't."

"That adds up to one hundred and three percent, and that's impossible."

His answer is meant to comfort me. "Then that is all we have to fear, my friend, the impossible happening." With great certainty, he says, "Nothing will go wrong—but one never knows."

I'm not embarrassed about being edgy and a bit testy. Athletes are like that before a big game, soldiers before a big battle. I try to instill confidence in myself. "Everything's going to be fine. I'll take care of Oswald. You just take care of getting me there and getting me back."

As he throws pieces of wire away in disgust he makes the grand promise: "Trust me. If I don't get you back, I'll give you one thousand dollars."

CHAPTER 8

I AWAKEN TO FIND LAURA, FULLY DRESSED, sitting in a corner staring at me as though she is trying to burn my image into her memory.

"I love you, David." She is very, very serious. This mood is a carryover from the previous night, when we had made love, at times almost desperately, as we strove to leave imprints on each other's souls, marks which no other lover could ever erase. With her legs encircling my back, and my hands grasping the cheeks of her behind, I would drive my length into her over her surrendering moans. There are moments between a man and a woman that are so intimate, so overpowering, so breathtaking, they literally become one body feeling the same sensations.

I say nothing. To merely tell her that I love her would only cheapen what I feel for her.

"David?"

"Yes, Laura?"

A momentary pause, then, as she rises, she says, "Nothing. I'll go make you some breakfast."

Her making breakfast is an ominous sign as to how she feels about my future.

Freshly squeezed orange juice is free of pits or pulps—rich, dark, hot coffee, whose aroma makes one think of distant mountain lands—bread toasted to a golden brown, onto which a pat of saffron-yellow butter gently melts—eggs basted to a delicate perfection—sizzling bacon strips that only the most obstinate pig would regret giving its life for.

It is a déjeunerian masterpiece, which saddens me. I look up at her and say, "You don't expect me to come back, do you?"

As she rinses a pan her evasive answer bespeaks her inner turmoil, her disquietude. "Will you just shut up and eat." It's obvious that as far as she is concerned, I am eating a memorial breakfast, my last meal in 1985.

We drive through an early morning drizzle on our way to the laboratory. It is always pleasant to gaze at a city as its imperfections are cleansed by falling rain. I have grown to love Dallas. Its skyline does not intrude on the vastness of the land beyond. Its population does not distract from individual identity. It has acreage, but without many of the aches that go with size. No subway has been surgically cut into its bowels. No overhead wiring system disfigures it like varicose veins on a shapely leg. Its people are courteous and hardworking—nothing like the spurious spectacle shown on television.

I have traveled the state and it belies its flat, barren reputation. It has prairies and high plains, rivers and mountain ranges. It is the land of the longleaf and the loblolly pine, the snow egret and the roseate spoonbill. White-tailed deer, minks, and gray wolves know its territory. The bluebonnets and ocotillas that come up from its earth look out on universities, museums, space centers, and research hospitals. With pride, it knows that no man can be elected President without carrying Texas. With shame, it knows that once a President was carried out of Texas— but that corruptive stain will soon be expunged.

One quick phone call to my parents just to hear their voices—familiar, loving, stoic—but without the resonance of people at peace with themselves.

The snows have comfortably settled in on the farm, determined to remain until the spring cleaning. From the imprint left on a fallen snowflake by a microscopic creature to the footprint of man and beast, that white carpet is an encyclopedia of life. All who walk it are forever recorded. The melting process is not a forgetting process. The snows will fall again, made of the same watered drops that fell and rose and fell again millennia ago. When one touches a snowflake one holds the very beginning.

So it is with my quest into the past. What once was, still is, but in unseen form. Somewhere in some dimension Dr. Koopman will transport me to, all who lived are still alive. To have those fallen heroes return—to have a brother, still alive, walking toward my parents' house, bringing young children to see their loving grandparents—that vision alone is worth all risks.

The tension shows on Laura as she grips the steering wheel. I can understand her conflicting feelings as she tries to relate to the situation. Just a few weeks ago she had it all—health, career, and a relationship that was predictive but still passionate. Suddenly she has been thrust into a realm of quantum mechanics, hyperspace, de Broglie waves, Z particles, and leptons—where what really matters are the quirks of quarks, which make up matter itself.

Thrust into a timeless arena of unmeasurable potential, yet filled with unknown perils, she has accepted mind-bending concepts as easily as she would approve my going out of town for the weekend. Women like Laura are the solid ground from which historical adventurers set forth into the unknown.

Now that the moment is near, I balance myself between two conflicting emotional states— elation, faith, and expectancy on one hand—apprehension, concern, and anxiety on the other. I feel I have courage equal to that of any other schoolteacher, but that is all I really am, a common citizen caught up in a majestic phenomenon. If all goes well, those now dead will be reborn. Those now infirm will be whole again. Those who grieve will rejoice again. And if I should fail, I can only take cold comfort in Charles Dickens's words, "Tis a far, far better thing I do."

Dr. Koopman has proved he can transport me from one location to another, but can he do so while he is also sending me back through time? Can he deliver me onto that roof at the prescribed time? And, though he returned me to the laboratory from the roof in 1985, can he also bring me back from 1963?

I will remain in 1963 for no more than half an hour, and when I return—assuming that Kennedy was saved, that he was reelected, that a divisive war was avoided—that Christopher, too, is still alive—I will be coming back to a better world. Dr. Koopman has told me that no matter what changes occur, he is almost sure that I will always be aware that I went back and am responsible for those changes—for when I go back to 1963 I will arrive there as the thirty-two-year-old man I am in 1985. I will be like an alien visitor who comes to earth from another star system light-years away. That alien is always aware of the planet he came from—aware that he is only temporarily visiting earth.

The scientist in him is fascinated at the situation. "You will be in 1963 at the same time that Laura and I are here in 1985," he has said. "We will all be coexisting in two different worlds at the same time." He is intrigued by this coexistence factor. "When you return to 1963 it does not mean that we will necessarily remember what you did after you arrived there. Not if we are coexisting. We can remember only *after* you have done something—only then can we be aware it happened."

And even after I have done something, when I return to the laboratory in 1985, Dr. Koopman has said that it is possible that neither he, nor Laura, nor I will be aware of what changes occurred during the years between 1963 and 1985—not until after we leave the laboratory. Only outside of the laboratory's walls will we become aware of what happened during those years.

"I do not say it will happen that way. I may be wrong," he has explained. "But it is a possibility." Indicating the walls encasing the laboratory, he has told us that they are reinforced with lead and metal alloys. "Creating an effect like a cocoon—and we will be inside that cocoon."

He feels there is the potential that once the immense volumes of energy are released within these walls—as the basic elements are propelled at faster-than-light speeds—as the four main forces of nature—gravitational, electromagnetic, strong nuclear, and weak nuclear—are themselves caught up in this vortex, it will create a whirlpool effect. While Laura and Dr. Koopman should be safe in the whirlpool's center, they may not be aware of what changes in the past have taken place—not until they leave the laboratory and go out into a world where all the forces they have harnessed and diverted are once again functioning within normal parameters.

To protect against this transitory inconvenience, to make sure it does not hold them up in case immediate decisions are needed, we take the entire MacVision setup out of the laboratory and place it in Dr. Koopman's office. We then place an Apple computer and readout screen in the laboratory and, by installing a telephone modem, create a visual network between the computer's readout screen in the laboratory and the MacVision in the office. In this way Laura and Dr. Koopman will have instant access to the newspaper's pages and to any changes that have occurred in them.

☆

Dr. Koopman's car is parked with the right front tire on the sidewalk. "Parked" may be the wrong word. "Abandoned" is more appropriate. Somewhere in Dallas there is a driving inspector who issues licenses who should be fired.

He stands behind his office desk struggling to open a bottle of champagne whose contents are questionable, for the bottle is covered with flecks of dust and the label is all but gone. On a sheaf of oddly assorted papers sit three small, bubbled glasses, the type that may once have held candles. "Come in, come in, my dear young friends." His cherubic looks are bolstered by an ebullient mood. Staccato sentences shoot out in nonsequiturs. "Champagne is for celebrating. Even if we fail, we have a right to celebrate. . . . If only Nikola Tesla could have lived to see this day. Such a scientist, and who really appreciated him? What you do, young man, will not go down in history, but it will change history. . . . Such a combination. A schoolteacher from New Mexico and a scientist from the Old Country. I was born in Volendam, a fishing village. That is what has made America great."

I am staggered at this confluence of thoughts. Laura, rather than trying to piece them together, is more practical. "Is everything all right, Doctor?"

"All right?" he asks with a mischievous smile. "Are you afraid something is wrong?" Then, trying to outwardly suppress some inner mirth, he says, "Do you think I cannot send him to 1963 and bring him back?"

"It's not that," she responds, assuaging him, "it's just that you just said it's possible we may fail."

As he pulls the cork out of the bottle he says, "You must not believe everything I tell you. Just believe me when I say everything is going to be all right."

Then, as he pours the contents into the small glasses, he reassures her. "Does one drink champagne like this to honor failure?" He holds the bottle out to me. "I gave my word it would be poured only on an occasion that was worthy of it."

I peer at the label. It is Mouton Rothschild, 1890.

"The Baron himself gave it to me. It was in Paris, after I had won my first Nobel Prize. He said, 'Doctor, on the day you feel you have reached the apogee of your skills, then drink the best the Rothschilds have to offer.'"

Holding that bottle has a calming influence on me. It, and the wine within it, are fellow time travelers. A century ago an earlier cellarmaster to an earlier Rothschild filled that bottle with the grape of 1890, and it survived that hundred-year journey—a good omen for me. It makes my voyage to 1963 seem like a walk across the street.

Dr. Koopman, with as much solemnity as his genial spirit will allow, says, "To President Kennedy. To Christopher Russell." Then, speaking to me: "To David Russell, who wishes the best for all men, and so will try to save the best of men." We drink that ancient brew. It tastes of success.

☆

The laboratory pulsates with the life inside the machines it contains. One can almost feel the hidden energies surging within them as they pour forth sounds that seem to blend into harmonious chords, into electronic melodies. It borders on the spiritual, as though we have entered a sacred chamber to perform a ritualistic ceremony where I will be the offering.

There are no emotional good-byes. We know how to say good-bye to warriors, to the terminally ill, to those about to be executed, but there are no past human experiences to draw from to frame a proper farewell in this situation. Tears are not called for, laughter is out of place, kisses seem a bit foolish.

Dr. Koopman just shakes my hand and pats my cheek. Laura, trying to appear unconcerned, casually says, "Don't make any plans for tonight. I'm going to cook dinner at home." For her to offer to cook two meals in one day is the worst of all signs. It signals her inner turmoil, her despair over ever seeing me again.

Now that there is no turning back, I suddenly find myself filled with a sense of peace and purpose. I'm coming, Christopher. You were always there when I needed you. Now that you need me, I shall be there for you. You will not spend the best years of your life in a grave.

☆

Once again I am encased in the sheath of tubings, then overwhelmed by brilliant coruscations, by ear-splitting, hair-raising decibel levels, by my body parts breaking loose from one another, by my mind being sucked into a vacuum. I feel my tens of millions of cells hurtling through a razor-thin slit of blinding light at speeds beyond the velocity of the light coming toward me. I am like a fish swimming upstream, but I am making headway against the natural flow. I flash past setting and rising suns, full moons, half-moons, quarter-moons, and no moons. I am assailed by images and sounds, multibillions of them, raspy and discordant, as though someone were playing a tape machine backward. Suddenly, without warning, the images are no longer blurred, the voices I hear are clear and distinct. I am standing on the roof of the Book Depository Building.

CHAPTER 9

FRIDAY, NOVEMBER 22, 1963 . . . 12:15 P.M.

I AM WHOLE AGAIN, BACK AGAIN. THE Hertz sign is on the roof again. I race to the edge of the building and peer down. The crowd is in the street again. It is 1963 again. Kennedy and Chris are alive again. I am staggered, almost faint with emotion.

I run to the roof door, pull on it, but it won't open. It is not locked, but stuck, either swollen shut or warped by rain. Panicked, I pull on it, wrench it, tug on it, bang on it with desperate fists, trying to work it free. "Open up, you son of a bitch," I both plead and curse. My jerking on it has loosened the bottom half of the door, but the top holds fast. I frantically try to dig my fingers into the slight opening in the lower half

77

so I can pry it open, but I can't get a firm grip. I am hyperventilating, wet with sudden perspiration, terror-stricken at this unspeakable catastrophe—to have come so far to be stopped by a balky door. For want of a nail a kingdom is lost—for want of a door opening, a President and a brother are re-lost. It can't be. It mustn't be.

In the distance I hear the police sirens of the presidential motorcade. The wedged door suddenly gives way and opens.

I vault down the stairs, taking three and four steps at a time. The sirens are almost upon me—I can hear the crowd beginning to cheer. I leap the final seven steps to the sixth-floor landing, fall, roll over, and come up on my feet. Oswald stands by the window, starting to raise his rifle to point it toward the approaching President. I race toward this sallow-faced psychopath, this hate-filled, hateful pariah who caused a generation of grief. He seems so slight, too insignificant to have been the genesis of such sorrow.

Mine is now a mad rush toward him. I am almost upon him as his finger embraces the trigger. I cry out, "No!" and fling myself at him. Instinctively he swings the barrel of the rifle around with all the strength he can muster. It catches me in mid-flight, crashing against my right temple. I am driven to the floor, onto my hands and knees by the force of the blow.

As I try to struggle to my feet, battling pain and double vision, Oswald turns toward the open window and fires two quick shots. I am on him with a brutal right-hand smash. He drops to the floor. I reach down and take the rifle out of hands that are now twitching as a nervous system, in shock from the punishment it has just absorbed, cannot command his fingers to hold on to his weapon. I quickly look out the window onto the familiar, fearsome scene below—the presidential limousine speeding away with a mortally wounded President.

I am stunned, dazed, overcome, momentarily crazed at this monumental irony, this indescribable failure. I turn and take my rage out on the repugnant life form groveling on the floor. I drive my foot into him again and again. "You dirty, miserable son-of-a-bitch bastard. You miserable piece of shit."

He rolls out from under the kicks, pushes himself to his feet, and starts to flee. Frenzied, inconsolable, unable to think, much less to think clearly, I want to kill, to smash, to destroy him. He is almost to the stairwell I came from when I fire. He screams in pain, grabs his thigh, and falls heavily to the floor.

Two burly workmen come up the stairs. Oswald points at me and cries out, "He just shot the President!"

☆

My mind is instantaneously as clear as a bell, and the bell is tolling out the terrible news— that I am in 1963, the President has been shot, Oswald has been shot, and I am being blamed.

As the two men cautiously approach me, Oswald, trying to stem the blood flowing from his thigh, yells, "Get him!" I point the rifle at the two men, which momentarily stops them. One of the men, obviously a Mexican, stands there with tears in his eyes. I know why he is crying. I, too, have shed tears over Kennedy. I grieve with him. All I can do is protest, weakly, "I didn't shoot him." Then, pointing the rifle toward Oswald: "He did."

"He's lying," Oswald shouts. "He shot Kennedy. Don't let him get away. Kill him."

I can tell that they are judging their chances if they rush me. I have nowhere to run. Even if I should get by them and make it up to the roof, it's unlikely my pursuers would then allow me to calmly stand in my prescribed area for three or four minutes while I waited for Dr. Koopman to return me to 1985. That dilemma is solved as more men start to come up the stairs. There is no way to get by all of them. The roof is out for the moment. I bolt toward the other staircase at the far end of the floor, then down the stairs, with the howling, cursing men behind me.

I am filled with one overpowering, all-consuming emotion—not to get caught. Escape is what life is about. How and where to is not important —only to avoid capture, to find a place to rest and think and to live on. Lungs and heart are called upon for performance levels beyond what they were created for. I now know the stark terror an animal feels as it flees the advancing hunters. But that animal has trees and mountains and burrows and caves to hide in. I have only the stairs and the street below.

Through the lobby area, as a few workers cower against the wall when they see a wild-eyed man running toward them, blood coming down the side of his head, a rifle in his hand. Out a side door of the building onto the sidewalk, and my frenzied flight continues down the street.

I am a quarter way down the block before the avengers swarm out of the building. By now they have become a mob, enraged, outraged, filled with righteous wrath. I throw my rifle down, insanely hoping they will stop to pick it up. Only a car, only wheels, not legs, can save me. At the corner a truck is pulling away from the curb. If I can just get into the back of it. I frantically race toward it as it picks up speed. I am in a living nightmare, seeming to run in slow motion as I try to close the distance between myself and the moving truck. I leap toward it, catch the handle of the open rear door, am dragged along for a few yards, then lose my grip. They are on me before I can regain my feet. One angry body after another piles on top of me. I am held fast by this avalanche of falling flesh.

☆   *OCTOBER 15, 1985*

At the precise moment agreed upon, Dr. Koopman activates the machinery for the return. He is serene, unruffled—Laura tense, expectant. Each piece of equipment faithfully follows its programming. There are no malfunctions, no miscomputations, no silicon solecisms, no flashing warning lights— but when the tubings lift there is no David.

Dr. Koopman, open-mouthed, stares in disbelief. Laura, trembling, face flushed, cries out, "He's not there! My God, he's not there!"

The scientist in Dr. Koopman immediately begins to check and double-check the machines, desperately searching for explainable errors, oversights, mishaps.

"Where is he? What happened?" Laura shouts, unable to control the horror of what she has just not seen.

"I don't know. I don't understand," he mumbles, his cherubic appearance having suddenly taken on a ghostly visage.

"Are you sure you did everything right?"

"I think so," he replies haltingly as he fumbles with dials and switches. Triumph has turned to tragedy, certainty to confusion. He is bewildered by an experiment he has already mastered.

"Maybe he was late getting back to the roof. Maybe he's waiting for you now. Try again."

His face lights up with the promise. "Yes, that's it. He was late. He's waiting." He resets dials and switches, knobs and buttons. He rereleases powerful floods of energy. The laboratory is bathed in blasts of blazing light, the walls shaken with the pounding of deafening decibels—but David does not return.

"Again. Please. Try again," Laura pleads.

Dr. Koopman once more unleashes the forces, sending them tunneling through the time barrier, opening a chute for David to slide back into 1985. His nonappearance confirms the grim reality that it is not the machines that have failed. Something unforeseen has happened in the past.

Laura screams, then cries out, "Oh, God, no!" She is looking at the readout screen on the computer, which shows the front page of the Dallas *Morning News*. Its headline still reads "Kennedy Assassinated"—but in the lower right-hand corner of the page, where once there was a photograph of the accused assailant, Lee Harvey Oswald, there is now a picture of David.

☆   *NOVEMBER 22, 1963 . . . 2:20* P.M.
I have been booked, fingerprinted, photographed,
and charged with the murder of the President of
the United States and the attempted murder of
Lee Harvey Oswald.

Hands manacled, in leg irons, I have been half
pushed, half carried through crowds screaming
for my death. Shrieking women and children
have tried to beat me with their fists. A charging army of media people push cameras and
tape recorders in my face, wildly shouting questions at me.

Safely inside the jail, I am in a bizarre,
surrealistic setting, surrounded by faces out of
the past, by men whose names I recognize from
books I have read. Homicide Captain Will Fritz
leads the interrogation. FBI agents Hosty, Bookhout, and Clements hover over me, pressing for
my confession. Fritz, a tall, taciturn lawman
with a Stetson and a sad face, has been forceful
in his questioning, but fair. The FBI men, look-
alikes with their trim haircuts, dark suits, shined
shoes, and ties neatly in place, are more intimi-
dating. Their eyes are piercing, their lips pursed,
their questions crisp. They are efficient, precise,
professional—and yet all those qualities did not
save the President. Their Dallas office has let
the home office down—something Mr. Hoover
will not soon forget. Their next assignment may
be near an ice floe in Alaska. They stare at me

as interns do a cadaver. I am a dead man they are trying to get information from.

"You shot the President," Hosty insists.

"No, I didn't," I protest in frustration. "I keep telling you, *I* didn't shoot him. *Oswald did.*"

"And then you shot Oswald when he tried to stop you," Clements charges.

"That's not true. *I* tried to stop *him.*"

"You had a rifle," Bookhout accuses.

"I took it away from him. It's not *my* rifle."

"He said you stole it from him."

"How could I steal it from him? I never saw him before in my life."

"He said he met you in a bar a little over a week ago."

"He's crazy. The man's a psychopath."

"He said he took you to his place and showed you where he kept it."

"He's a fucking liar." I am emotionally drained, physically exhausted, at the breaking point. Without thinking, I cry out, "He didn't keep the rifle at his place. He kept it in the garage of the house where his wife's living. He and his wife are separated. *He's* staying in a boardinghouse in Oak Cliff, under the name O. H. Lee."

Fritz quietly says, "If you never met him before, how do you know all those things about him?"

I stare at him blankly—the stupidity of the blunder just starting to be absorbed by a mind numbed with what has happened, narcoticized by a vision of myself hanging from the gallows for a crime I tried to prevent—tortured by the thought of having to watch a President slain a second time. I am losing the ability to differentiate between 1985 and 1963.

Fritz's voice easily penetrates a porous, crumbling wall of mental alertness. "You shot the President."

"No, I didn't. I swear it. You've got to believe me. That's not why I came back."

"Came back? Came back from where?" Clements asks.

I am losing concentration, stumbling between generations.

"Why did you kill the President?" Hosty asks again. It is not the accusation but the repetition that wears one down.

"I didn't kill anyone," I reply wearily.

"What's your name?" Bookhout now tries for a minor concession.

"It doesn't matter," I mumble.

"We're going to find out anyway," Clements cuts in. "We're running a check on your fingerprints."

Depleted as I am, I still have to smile thinly at their trying to trace my fingerprints. Hosty takes the smile as arrogance and defiance. "Bastard," he snarls, and hits me across the face with an open hand. Fritz grabs his arm before he can strike me again. Hosty defends his action. "Son of a bitch is playing with us."

How can anyone look at me sitting there, disheveled, defeated, defenseless, and think I am capable of playing anything?

I am taken to an identification lineup, where I am identified by the two workers who saw me on the sixth floor with the rifle. Other witnesses confirm I was the man fleeing down the street. Then I am taken back for further interrogation. More men crowd into the room—Dallas police, Secret Service men, and a postal inspector. I am too weary, too beaten, to even try to figure out what the post office has to do with this. It's much too early for a commemorative stamp.

They encircle me, their staccato questions a battering ram. Why did I shoot the President? ... Who helped me? ... Who am I? ... Where do I live? ... Am I a member of the Communist Party? ... Have I foreign connections? ... Was I paid to do it? ... And a most damning accusation: "If you didn't plan to shoot the President, what were you doing on the sixth floor of a building you didn't work in?"

These men are under enormous pressure to get answers. A stunned world, a reeling nation, waits. Cronkite and Reynolds and Huntley and Brinkley wait. I am delaying the evening news. A new President on Air Force One, on his way back to Washington, with the old President riding in the cargo hold, waits. A freshly widowed woman, her dress spotted with blood, waits. A younger brother, who will watch his older brother lowered on a forklift, waits. Two orphaned children, staying up past their bedtimes, wait.

Captain Fritz again reminds me that I have a right to legal counsel. "Don't want one," I mutter. No lawyer can help me, for the truth won't set me free. Truth is only relative to the extent of a society's belief system. Would an aborigine in New Guinea believe me if I told him I talked to a man who had walked on the moon?

Inculpating voices have become a drone. It is difficult to focus my eyes, which is why I have not noticed the man being brought in in a wheelchair, his thigh heavily bandaged. Suddenly I am face to face with Lee Harvey Oswald.

Narrow-faced, slack-jawed, thin-lipped, less than ordinary, he points a stubby finger, topped by a well-bitten fingernail, at me and says, "That's him." Only I see the sly smile which conveys the pariah's message: "Fuck you, buddy."

Literally driven mad by this historical injustice, I let out a primordial shriek of outrage and leap toward him, wanting to smash him back into the hell I released him from. A dozen hands grab me. As I am roughly thrown back onto my chair, I cry out for the ages to remember, "*He* shot the President! *He* killed Kennedy!"

☆

I am carried, struggling, cursing, to an infirmary where I am held down as a tranquilizing liquid is forced into my nervous system. It is administered by a nurse who seems to float in the air above me. Her six-foot body carries less than a hundred pounds of weight. Spindle legs resemble stockinged broomsticks, and a concave body admits it would bend before a strong wind. I keep imagining her spreading her long, thin arms and flying out between the bars of the window. Nature meant her to be a huge bird standing on one leg in some African marsh—but in some cosmic mix-up she has been given human form—and somewhere, on some remote, third-world jungle lake, there lives a huge bird who looks like a nurse.

I don't know why I have zeroed my thoughts in on this thin lady. Perhaps it is the shot she gave me, which has taken hysteria, anger, and frustration and blended them into a serene, subdued stew. I placidly hallucinate as I am led to an isolated holding cell. I fantasize my escape. I will get Captain Fritz to put an ad in the *Morning News*, addressed to Uncle Hendrik, in which a time will be set for my departure. I will then get them to take me up to the roof of the building, from which I will disappear back into 1985. It all seems so simple, I even smile tolerantly at the two guards who are assigned to see that I do not attempt to harm myself. They are massive men who look like Dallas Cowboy linemen. Large heads, with widely spaced eyes, give them a slightly retarded, almost menacing look. Police departments generally keep men like this off the streets, assigned to inside work, for public peace of mind.

They dispassionately watch as I eat, then sit on the toilet seat. It is a degrading, humiliating experience to be studied as one voids waste and wipes up afterward. Do household pets feel that demeaned when we walk them?

At a little after nine at night I am taken from the cell and told I am being transferred to the county jail. I am handcuffed to the left wrist of Detective Leavelle. A second detective, Combest, holds my left arm with both his hands. We take the elevator down to the basement, which is filled with police and reporters. As I am led to a waiting car I notice a heavyset man in a dark suit and a gray hat step toward me. I've seen him before, but where? Terrifying recognition sweeps through me at the very instant he draws a gun, points it at me, and fires. I barely have time to cry out, "Jack Ruby," before paralyzing pain and darkness envelop me.

CHAPTER 10

THE MOMENT LAURA AND DR. KOOP-
man step out of the laboratory building
onto the street they are battered by incoming waves of remembrances which flood over
them in a sea of shocking, grievous, unbearable
memories. Ill tidings wash over them, each revealing an additional horror.

Dr. Koopman recoils as though scourged with
a whip. Christlike, he accepts the lashes, but
with those stripes he is not healed. This genial,
jovial scientist has become an old man, confused, self-deprecating. "We meant well . . . a better world," he stammers in self-ablution. Then,

in convoluted rationale, he regretfully concludes, "Sometimes better is worse."

Laura, pale, shaken, tries not to be felled by each new recollection—David on trial in 1964 for the Kennedy killing—the historical trial of a man who never admitted his name—who became known as the "John Doe Killer." Found guilty, his only statement before receiving a life sentence was a passionate appeal for a nation not to become involved in a war in a place called Vietnam. After that he fades into the prison population of the Federal Correctional Institute at Marion, Illinois. The only mention of him comes on November 22 of each year, telling a forgetful nation that he still languishes there, bitter, broken, uncommunicative.

Memories flash by, stitches in a colossal tapestry. A stitch here is a bit different, a seam there slightly altered, but the tapestry itself has not changed. There is still Martin Luther King and Memphis, Robert Kennedy and Los Angeles, Johnson and Vietnam, Nixon and Watergate, Carter and Iran, Reagan and Nicaragua, Mondale and Ferraro.

It is a bitter, acrid pill to taste, much less to swallow. The magnitude of the misfortune is compounded by a grotesque burlesque of fate. The past that she has remembered in moments, David has had to suffer in years—imprisoned, alone, in despair. While death deserves grief and lamentation, David's fate calls for an emotion that would panegyrize this inexpressible calamity. Yet all she can offer is a soul in sackcloth and ashes.

Dr. Koopman gently rests a hand on Laura's shoulder with a comforting paternal touch and, assuming parental guilt, says, "I should never have let him go."

Laura, stunned, almost immobilized, stares at the cars going by, their drivers unaware of the historical calamity that has taken place—a man called "John Doe" is imprisoned for Kennedy's murder, another man called Oswald is a hero for having tried to save the President. Honored, respected, a public park has been named after him. Laughing children play on swings, on slides, in sandboxes, in a happy place named the Lee Harvey Oswald Park.

"Oh, God," she agonizes, "all those years. All those years—and for nothing—nothing really changed."

"We will go to see him," Dr. Koopman says, not pausing to give thought to the kind of man they would be seeing—a man in his fifties, graying, transmigrated by a martyred incarceration.

Laura takes a deep breath, trying to inhale a strength that had been momentarily lost. A thought that had been fleeting is now a commitment. "I don't want to see him," she says. Before Dr. Koopman can object, her decision becomes immutable. "Not in prison. Not the way he is today." Every instinct has told her that such a meeting would be unbearable for each of them. "I want David the way he was." The potential of the possibility begins to intoxicate, to impassion. "I want him never to have failed, never to have been jailed." Her breathing is now becoming rapid as a once more happy heart pumps its victory news to distant body parts. "David alive—Christopher alive— Kennedy alive. It can still be done, Dr. Koopman. Can't you see that?"

Dr. Koopman peers into her eyes, trying to get a glimpse at what she is seeing.

"I'll go back. Send *me* back."

Dr. Koopman, still not sharing the vision, will not share the risk. "Send *you* back? No. I can't. I won't."

She grabs both his hands in hers, pleading, "Send me back—not to November twenty-second —but to November twenty-first—*a day before David arrived."* Her face is flushed at the thought. "Don't you understand. I'll warn them— the police, the FBI. The FBI was already suspicious of Oswald. They were trying to find out where he lived. I'll give them his address. I'll tell them he'll be on the sixth floor waiting to shoot the President. They'll stop him." Her eyes are now glowing with the promise. "When David gets there Oswald will already have been arrested. David will return to the roof, and you'll bring him back. Then you'll bring *me* back."

Dr. Koopman stands there, mouth open, almost gaping at her as he absorbs the concept, its daring, its staggering rewards. Yet somehow he must try to resist this siren call. "What if something goes wrong again?"

"At least David and I will be together. That's all I want. I love him. Everything David ever did, he did for love. He deserves more than a lifetime in prison. It means all those terrible years will never have happened. We owe it to him."

Whatever his doubts, whatever his fears, she has touched an ancient sense of gallantry, honor, and obligation. "Yes," he admits, "we owe it to him."

☆

Both Laura and Dr. Koopman realize she cannot be returned to the roof of the Book Depository Building. She will need a place to make her phone calls to the authorities, a place to spend the night. She will need a safe place to be returned to, a safe place to stay, to do what has to be done, and that safe place does exist—Dr. Koopman's home.

As he drives toward his house, miraculously avoiding two sideswipings and one head-on collision, he says, "I was at a science seminar in

95

San Francisco the week President Kennedy was shot. I did not get back till November twenty-seventh. You will have the house to yourself. I will show you where I kept the spare key so you can get in." As he ignores the wail of the siren and crosses an intersection just seconds ahead of the oncoming fire truck, he emphasizes that safety must be a major part of their plan.

Dr. Koopman's house stands surrounded by trees, bushes, shrubs, plants, and flowers, none of them ever having known a cutting tool. A narrow driveway remains passable. Birds claim the trees and small animals wander the grounds, not as visitors, but as landlords.

The car skids over a pile of fallen leaves and stops outside a small carport next to the house. Very few houses have ever blended in better with their surroundings. It is Hansel and Gretel in appearance, built of cocoa-colored wood and red and white bricks. Emerald-green shutters and yellow window curtains hide what is going on inside. The only thing missing is the sound of calliope music.

Dr. Koopman squeezes out of the car and, indicating the spot of ground he has stepped onto, says, "I will bring you back right here." Then, pointing toward a shelf in the carport, he confides, "The key to the house is in that empty coffee can."

Even though it is no longer a barrier, time is still of the essence. It is not for David's sake, but for their own peace of mind that they are proceeding as quickly as possible to redeem and restore. At City Hall they obtain copies of the needed blueprints; acreage is geographically pinpointed; holographic images implanted into computers, where numerical triangulations and coordinates are then fed into digit-crunching and programming components, guaranteeing that Laura will reappear on that specific parcel of ground in front of the carport.

Laura, as David did before her, divests herself of all identification, of all material objects that might attach her to a future year, like a mother to a still unborn child.

With Laura alerting the authorities on November 21—giving them a precise rundown of Oswald's whereabouts—of the rifle wrapped in a blanket in the garage—Oswald will be apprehended and in custody before the President's plane even touches down at Love Field. Certainly David will be shocked when he returns and doesn't find Oswald on the sixth floor of the Book Depository Building, but he *will* see the President's motorcade go safely by. Explanations can come later.

☆   *OCTOBER 16, 1985*
As Laura takes her place beneath the tubings an anxious Dr. Koopman fusses with the dials on a

nearby panel. "If you get hungry, there's food in the refrigerator."

Laura, composed, almost serene, with a smile, repeats, "Food in the refrigerator."

Then, as Dr. Koopman steps over to position her, he cautions her, "And be careful with the stove. Sometimes you have to kick it to make it work."

"Kick the stove," she dutifully records the instruction.

"And if you need money, there's some in my green suit in the closet."

She puts her arms around him, hugs him, and kisses his cheek. "I love you."

He unconvincingly waves the kiss aside. "Smooching is for later on. Now is for remembering," he reminds her. "And don't answer the phone. It's me calling from San Francisco. If someone answers, I know the house is being robbed."

"I won't answer the phone," she promises.

He looks at her, desperately trying to think of one more delaying tactic. Like a papa bear about to see his baby cub go out on its first solo walk in the forest, he wants to warn of all the hidden dangers. And, like the papa bear, all he can come up with is, "You be careful now."

This time it is he who delivers the hug and the kiss—then he turns and is gone. As the panel door slides shut Laura takes a deep breath, not in fright, but in anticipation, much like an athlete does before the game commences, before the stadium's silence is shattered by the roar of the crowd.

She is enclosed in the tubings womb, which turns silver-white as titanic megaforces deliver Laura's parts into another time, another place, where she will be reborn to give David a second chance.

☆ *THURSDAY, NOVEMBER 21, 1963 . . . 11:15 A.M.*

Laura rematerializes at the very instant the Buick shoots out of the carport. She has no time to scream, the car's driver no time to stop. Only the fact that it is a glancing blow prevents her death. Struck by the right front fender, she is hurled backward, hitting her head against the trunk of the tree.

As the terrified nineteen-year-old driver leaps from the car, he calls out, "Are you all right, lady?" He runs up to her, kneels by her, apologizing. "I didn't mean to hit you. Honest, I didn't see you." Getting no response, he gently shakes her shoulder and anxiously asks, "Lady, are you okay?" Laura moans softly. Starting to panic and to stammer, he cautions her, "D-d-d-d-don't move. I'll be r-r-r-right back." He races down the driveway toward the street.

☆   *3:05 P.M.*
Sergeant Okrand curses a karma that has sent

him to the Parkland Hospital just twenty minutes before he was to get off duty. He could have been home, opening up a bottle of beer, getting ready to go to his son's high school football game. All he can envision now is a mound of paperwork to be filled in over another dumb car accident.

"How do you spell your last name, Teddy?"

"P-a-l-m-i-e-r-i. Palmieri."

"And you work at the Gregson Brothers Garage?"

"Yes, sir. When Dr. Koopman is away, we always p-p-pick up his car to service it. He doesn't t-take very good care of it. He's n-not a very good driver."

"*Dr. Koopman* is not a very good driver?" Sergeant Okrand comments sarcastically. He then focuses on the object of his cynicism. "How the hell can you hit someone coming out of a carport?"

"I didn't see her. She wasn't th-there, and then she was."

"She just appeared like magic, right?"

"Yes, sir."

"People don't pop up out of nowhere."

"Sh-sh-she did."

"How long have you had that stuttering problem?"

"All my l-life, when I g-get nervous."

Sergeant Okrand realizes he's being a bit unkind, pressing the boy about his speech impediment. The kid doesn't deserve it. He's really a nice enough young man. How many teenagers today would even bother to call the police after they'd run someone down? Chances are they'd have a pizza, then go back and run over the victim a second time.

"Are you sure she didn't have a handbag or some kind of purse with her? It might help us find out who she is."

"No, sir. I'm sure."

"It's not natural, a woman going out without something to carry all her junk in," he lectures. Then, to prove his point, he confides, "The last airplane trip my wife and I took, her handbag alone was over the weight limit." The boy smiles at that, which reinforces Okrand's opinion that he really isn't such a bad kid.

Teddy then comes up with a motive for Laura being where she was. "Maybe she's a burglar."

Sergeant Okrand ponders that for a moment, then overrides it with his own theory. "It's probably just a domestic argument. She and her husband have a fight—she storms out of the house—has a few drinks—wanders onto this doctor's property."

"If she has no handbag, where'd she g-get the money for drinks?" Teddy asks innocently.

Sergeant Okrand gives the boy a hard look. Before he is trapped into an embarrassing answer, he is saved by the appearance of the young intern, who hides his youth behind a receding hairline and an advancing pretentiousness. Dr. Leonard Nazworthy is full of himself and his calling. He is immersed in the magical mystique of the physician. He has quickly learned that his smile is his patients' joy, his frown their fear. His words can give them a sense of well-being or cause them to walk softly and speak in hushed tones.

"She is a very lucky young lady. Very lucky indeed," he announces in stilted, professorial tones. "Some bruises, abrasions, and possibly a slight concussion."

"Can I go up to talk to her?" Sergeant Okrand asks.

"I think not, Sergeant," Dr. Nazworthy pontificates. "She hasn't regained full consciousness yet. She sort of slips in and out of it. It's best to let her sleep it off. I'm sure anything you have to ask her can wait till tomorrow."

To wait till tomorrow. Those words are lyrical to Sergeant Okrand. It means he might still get home, if not in time for the beer, certainly for his son's football game. It isn't every father who has a seventeen-year-old boy who stands six two, weighs two-thirty, and can pick an opposing quarterback up and slam him into the ground. That was the part Sergeant Okrand always liked best, to see his son pounding the enemy into the earth.

"Tomorrow. Right. I'm much obliged, Doc." Then, almost as an afterthought: "Did she say anything, like what her name was?"

"Nothing I could understand. Just a lot of mumbling. Something about someone called Oswald."

"Oswald? Could be important. Might be her name. I'll run a check on it tomorrow."

"Oh, *I* almost forgot," Dr. Nazworthy recalls immodestly, as though his forgetting anything was an event to remember. "She also mentioned President Kennedy's name a couple of times."

Sergeant Okrand is not too impressed with that. Lots of people were talking about his visit the next day. "She may have been planning to go see him."

"I doubt if she'll be in any mood for President-watching tomorrow," Dr. Nazworthy prophesies as he starts to walk off fingering his stethoscope, the source of his machismo.

"Thanks again, Doc," he hears Sergeant Okrand calling after him. "Sure do appreciate all your help." It feels good to have people thanking him, appreciating him. It fills him with a sense of well-being, knowing such deference will follow him the remaining days of his life.

CHAPTER 11

S HE HAS BEEN MOVING, SNAIL-LIKE, through a dense fog, so thick it has jelled into an almost impenetrable mass. It can't be pushed aside, for her hands slowly sink into it. She has to force her way through, taking one labored step at a time. Far ahead, there is a light. The fog's viscosity causes reflections and refractions, so that the true source of the light seems to come from many different directions. As she draws nearer to it she is aware of the shimmering silhouette of a human figure. "Am I still in 1985?" she asks.

The nurse smiles. A disoriented patient is common in situations like this. She pats Laura's hand to soothe her and reassuringly replies, "No, dear, it's not 1985. It's 1963."

"Thank God," Laura whispers, trying to smile through her throbbing headache. She's in 1963. It worked. But why is she lying on her back? Why does she find it so difficult to move? Struggling to break free of the glutinous encirclement, she tries to sit up. The nurse gently forces her to lie back. "Easy now, dear."

"Where am I?" Laura asks as distant alarms start to sound.

"You're in Parkland Hospital."

"Hospital," Laura murmurs in semiconscious confusion. "It's not where I'm supposed to be."

"You were in an accident. You were hit by a car."

An accident? Something must have gone wrong. Why can't she remember? It's all just out of mind's reach. If only her head would stop hurting so she could think.

"What's your name, dear?"

What was her name? If she can remember her name, she can remember other names. Names are important. It is why she is here.

"Is it Oswald?" the silliouette asks, trying to be helpful.

Oswald! That's it. Suddenly other names are deposited into her memory bank. David, Dr. Koopman, Christopher, President Kennedy. "Got to stop him. Got to stop him," she cries out as she again strains to sit up.

The nurse puts her hands on Laura's shoulders and as she eases her back onto the bed inquires, "Stop him? What's he going to do?"

Laura feels herself tumbling backward in a sort of free-fall. In desperation, she shouts toward the receding silhouette. "President Kennedy. I've got to save President Kennedy."

The voice that answers her is distant but tranquilizing. "The President is fine. Just fine."

With those comforting words, Laura relaxes and begins to enjoy her fall into the noiseless, sightless void.

The nurse rearranges the sheet over the sleeping woman, mentally making a note to herself that if she wants to see Kennedy go by, she'll have to skip lunch.

☆   *12:07 P.M.*

Like a swimmer coming up and breaking the water's surface, Laura bursts through the shrouded enclosure into full consciousness. A throbbing headache does not diminish her recall of that split second between arrival and accident. She is in a hospital bed, but better injured in 1963 than in mourning in 1985.

The exhilaration of having traversed that great divide eclipses head pain and body soreness. Her mishap was bad luck, her survival good fortune, her mission still possible. Phone calls to the authorities will be as effective from the hospital as from Dr. Koopman's house. How she will get back to his house for her return to 1985 is a problem to be solved afterward. Stop Oswald first, stop the headaches later. Save Kennedy, then save herself. Deliver David from a lifetime in prison, then deliver herself into David's arms.

She sits up and swings her feet off the bed. There is a brief sense of dizziness, but that soon passes. She then stands. Momentarily unsteady, she rests her hand on the edge of the bed. As an orderly passes the open door to her room, he glances in, sees her trying to balance herself. "Are you all right, ma'am?" he asks as he steps in to help her.

It's embarrassing to stand there in a loosely tied hospital gown that exposes her bare behind, but coyness is not a luxury a time traveler can afford. If it would help save David, she would gladly drop both gown and modesty. The main thing is for her not to arouse suspicions, not to cause concern or alarm in the hospital staff.

"Thank you, but I'm fine. I was just going to the bathroom."

Solicitously, the orderly suggests, "If you want, I'll get you a bedpan."

A decent man, he still can't help glancing at her exposed rear. It isn't often one sees such well-shaped buttocks, much less such healthy-looking ones on the third floor.

Laura draws the line at the suggestion. Being seen naked is one thing, but she does not intend to try to pee into a pan in front of a total stranger.

"The doctor said the more I'm on my feet and move around, the better it is," she explains.

"Yes, ma'am."

"What time is it?"

"Almost ten after twelve."

As she heads toward the bathroom she points to an overhead television set. "Would you mind turning on the television for me?" It is important that she portray a person who is preoccupied with ordinary, everyday habits.

As the orderly reaches for the remote-control box he says, "I sure do wish they'd televise the President coming here. Most of us can't take the time off to go see him."

Laura, at the bathroom door, drops a helpful, medical hint. "You can always call in sick tomorrow."

"Tomorrow?" he answers with a smile. "You lost a day somewhere, ma'am."

Laura has to hold on to the door handle to keep from sinking to the floor as life-sustaining blood suddenly abandons expendable extremities and rushes to protect more valuable organs. She has to force the words out of a rapidly constricting throat passage. "Today is Thursday, the twenty-first," she declares, demanding her declaration be acknowledged as fact.

"No, ma'am," he corrects her, demolishing declaration and deliverance with a single, cutting sentence. "Today is Friday, the twenty-second." As he leaves, he reveals the reason for her miscalculation. "You slept for twenty-four hours, ma'am."

Transfixed, shocked into immobility, she is frozen fast to the terrible tidings. She slept for twenty-four hours. It is ten minutes after twelve. David will be on the roof in five minutes. Kennedy will be dead in twenty.

Deep within the genetic core of every living creature there is a survival instinct, an impulse, independent of reason, of the mind's ability to understand. In times of crisis it floods the body with a chemical composition which makes the timid valorous, the weak strong. It is what enables a mortally wounded soldier to literally rise up from a grave and continue the battle, with a strength beyond any he ever knew.

It is these survival juices that now flow like a torrent through Laura, overriding pain and fear. She has lost all her hours, is down to her last twenty minutes, but, spent wisely, they can buy the lives of David, Christopher, and the President.

The phone next to the bed is like an ebony lighthouse showing the way. She takes the receiver off the hook and is greeted by an impersonal, put-upon voice: "Operator."

Laura tries to mix composure with urgency. "Would you get me the Dallas Police Department, please?"

"Are you a patient here?" the voice asks, following orders.

"Yes, I'm a patient. Would you please call them?"

"May I have your name and room number?"

"My name is Laura Watkins. I don't know my room number."

"What floor are you on, ma'am?"

"I don't know what floor I'm on. Would you please call the police? It's urgent."

There is a brief silence, then the voice returns, slightly suspicious. "We have no Laura Watkins registered here."

Pressured, composure cracking, Laura shouts, "That's because I didn't tell them my name. I was brought in here unconscious. Now will you call the police?"

"I'm sorry, but we are not allowed to make outside calls unless you are a registered patient."

"You don't understand. This is an emergency. President Kennedy is going to be shot."

It is only after the silence at the other end lasts more than a few seconds that Laura realizes that security guards will soon be searching the hospital for her. She drops the phone, turns to the closet door, opens it. Her clothes are in it. She pulls them off the hangers, picks up her shoes, and rushes out of the room. Except for a nurse behind the nurse's desk, reading, the corridor is empty. Laura quickly crosses to the stairway. She stops between floors, slips out of her gown and into her clothes. The vanishing seconds are too precious to waste with brassiere and stockings.

Out onto the ground floor. A wall clock reads 12:15. David is on the roof. Each passing minute is an additional finger wrapped around her throat, choking her. She starts down the corridor toward a lobby pay phone and is stopped by a thought and a vision. The thought that she has no coins—the vision of two security guards talking to an orderly, the one who was just in her room. He turns, sees her, points toward her, and calls out, "There she is."

She turns and runs toward a rear exit. As she passes a small waiting room she sees a middle-aged couple sitting there. She stops and cries out, "Call the police! Tell them that President Kennedy is going to be shot—from the sixth floor of the Book Depository Building! Call the police! Kennedy is going to be shot!"

After she runs out, the man, puzzled, turns to his wife and asks, *"Que digo Ella?"* His wife shrugs and says, *"No lo se. Digo algo del Presidente Kennedy."*

☆

The young, anxious, soon-to-be father helps the young, serene, soon-to-be mother out of the blue Studebaker and carefully guides her toward the emergency entrance. "Don't walk too fast," he nervously cautions her, "something might happen to the baby."

"Stop worrying," she assures him. "It won't fall out."

They do not see Laura run out into the parking area and get into their car in which he has left the keys. They turn only when they hear it being driven off, burning rubber.

"She's stealing our car," the woman gasps.

The man, weighing car against child, warns her, "Don't get excited, Cheryl. It'll give the baby emotional problems."

☆

The Studebaker swerves onto the boulevard, barely managing to swing around the slow-moving beer truck. Down Camelia, onto Motor Street, toward the Stemmons Freeway, veering around cars, between cars, past cursing drivers and blasting car horns. The St. Christopher medal hanging from the rearview mirror gyrates wildly as this patron saint of travelers desperately tries to escape from the car with his life.

Fortunately for the freeway's drivers, they are all exceeding the speed limit so that Laura has time to cut around them as she passes. Catastrophic pile-ups are avoided only by the failure of the law of averages. The victim of great misfortune, she is now the recipient of small blessings. The dashboard clock has stopped at 8:15.

Somehow, racing a stopped clock gives one the hope it can be beaten.

She is being drawn, as are David, Oswald, and Kennedy, toward a cataclysmic confluence, a gathering of destinies, where history will be rewritten or repeated.

Battered into insensibility on her arrival, awakened to paralyzing realities, propelled by blind panic, she has not had time to absorb what a difference two decades have made. Subliminally she is aware that the skyline is shorter, the cars longer, and the people unchanged. Like colonies of bees, they fit into the hives of any generation.

As she nears the Main Street exit she sees the Book Depository Building, the lair of the rifleman. She barely negotiates the curved off ramp, leaving dark skid marks to bear witness to a desperate journey. Like ill-starred ships that pass in the night, as the Studebaker circles the overpass the President's limousine crosses on the underpass below, rushing a dead President to Parkland Hospital.

CHAPTER 12

FRIDAY, NOVEMBER 22, 1963 . . . 12:37 P.M.

OUT A SIDE DOOR OF THE BUILDING onto the sidewalk, and my frenzied flight continues down the street. I am a quarter way down the block before the avengers swarm out of the building. By now they have become a mob, enraged, outraged, filled with righteous wrath. I throw the rifle down, insanely hoping they will stop to pick it up. Only a car, only wheels, not legs, can now save me. At the corner a truck is pulling away from the curb. If I can just get to the back of it. As I race toward it a blue car careens around the corner and screeches to a sliding stop between the truck and me. The driver is a woman with Laura's face. She reaches over, pushes the passenger door open, and, with Laura's voice, cries out, "David! Get in!"

I stare at her blankly, stupidly. Driven mad by failure, I have started to hallucinate.

"It's *me*, Laura! Get in!"

Having lost touch with reality, obeying the illusion's command, I open the car door and throw myself into its front seat. The car's wheels spin uselessly, then they catch hold of the concrete and we are catapulted forward, just ahead of the charging crowd. The wild-eyed woman impersonating my fiancée sends the car forward with such velocity, it pins me back against the seat. One man, with a belly almost bursting through his shirt, somehow manages to leap onto the hood of the car. Our eyes lock. We are the subjects, he is the camera. Shutters click, instantly recording our images for future identification. He then slides off the car.

We brake around the street corner, scraping a parked station wagon whose driver, a priest, looks out the window at the damage and then asks God to do ungodly things to the offending car.

Hyperventilating, I must make sure this woman is Laura—that she is not an apparition, not some theurgist holding me spellbound—so I make the most banal inquiry: "What are you doing here?"

"What am I doing here?" she replies sarcastically as she turns the wheel sharply, so that we whip around another corner with the car's rear end swinging in an arc. "I don't answer dumb questions."

It *is* Laura. Witches are much more diplomatic. As we cut into an alley she reveals the scope of the tragedy in short bursts of half sentences. "Kennedy was shot . . . you were blamed . . . sent to prison . . . I came back to change it . . . everything went wrong."

Her broken phrases have adhered to each other in a sorrowful summary, a sad obituary to a noble undertaking. I failed, and with that failure I dragged Laura into attempting a desperate rescue. Now, as we flee through Dallas's back streets, I will still be blamed for the President's death, and she will be damned as my accomplice. She has become an additional victim. I am suddenly filled with all-consuming anger. To have come this far on such a miraculous journey, only to have been stopped by unforeseen, uncontrollable, freak mishaps—it is an unforgivable miscarriage of justice.

Anger is the high vantage point from which I can look down on the calamity and somehow feel above it, somehow feel I still have some control over my destiny.

"You shouldn't have come," I say, irritated.

"I love you," she replies simply.

Her simplicity is not acceptable. "You didn't have to be so damned self-sacrificing," I snap back.

Bristling, she comes right back at me. "What

117

was I supposed to do, let you spend the rest of your life in prison?"

"You shouldn't have come," I repeat. "I don't care what happened."

"I don't want to argue, David. I've had a hard day. I'm beat. I have a terrible headache." Then, as she pulls the car over to the curb, she says, "Hey, look, you want me not to have come, just make believe I didn't." Then, indicating the door, she says, "Go ahead, leave. Don't forget to write."

Having a normal, domestic-type argument like any other average, everyday couple brings a certain sense of reality to an unreal situation. Letting off steam has aged us over twenty years, so that we feel as if we are again in 1985 and not marooned in 1963.

Resting her hands on the steering wheel, she summarizes this larger-than-life experience in mortal terms. "We tried."

"We tried" is a statement you make when you have just lost the World Series or come in second in the Boston Marathon. It is not profound enough, or powerful enough, to describe what has happened to us. We have transcended ordinary comparisons. Too exhausted to rise to oratorical eloquence, I draw on whatever residue I possess of the Camelot covenant. "It could have worked. It could have worked."

She realizes that I may still be irrationally dedicated to a lost cause, like a soldier continuing to fight long after his country has surrendered. "Maybe it just wasn't meant to be." Then, resting her hand on mine, she says, "Let's go home, David."

Home. After love, mother, father, child, and God, it is the sixth most graceful word in the human language. It is also a word of multiple meanings. There is the home I share with Laura. There was the home I shared with my parents and Christopher. Hidden in as yet undiscovered recesses of my mind, new thoughts are formulating, new faiths being born. They are still obscure; I cannot penetrate them. All I know is that they are like tiny mountain streams that will flow down to form some mightier waterway. Even if I did know their purpose, I would not tell Laura, for she has come here to return, not to remain. I am again aware of her voice explaining our deliverance. ". . . Dr. Koopman's house . . . it's on La Sierra, off Central Expressway . . . he's not home . . . we can use his house . . . take an ad out . . . tell him to contact us there . . . return us from his house."

Three police cars, sirens blaring, roar down the street on their way to the killing ground. They are like white corpuscles racing through the bloodstream to the point of injury, ready to attack the invading force that has caused the body such grievous damage. Soon we will be recognized as the invaders.

First we must divest ourselves of our most obvious liability, our transportation. It will take

some time before witnesses describe us and artists draw our composite pictures. Until then their
best lead will be the blue Studebaker.

"Get out of the car," I tell her.

I can see that she is in pain. There are dark
shadows around her eyes, her teeth are clenched,
her face is pale and perspiring. She won't last a
mile. Out of the corner of my eye I notice the
small suitcase lying on the backseat and the
woman's tan raincoat next to it. Reaching back
and grabbing the raincoat, I hand it to her. "Put
this on."

"Why? It's not raining."

"Just put it on," I insist. To our pursuers the
assassin team is composed of a man in a brown
suit and a woman in a pink wool dress. The less
resemblance to that image the better. A lone
woman in a raincoat will receive no attention.
Safety lies in us reaching Dr. Koopman's house
separately.

As Laura steps out of the car I open the suitcase. It contains a woman's bathrobe, under-
things, slippers, a makeup kit, a book on infant
care, and a small change purse. I open the purse.
It contains two five-dollar bills, two singles, and
a half dozen or so coins.

I realize I have the gold doubloon, but I don't
have the time to find a coin dealer to sell it to.
These twelve dollars are a godsend. Money. How
easy it is to melt into any generation if you wear

its clothing and possess its currency. Money—
the cement that holds the centuries together.

I remove the keys from the ignition, and as I
get out of the car Laura stands on the sidewalk
buttoning the raincoat. "It's too big," she grum-
bles.

"So belt it in," I suggest. "You're not going to
a fashion show." It may sound foolish for her to
complain about the fit, but placing such importance on trivialities makes this nightmarish
trauma more manageable.

I go around to the rear and open the trunk.
There is a windbreaker lying on top of the spare
tire. It has a Washington Senators patch on it. I
feel a fleeting sense of pity for the owner of this
Studebaker. He has a car no longer being manu-
factured and he roots for a baseball team no
longer in existence.

Quickly removing my jacket, I put on the windbreaker, then fold the jacket into a bundle, which
I will drop into the nearest trash basket. The
sidewalk, which was almost deserted a moment
before, has started to fill with people—many of
them exiting the office buildings and entering
nearby restaurants and bars—others leaving the
bars and restaurants and returning to the buildings—all of them looking as though they are
trying to find someone to share the moment
with. Their movements are not aimless, but neither are they purposeful. Many are subdued,
others stunned, some have tears in their eyes, a

few are flushed with anger. One thin man in his late fifties hurries by, a sly grin on his face. He is glad. I resist an impulse to throw a punch at him. I am in enough trouble without getting into a street fight with a man who would probably hide me out if he knew who I was thought to be. A balding, overweight young man brushes by me, and instead of excusing himself, just blurts out, "They shot the President."

There is not panic, but there is confusion—a moment when people are obsessed with what they've heard, not with what they see. Crowds are our best cover—out in the open our best hiding place. Being on a bus filled with bewildered people will be much safer than being alone on a street and seen by alert police officers.

"Are you sure his house is on La Sierra?" I ask, double-checking just to be sure. It's no time for us to break into the wrong home.

"Positive. It's the fourth house from the corner."

Pointing toward a bus stop at the next corner, by a theater—a bus stop that will still be there in 1985—I hand Laura precious dollars and precise instructions. "Take a bus going toward North Park—get off a few blocks beore La Sierra—then walk the rest of the way."

"What about you?"

"Don't worry—I'll be on that bus too."

As Laura heads for the bus stop I follow at a discreet distance. The enormity of the aborted attempt starts to sink in, to weigh me down, but I must pull myself out of that pit of self-pity. I must block out self-reproachment, self-condemnation.

I am walking down a street in 1963 that I know so well in 1985—but it is as if someone has erected false facades in front of the buildings. I see a six-story structure where I know a twenty-story high rise now stands. I see small restaurants and bars, spaces now occupied by computer centers and stockbrokerage houses. The movie house on the next corner has been replaced by a multitheater complex. The first-run film it is showing, *Tom Jones*, still sometimes plays on late-night television.

It is like stepping into an old, faded snapshot in which the once frozen figures have suddenly come to life. The most difficult part is relating to them. They are not wax museum imitations, but very real flesh and blood beings. I must be careful to rid myself of that disquieting sense of superiority. Yet, if knowledge is indeed power, Laura and I are the power of the planet, for we know what no one else knows.

What happened to all these people I am walking with? Is that old couple still alive in 1985? Did that young soldier go to Vietnam ... and did he return? Did that black woman live to see the progress we've made in civil rights? Would that Mexican man believe me if I told him the

Texas city of San Antonio now has a Hispanic mayor?

As I stand under the theater marquee Laura waits at the bus-stop bench with a half dozen other people. She turns and takes a quick, anxious glance toward me. I nod, reassuring her. As fatigued as she is, without any makeup, she is still one of the most beautiful women I have ever seen. It is a comeliness that is admired in all generations. She has the classic features that make young men stare and old men remember. But beauty so finely formed can often carry with it a harshness of character, a selfishness of spirit. It is Laura's eyes that belie any of those negative qualities. From them there shines forth a warmth, a gentleness, a humanity, a feminine aura so magical it makes being loved by her an Olympian honor. I must get her back to 1985, for I owe so much to her. I failed Kennedy and Christopher; I must not fail Laura.

As she boards the bus I wait until the other passengers enter before I follow—and just in time, for as I get on I glance down the street and see the police car stopped alongside the Studebaker and the two officers, guns drawn, approaching it.

For us the bus is an infinitely safer vehicle. In it we are but two people in a crowd of thirty or forty—none of them speaking to one another. Aware of the shooting, they are silent, passive, staring vacantly into space, almost in a state of suspended animation. Each is father confessor to his own thoughts, which he cannot share with others. If on the outside the public is being warned about the culprit couple, there is no blaring radio aboard the bus to point an accusing kilowatt finger at us. It is carrying us through the storm that rages outside.

From the hub of the Dallas transportation system we move through a transit spoke to the city's outer regions. The route is almost the same as it is in 1985, which proves that old bus routes never die, they just become more congested. The bus itself is like a mobile picture frame within which a human mosaic slowly changes as new passengers enter and old ones depart.

The passing landscape is familiar, although diminutive in size in some areas. It is like seeing the boy after you have already met the man he will grow up to be. Only the landmark buildings stabilize this slightly out of focus panorama. There is a sense of well-being as we pass the campus of Southern Methodist, its rectangular buildings as pristine as they will be in 1985—its red brick threads firmly attaching one generation to the next.

The gray-haired black man with the white cane gets on at Park Lane. His movements are slow and cautious. He may still have a bit of sight left, but obviously not enough to disqualify him from using that cane. As he works his way up the aisle he abruptly stops and looks at me. I do not know what mysterious forces have guided him to single me out, but it is a terrifying feeling to be stared at by a blind man. Eye contact is bone-chilling, for the liquid in his pupils has spilled out onto the whites of his eyes. In a broken, choked voice, which I fantasize as also being accusatory, he says, "President Kennedy is dead."

☆   *1:32 P.M.*

The blind man also gets off with Laura, the stop before La Sierra. I will stay on until the next stop, then I will double back. As we pull away I see Laura helping the man cross the intersection. The longer she can walk with him, the better. No one will suspect a blind man of shooting the President.

I step off the bus at Charleville, deposit the folded brown jacket in the wastebasket, turn and see the police car come to a stop behind the bus. Affecting my most casual posture, I innocently stroll by it. As I do the officer inside leans over and calls out, "Hold it, mister."

I am torn between fought and fight, and it *will be* one or the other, for I will not allow myself to be taken. Fight wins out. As I step over to the police car I weigh the odds of going for his gun if he should start to reach for it. My chances of grabbing the gun far outweigh my chance of outrunning the bullet it fires. That officer may be seconds away from a medal or an obituary. That I am even thinking of killing a police officer is unsettling, but nevertheless a definite possibility.

"What's wrong, Officer?"

"We're looking for a man and woman. He's around six feet or so, about a hundred and eighty pounds, dark hair, and has on a brown suit. She's around five eight, about a hundred and fifteen pounds, blondish hair, and is wearing a pink dress."

He has just described me, but he has been betrayed by his training, which stresses image retention—and that demands I be wearing a brown jacket and have a female companion.

"No, sir—ain't seen anyone like that," I say.

"Keep your eyes open," he cautions as he drives off. "They just shot the President."

I am annoyed to see Laura standing on the corner. Why hasn't she gone down the street to Dr. Koopman's house? Why just stand there? I want to call out, "The house, damn it, get to the house."

As I come to the corner across from her I can see fear and confusion on her face. I look down the street to a heart-stopping sight. There is a police van parked in Dr. Koopman's driveway.

Sergeant Okrand points toward the ground out-side the carport. "You're sure this is where she was?"

"Yes, sir," Teddy Palmieri responds. "One m-minute she wasn't th-there, the next sh-she was."

Sergeant Okrand tries to piece together this ever-more-mystifying puzzle. A woman suddenly appears—is run down—escapes from the hos-pital—steals a car—picks up the man who shot the President. It's the sort of case every police officer dreams about, but not on the day his son is playing for the football championship. You wait all year for that game, and then something like this comes up. It's not that he isn't pissed off about the assassination, it just came at one hell of a rotten time. People might not have agreed with Kennedy, but they had no right to take out their frustration with a gun. There are laws, and they're made to protect everyone, even the President. Somehow he had always felt a kind of grudging admiration for Kennedy. Maybe it was all those stories he heard about him get-ting laid a lot. Anyhow, Lyndon Johnson was now President, and he was one good old country boy who wouldn't be taken in by those Eastern liberals. Johnson was a change for the better, but it did not excuse what had happened. You catch the sons of bitches who did it and introduce them to a Texas tree.

A lanky, perspiring patrolman, still young enough to be shaken by a shooting, runs up to Sergeant Okrand. Somehow walking would denigrate the gravity of the moment. Running shows the proper respect. "Hey, Sarge, they got in touch with Dr. Koopman in San Francisco. He said he didn't know who the woman was. He wasn't expecting anyone."

Sergeant Okrand frowns. Then what the hell *was she doing* at the house? The burglar theory that the stuttering kid advanced didn't hold up. People don't break and enter the day before they're going to shoot the President.

"Call headquarters and tell them to have someone pick him up at the airport and bring him home. And make sure they're real nice to him." It never hurts to be nice to a Nobel Prize winner. Someday he might write a letter of recommendation when your son's applying for college.

Sergeant Okrand turns to Teddy. "Show me exactly where she was standing when you hit her."

Teddy takes a few steps toward the carport, then stops. "It was right here. I'm s-sure of it."

A nagging incertitude keeps prodding Sergeant Okrand. Hadn't he been told that the woman had mentioned Kennedy's name a few times? Why didn't he question her about it? She was semiconscious. She might have accidentally told him what was going to happen. He grits his teeth at his lack of professionalism, but it's something he won't mention in his report. Three years away from retirement, there's no sense in making waves that might wash away a damned good record.

As Sergeant Okrand turns to look toward the house he has his back to Teddy, who suddenly disappears.

☆   *OCTOBER 16, 1985*

The tubings glow an irradiated silver-white as a tense Dr. Koopman looks on. Why hasn't he been able to bring Laura back from his house? Why hasn't he been able to bring David back from the roof? He has been reactivating the machines every few minutes. There are no equipment malfunctions. The problem lies in 1963, with David and Laura. Each time they fail to return, the odds against them grow greater, for he is using up enormous amounts of energy with each attempt. If any of the delicate component parts should be overloaded and break down, it would take weeks to replace them. Certainly a Providence that blessed him with the wisdom to flee the Nazis, and the ability to win world honors, will not begrudge him the good fortune of bringing back his dear friends.

As the tubings rise he sees legs—but the legs are in blue pants and Laura wore a dress. The legs are followed by a short, thin body, and the head of a teenager, who stands there terrified, eyes bulging. It's been many years, but Dr. Koopman recognizes him. It's Teddy, the boy who would come to pick up his car when he was out of town.

A petrified Teddy, near collapse, hears a voice say, "What are you doing at Dr. Koopman's house?" He manages to stammer out, "I w-w-was sh-showing the police wh-where the l-lady c-came from."

"What happened to the lady?" the voice asks.

"I h-hit her b-b-by mistake."

Like a Rubik's Cube that has been impossible to align, all the colors suddenly fall into place. But they are dark colors that tell a most ominous story. Laura has been hit by a car—the police are at his house—escape back into 1985 may be impossible.

Teddy, in a faint voice, cries out, "Wh-wh-where am I?"

Dr. Koopman resets the power thrust. The tubings lower over the trembling boy.

☆   *NOVEMBER 22, 1963 . . . 1:52 P.M.*
Teddy reappears behind Sergeant Okrand an instant before Okrand turns around.

131

"Hey, what's wrong with you?" Sergeant Okrand asks as he sees that the boy's face is a ghostly gray and that his whole body is shaking in some kind of seizure.

"I w-w-was j-just here."

"Of course you were just here."

"And th-then I w-wasn't."

"Where were you?" Sergeant Okrand asks, his face darkening with suspicion.

"I d-don't know."

"Take a guess."

"S-somewhere f-far away."

Sergeant Okrand closes his eyes. November 22 is going to be a day to remember.

CHAPTER 13

NOVEMBER 22, 1963 . . . 2:04 P.M.

T HE COIN DEALER STUDIES THE GOLD
doubloon. Sitting on a counter behind
him is a small portable television set.
There is a film clip of Lee Harvey Oswald being
taken out of the ambulance. As he is wheeled on
a gurney to the hospital he re-creates the death
scene for the cameras. The little bastard is a
good actor. There are actually tears in his eyes
as he tells what a hero Kennedy was to him.

The coin dealer points to the television set
and solemnly says, "It's terrible. Just terrible.
Terrible."

"Terrible," I reply. It seems a safe word to use
with him.

Then there is an interview with the owner of

the getaway Studebaker. His car an accessory, his wife in labor, he is a nervous wreck, but not so distraught not to know he may never again have a television camera on him. He declares, "If it's a boy, I'm going to name him John Fitzgerald Cohen."

There are scattered shots of people in the streets. Many of them are crying. Little children seem to hold on a bit tighter to their parents.

Captain Will Fritz and other law-enforcement people stand in front of the cameras. Their faces bear the burden of the failure of their collective agencies. Fritz, close-mouthed, tight-lipped, hangs on to each word an extra beat before releasing it to a stunned world. It is a painful, humiliating moment for him. It is like a pitcher giving up the game-winning home run and then announcing that he will make an all-out effort to find the ball.

His words are familiar: ". . . all-points bulletins . . . the most massive manhunt in history . . . leads being investigated . . ." And then the most cutting statement of all: "We have talked to Lee Harvey Oswald, who has provided us with valuable information."

Huntley-Brinkley come on, and in that low-key, understated manner of theirs, as if someone has wound them down, they discuss a President's death with the same intensity they would give to the naming of the new Miss America.

"It's strange," the coin dealer muses, "but

when terrible things like this happen, business always get better. People start to sell coins, gold, silver, like the world's coming to an end." Then, holding up the doubloon, he says, "They sell things for maybe half of what they're worth."

In so many words he's told me I'll get half of what the coin is worth.

"How much?" I ask.

"Seventeen hundred."

"It's worth three thousand," I protest.

He shrugs, uninterested. "In twenty years it'll be worth twenty thousand. Come back and see me then. I'll be here."

Oh, how I'd like to tell him that in twenty years this store would be a pizza parlor. Instead I say, "Okay, seventeen hundred." It will buy food, clothes, a car to get around with, an ad in the Dallas *Morning News*, and a room at the Adolphus Hotel. It is from the Adolphus Hotel— that grand old landmark building that hasn't changed in seventy years—that Dr. Koopman can return Laura to 1985. As for myself, I cannot shake off a persistent thought that somehow there is still something I can do—that all is not lost.

☆   *3:10 P.M.*

The more familiar the surroundings, the better I will function, which is why I go to Neiman-

Marcus. I have been there a hundred times in years to come. I am aware of the location of its exits and entrances, its emergency stairways, all of which could serve me well. It also has the advantage of being just a few blocks from the Book Depository Building. The closer to that damned spot, the further away I am from capture. The search is for a couple who took off in a blue car and then abandoned it—a desperate couple who are fleeing the city, not circling back so one of them can go shopping at Neiman-Marcus.

All those customers must know what happened. Do they still go shopping because they don't care or have they been driven there by their helplessness to do anything about it? It must be the latter, for neither the customers nor the salespeople seem motivated to buy or sell. It all resembles a social ballet being performed in slow motion, with each person assigned a role and, in the tradition of the show having to go on, each continues to play his part. Each may be overcome by shock, fear, rage, grief, or tears, but not by immobility. I remember once, as a small boy, seeing hundreds of ants going out of and into a hole in the ground. I put a firecracker into that hole. It must have been a horrifying moment for those ants, their Hiroshima. I then dug away part of the earth with a stick and saw the dead, the dying, the mangled bodies. Other ants were already carrying them away to wherever ants take their casualties, while still others were going about the job of finding food, of rebuilding their shattered society. I felt power, guilt, loss, and a helplessness to undo what I had done, so I moved on. Movement means survival, just as shopping for these people verifies their existence. Life is not always symbolized by grand and stately actions.

I purchase a small Louis Vuitton suitcase from a young salesgirl whose eyes are still red from crying. I really cannot afford to spend the $125 for it, but knowing that the suitcase will cost $700 in 1985 makes it a bargain I just can't pass up.

In the men's department I buy some shirts, underwear, socks, and two pullover sweaters. I will have to have some weight in the suitcase when I check into the hotel.

In the men's room I put the clothing into the suitcase and then I take the escalator up to women's wear. I confess to a saleswoman that I'm a little embarrassed to be shopping on a day like this but it's my wife's birthday. The saleswoman, in her early forties and married, is very understanding about my predicament. In a way I feel she secretly admires me for thinking of my wife at a moment like this. She helps me select a dress, shoes, and makeup kit.

Before leaving the store I buy a wallet and a Stetson. Out onto Ervay Street, right on Commerce, one block to Akard, and there she stands, right where she's been since 1912, the Adolphus Hotel. This once grande dame of grand hotels, a bit faded now, in need of some cosmetic repair, a bit out of vogue; she has to gracefully take a backseat to the new debutantes on the block, the Statler Hilton and the Sheraton. In 1981 she will be restored to her former splendor. Aging but still proud Greek figures look down from lofty granite casements. Her tower is crowned with antique bronze. Terraced gardens rise toward the city skyline. From this once elegant lady, my lady will find her way home.

As I walk up to the doorman I breathe a bit heavily in exasperation and complain, "Damn cab broke down about three blocks away." Taking my suitcase, the somber doorman replies, "Yes, sir, it's been a bad day all around."

The harried desk clerk searches through his bookings list for my reservation. In crisis it is the hotels and the airports that reflect the prevailing anxiety level. The Adolphus mirrors Dallas's trauma. There are canceled bookings, an exodus of guests who no longer find the city a place to spend the upcoming holidays. Business meetings have been changed, dinner engagements broken, theater tickets forgotten. Offsetting all that is the flood of new reservations as Dallas is about to be invaded by the thrill-seekers and their cameras and the truth-seekers and their questions. Hordes of government investigators and armies of domestic and foreign journalists will be encamped here for months to come. A hotel room near the execution street will be harder to find than a witness who can lucidly recall the event.

"We don't seem to have a reservation for you, Mr. Russell," the desk clerk apologizes.

"My secretary confirmed it this morning," I insist. It is absolutely imperative that I get a room. "Look, I know how confused everything has been down here, with what's happened."

"It's been chaotic, sir," he admits, accepting this opening I've given him to excuse what might very well be a clerical error.

"I had a reservation confirmed. I expect you to honor it."

He fumbles for words. "We're booked up solid, sir."

I know that all hotels always hold a few rooms for emergency situations. Unfortunately I can't tell him the scope of this emergency. Instead I take out a fifty-dollar bill, and as I set it down on the counter I say, "I've had a rough plane trip, my cab broke down, and my ulcer's acting up. I need a room."

A bit uncertain, he stares at me for a moment, possibly trying to measure my need. I must measure up, for he pulls a card out of a file and says, "I think Room 311 might be available." Then, to his everlasting credit, he pushes the fifty-dollar bill back toward me. "That won't be necessary, sir." If I should ever get back to 1985, and he is still working at the Adolphus, I will make it a point to see that he is properly rewarded.

☆   4:25 P.M.

At the classified department of the Dallas *Morning News* I hand the sales representative my ad, which she assures me will appear in the Sunday edition. The ad reads, "Uncle Hendrik, arrived in Dallas. Checked into the Adolphus Hotel. Please contact us on Saturday at 10:30 A.M. in Room 311. Love, David and Laura."

☆   4:45 P.M.

The Majestic Theatre is on Elm Street. A legitimate theater in 1985, it was a motion-picture house in 1963. Laura has been inside, waiting. As my eyes adjust to the dark, on a quick count there seem to be about a hundred people in the audience. Does watching *Beach Party* give them a sense of security? Do Robert Cummings, Dorothy Malone, and Frankie Avalon provide some kind of celluloid bridge that will help them get over this day?

I sit down next to Laura, and as I hand her

some money and a spare room key, which she puts in the pocket of her raincoat, I whisper, "Take a cab to the Adolphus. Room 311." I then move to another seat.

A moment after Laura gets up and leaves, I follow. While she waits at the curb for a cab I stand in the lobby making believe I am studying a poster for their next attraction, *The Pink Panther*. As soon as she is in the cab I start walking the five blocks to the hotel. I can see the sun setting behind the Book Depository Building. This ugly day is finally hiding its scars in early evening shadows.

☆   *5:05 P.M.*

I stop at a drugstore across the street from the hotel and buy toilet articles I think we might need—toothbrushes, toothpaste, scissors, needles and thread, combs, things like that. The only mistake I make is when I ask the clerk for some Advil.

"Advil? I never heard of it, sir. What is it?"

I must be more careful not to forget that I have been using products during my adult life that were unknown in 1963. I tell the clerk that Advil is a new vitamin, then ask for a bottle of Bayer aspirin.

I leave the drugstore, stop at the corner, look

141

around, and it is as if I have been struck by a bolt of lightning. There, not ten feet away from me, is Dr. Koopman.

He is sitting in the back of a police car. A new plaid suitcase, which I remember as a battered plaid suitcase, lies on the seat next to him. His suit spans all generations, for it is the same wrinkled blue suit he wore when we first met. In his middle forties, he is a middle-aged version of the lovable old man he will become. His hair and beard are an equal mixture of brown and gray—those undersized, rectangular glasses still sit precariously on the end of his ample nose—that cherubic countenance still conveys images of Christmas trees, a fireplace, and family He turns his head, our eyes meet, and I am bathed in that holiday spirit. I want to rush over and take him in my arms and tell him we will someday meet, someday share in a great adventure. The light changes and he is gone. Whether the future remains is still to be seen.

CHAPTER 14

A S I SHAVE, LAURA LEANS BACK IN THE
tub of hot water, eyes closed, in a state of
relaxed ecstasy, as aching muscles and
bruised bones respond to the soothing heat.

"I love the dress you bought me, David. And
the shoes. You remembered my size."

Again, by simply acting like we have come
here for a weekend of pleasure, we avoid facing
the compactorlike pressures that can easily crush
us. It would be suicidal to continually discuss
our predicament—trapped in 1963—being sought
for the murder of the President—relying on a
pixie-like man to find our ad in the classified
section of an old newspaper.

The waiter brings up the dinner I have ordered from room service. It is the biggest meal I could order and still have them believe one person could eat it all.

After the waiter leaves, Laura comes out of the bathroom, a large bath towel wrapped around her. I have turned the television set off. I cannot allow our first meal in 1963 to be rendered indigestible by us having to hear and see Lee Harvey Oswald being given a hero's accolade.

Although Laura is still exhausted, and still hurting, she eats well, and the color has come back into her face. Her thought processes seem stabilized and her goals are clearly defined. She has locked out the past we are temporarily sharing and zeroed in on the more realistic future. "As soon as we get back we're getting married, David."

I nod. I'm not about to tell her I've made other plans. Then, softly, she says, "I hope I'm pregnant."

I give her my best pregnant smile, for I, too, remember our last night together in 1985. In a way I hope she *is* carrying our child. It may be all of me she will have when she returns.

"If it's a boy, we'll name him Christopher," she says.

I nod again, not confiding that it is possible that Christopher may be around to be the godfather of the baby. Ever since I saw Dr. Koopman in the police car, what was once a persistent thought has evolved into a plan. It is a wild plan, a desperate plan, but a plan nevertheless. I have failed to save John Kennedy, but I have not yet failed to save Christopher. I have not failed to stop a wicked war.

☆   *8:25 P.M.*

Laura has put on one of the pullover sweaters to go to bed in. Her breasts move sensually beneath the cable stitches. It does not fully cover her behind, so that part of the cleavage shows.

God forgive me—we are on the run for our lives—she is not that well—and yet I feel myself hardening. As she bends over to pull the bed sheets back, I see past those magnificent buttocks to the erotic breach between them.

Under the sheet, eyes closed, she holds her hand out toward me. "Lie down," she whispers, almost asleep.

I lie down next to her, keeping the lower half of my body away from her.

"Hold me, David."

I am ashamed of myself. Here is the woman I love, who only wants to be held, cuddled, protected, and I am almost overcome with a primitive urge so strong it rises above sensitivity, morality, and compassion.

With a contented sigh, she turns toward me, and as she does so her hand accidentally touches

145

my erection. To her everlasting credit, she does not react with outrage at my lack of understanding. She gently closes her fingers around my rocklike protrusion and, with a sleepy smile, says, "Shame on you." The woman in her comforts her self-indulgent lover—"Let me sleep a little while"—a promise that soon she will be available for his pleasure. She falls asleep holding me lovingly, possessively, in her hand.

Somewhere deep within the psyche of women there is an inner sense of satisfaction that they are desired, that they can cause this hardness in a man. More important, somewhere within woman's nature there is an almost supernatural understanding and acceptance of the innate baseness of men.

☆

About ten minutes later I carefully get out of the bed, taking pains not to disturb Laura, although a gun going off at this point would probably not wake her.

Why can't I remember the phone number of my house in 1963? Is it natural to forget something that was once second nature to me? Why do we remember embarrassing moments and not pleasing ones? Why do we remember the bad words told us and not the kind ones? Why can't we forget the harsh voices and not the gentle ones?

After a moment of concentrated thinking, of numbers tumbling through my mind like falling pellets, the right combination locks into place. I pick up the phone. "I'd like to place a long distance call to Linnett, New Mexico. Sheffield 3-4285."

I am filled with the expectation and dread you feel as a doctor examines your X ray.

"Russell residence," says the gruff voice I will never forget. It belongs to Chief Willoughby. What are the police doing at my parents' house?

"May I speak to Mr. Russell?"

"Who's calling?"

"A friend. Is he home?"

"They're at the funeral home. Their son, David, died."

My mind struggles to accept the news of my death. Only a deathly silence can cope with it. Chief Willoughby's voice fills the void. "They say it happened right about twelve-fifteen. He was eating lunch in the school yard and he suddenly fell over."

Twelve-fifteen. Exactly when I returned to 1963. Dr. Koopman was right to be concerned about it. The same life force cannot exist in two bodies at the same time. For whatever reason, the older life force has survived—the younger one hasn't.

I hang the phone up, then turn and look at

Laura. It has been a double disaster. If I, as a ten-year-old, died, then so did Laura as a seven-year-old. Why have we lived and our younger selves not? We have broken natural laws, slipped through the firmament, revised the canons of creation, reversed the flow of time. We have returned to yesterday, defying a universe that is hurtling toward tomorrow. What unalterable life cycles have we altered and recycled? Laura and I are merely voyagers, momentarily trapped halfway through our journey. I must get Laura back to 1985, and I must save Christopher. I cannot leave my parents childless. So long as I have a breath in me, my death must not have been in vain.

CHAPTER 15

OCTOBER 16, 1985

THE PANIC THAT ENGULFED DR. KOOP-man when he looked at the computer's screen and read about the search for the couple believed to have killed President Kennedy has subsided. A hopeful flush of triumph surges through him as he peers at the classified-ad page in the Sunday edition of the Dallas *Morning News*. The ad reads, "Uncle Hendrik, arrived in Dallas. Checked into the Adolphus Hotel. Please contact us on Saturday at 10:30 A.M. in Room . . ." Dr. Koopman squints, trying to make out the room number on the screen. It is blurred. It is either Room 311 or 317. The rest of the words are clear: "Love, David and Laura."

He can decide the room number later. First he

must get to the Building and Safety Department at City Hall, where he can secure the original blueprints of the Adolphus Hotel.

As he walks out onto the street it is as though he has walked into a brick wall. He is staggered by a returning memory, a recall of a past event so frightful it is painful just to be aware of it. A police officer by the nane of Sergeant Okrand came upon the suspected assassins at the Adolphus Hotel. They fled, stole a car from the hotel garage, and were pursued. In a wild chase, they crashed, and while attempting to escape on foot were shot. Never identified, they nevertheless went down in history as the slayers of the President. Sergeant Okrand and Lee Harvey Oswald were flown to Washington, where President Johnson gave them appropriate medals to show a nation's appreciation of their efforts.

☆ *SATURDAY, NOVEMBER 23, 1963 . . . 7:40 A.M.*
Laura is already awake, still wearing the pullover sweater. She sits on the edge of the bed, her hand on my chest, studying me with a smile. There is a physical intimacy so intense it is almost electrifying. Nothing we feel is preplanned but simply a matter of allowing ourselves to be carried along by the dynamics of the moment. We are trapped in a hotel room, isolated and

momentarily protected from a dangerous, hostile outside world. Salvation, if it does indeed exist, will come from inside this confined area, within these few square feet. Just as wartime conditions are often the basis for great love stories, immediate danger and possible death act as powerful aphrodisiacs. Two people confined this closely have all their senses heightened. They are aware only of each other, of the need to show or to prove their physical humanity. I reach beneath her sweater to cup her breast and feel her nipple grow taut in the palm of my hand. She runs the fingers of one hand up along the inside of my thigh until they are cradling and gently massaging more sensitive areas. Then, on her knees, straddling my body, with a sharp intake of breath and a soft moan, she slowly lowers herself onto me. The deeper I am drawn into her, the safer I am, and the further away a threatening world.

☆   *9:43 A.M.*

Sergeant Okrand arrives at the Adolphus Hotel. He is tired, frustrated, annoyed. He didn't get home till almost two in the morning, what with waiting for Dr. Koopman to be brought home from the airport, getting a statement from him, then having to file reports with the Dallas Police Department, the FBI, and the Secret Service. Now he has to pick up these government investigators, take them to Dr. Koopman's house, where the kid ran the woman down, then to Parkland Hospital, where she stole the car, then to Elm Street, where she picked the assassin up, then to Live Oak Avenue, where they abandoned the car. Damn, he's already told everyone everything he knows. Where the hell were they when it counted? They've come here a day late and a President short. He's going to have to chauffeur them all over Dallas, and the part that really hurts is that they're probably getting time and a half. Christ, wandering around Dallas looking for this couple is about as smart as searching your house for the guy who made it with your wife. They're probably a thousand miles away by now.

☆   *OCTOBER 16, 1985*

There are beads of perspiration on Dr. Koopman's forehead. This time it is a bit more complicated. First he will have to let David know the exact spot in the hotel room where he wants them to stand. He can accomplish this by sending some object back. Wherever it appears in the room, they will know that is the point of return. It must be an object so different from anything in

1963 that they will in no way be able to overlook it.

He picks up a silver-framed, eight-by-ten photograph of him and then-President Jimmy Carter, taken when he went to Washington to receive the Medal of Freedom Award. Onto it he Scotch tapes a piece of paper on which he has written, "Laura at 10:45. David at 11:00."

He takes one last concerned look at the laboratory's machinery. The accelerator and its heavy-duty parts, which have created the massive surges of energy, have stood up well. Some of the smaller computer components, however, are beginning to buckle under the overloads placed on their delicate silicon systems. Too many warning lights have been flashing. He is down to patchwork repairs. How many more times he can successfully reach back in time now becomes less a matter of science and more a matter of luck.

Just one final decision—to decide which room to return the photograph to, 311 or 317. His lucky number is 7. Why shouldn't it be their lucky nunber too?

☆   *NOVEMBER 23, 1963 . . . 10:20 A.M.*
I have removed the back panel of the television set and fitted the pink wool dress into it. As I

start to replace the panel, Laura comes out of the bathroom wearing the dress and shoes I bought her at Neiman-Marcus.

"Why are you hiding the dress, David?"

"So no one will find it for a while."

"It won't matter if they do, will it?"

As I tighten the screws I casually say, "It never hurts to be sure."

After a momentary pause, as though she is weighing different, disturbing possibilities, she says, "Sure of what, David? We won't be here, will we?"

"I never said we would be," I reply, focusing my attention on the job at hand.

"Look at me. . . . I said look at me, David."

It is almost impossible to look someone you love in the eye—someone with whom you have shared the most intimate passions, the most secret thoughts—and then lie to that person, but I will try. To leave, with Kennedy dead, Oswald alive, Johnson's Asian misadventure about to begin, Christopher lost in that conflict's cauldron, our younger selves sacrificed—*that* is impossible.

I must placate her until she is returned. "You're getting all upset for no reason, Laura. Of course we're going back. Just trust me."

Casting my words aside like so many corrupt particles of deception, she comes over to me, kneels down, and, stroking my cheek, gently consoles me. "There's nothing more you can do, David."

My silence tells her I don't agree.

"If we could still save Christopher, save all those other lives, I would try—but we can't. If we remain here, we can't change anything. If we're caught, we spend the rest of our lives in prison. We don't deserve that, David. Just tell me," she pleads, "just tell me what there is you think you can *do*?"

I cannot tell her, for then she might want to stay with me, and it is far too dangerous to allow that.

She then uses the only weapon she has left— the only roadblock she can throw up that can keep me from starting on this desperate journey. "As God is my witness, David, I will not go back without you."

☆

Sergeant Okrand, pacing in the lobby, looks at his watch, his irritation turning to anger. Where the hell are they? They tell him to be here at 9:45 sharp and here it is after 10:30. Damned bureaucrats, all of them lazy fat-asses, wasting taxpayers' money, and there's no way to fire them. As long as it's one bureaucrat, one vote, no congressional committee will have the balls to dismantle their agency. He picks up the house phone. "Would you please ring Room 325?"

☆

Something must be wrong. The small clock on the night table reads 10:40. Dr. Koopman should have contacted us ten minutes ago. I stand by the door, Laura by the window, so that we view every part of the room.

"Maybe he didn't find the ad," she says.

I realize what a tenuous umbilical cord connects us to Mother Earth of 1985. Our rebirth depends on a dear old man, brilliant and lovable, but also an old man with questionable eyesight and the spirit of a leprechaun.

Each extra hour we are bound to this room increases by tenfold our chances of being caught. I temporarily put aside my problem of how I will induce Laura to leave ahead of me. The more immediate problem is that *no one* can leave without Dr. Koopman.

There is a knock on the door. Every unexpected sound sets my teeth on edge, starts the adrenaline racing to protect organs that may not need it. Will I be like the boy who cried wolf? Will I one time really need that adrenaline, and it will refuse to leave its adrenal home, thinking I am lying?

"Who is it?" I call out.

"Maid. Room service."

I open the door partway and tell the heavysct, middle-aged black woman, "Thank you, but can you come back after lunch?"

"Yes, sir."

As I am about to close the door my senses are jarred by a silver-framed photograph that lies atop the towels on her cart. It's of Dr. Koopman and Jimmy Carter.

This time my adrenaline has a true emergency to respond to. Trying to keep my hand from trembling, I point to the photograph. "Where did you get that?"

Puzzled at my obvious interest, she replies, "Room 317. That lady done left it when she checked out this mornin'."

Dr. Koopman *has* contacted us. He *has* shown us a point of return. But he has done so in the wrong room. It's a mistake that Dr. Koopman can explain afterward. Stepping out into the hall, I pick up the photograph and say, "Are you sure it was Room 317?"

"Yes, sir, it was just lyin' in the middlle of the floor, near the bed. Folks go off forgettin' things all the time."

Laura has joined me. The maid gives her a quick glance, but not a suspicious one. Guests who register by themselves at night often leave with a friend in the morning.

"Can you show me exactly *where* it was lying on the floor?"

Before she can protest I hand her a fifty-dollar bill. A magnanimous tip in 1985, it is a week's salary in 1963. "Yes, sir," she beams as she puts the bill in her apron pocket. "I sure do remember where I saw it." Then, reaching into a waste-paper basket on her cart, she takes out a folded piece of paper. "This here was stuck to it."

I unfold the paper, revealing the magical words "Laura at 10:45. David at 11:00." A quick glance back toward the clock on the night table reveals we still have almost two minutes.

Room 317 is just a few doors down the hall. The maid opens the door, steps in, and lays the photograph down on the floor. "Yes, sir, it was layin' right here. I'll never forget it."

I pick the photograph up, not wanting it to suddenly disappear in front of the maid's eyes. I also step back a few feet from the spot, and with a slight movement of my hand motion Laura to do the same. It wouldn't do for one of us to disappear either. My plan is to let the 10:45 return go by—get the maid out of the room—then somehow convince Laura to return at 11:00.

☆   *10:44* A.M.

Sergeant Okrand, in a nasty mood, steps out of the elevator and starts down the hall toward Room 325. He is even annoyed by the maid's cart, abandoned in the middle of the hall. He throws a quick look at the three people standing in the room—and then his heart fairly explodes against his chest, his head seems almost to burst with the pressure of the suddenly rampaging blood. Jesus Christ Almighty God—it's her! It's her! He draws his service revolver.

☆

"Don't move! Don't anyone move!" this man is yelling as he bursts into the room pointing a gun at Laura. The maid screams, "Lord save me" as I hurl the framed photograph toward his face. Its silver-framed edge catches him on the forehead, cutting through the flesh, knocking him backward as he fires. The bullet tears through the wall behind Laura. I lunge at him and catch his gun hand, immobilizing it. Then, jamming my foot into his stomach, I fall over backward, flipping him over my head. Having managed to hang on to the gun, he lands on his back near the bed, twists around in a crouched

159

position, and aims the gun at me. There is no way he can miss, except for one unexpected development. He disappears.

☆

Sergeant Okrand will relive the moment the rest of his life. One second he is aiming at this man's heart and just as he starts to squeeze the trigger he is sucked into a maelstrom of brilliant, blinding light patterns. He feels himself disintegrate into millions of parts, and when he comes together again, and the lights lift, he is standing in a chamber whose walls are filled with all sorts of machines—and he is aiming at an old man's face that peers at him through a thick round window. His finger finishes squeezing the trigger and he fires. A thousand jagged cracks appear in the window, but it does not break. A voice with a foreign accent calls out, "Don't shoot or I can't get you back." As he turns, wild-eyed, to see where the voice is coming from, he is again enveloped in the radiant coruscation, again rendered into uncountable fragments, and again on the floor of the hotel room. As the screaming maid points at him Special Agents Kimbrough and Allison leap on him, pin his arms behind his back, and snap handcuffs on them. Sergeant Okrand hysterically cries out, "Not me! I'm a police officer! Stop them! They killed the President!"

☆

While the maid screams "Lord, save me," Laura and I try to find salvation in our feet. For some reason, as we run out I pick up the photograph of Dr. Koopman and Jimmy Carter. Across the hall, down the stairs to the second floor—past the Kings' Club, a meeting room devoid of meeters on this solemn Saturday morning—then down the next stairway to the garage, where many dozens of cars are parked. To my eyes, still unpracticed in evaluating 1963 objects, it looks like a huge antique-car show. A parking attendant drives a Cadillac toward the exit.

"Find one with a key in it," I tell Laura as we fan out, going from car to car. I know we have only minutes to work with. As soon as Dr. Koopman returns that man with the gun, as he will, this hotel will be surrounded and our escape cut off.

"Over here," Laura calls, pointing to a gray, four-door Rolls-Royce, which is parked in the front row with a clear path to the exit. I wanted a more conservative car, one which would blend in with traffic, but beggars can't be choosers, so I accept the Rolls-Royce.

161

Out the exit, past the attendant who is holding the door open for the Cadillac's owner, a short, thin man in cowboy boots and hat. I miss him by mere inches, which prompts him to give me the time-honored finger of frustration.

As I turn onto Field Street I see the attendant in the rearview mirror as he runs out into the street, shaking a fist at us. It is always a relief to see any threatening figure receding in the distance.

Onto Elm and toward the freeway. We are caught in an evertightening vise, which has slowly pressed us into a stolen Rolls-Royce, highly visible, highly vulnerable. It is like a giant chess game where we have inexorably lost all our major pieces. Room 311 was our Queen, Dr. Koopman our King, both now gone. Laura and I are the two remaining pawns, frantically moving from Dealey Square to some unknown square on this huge chessboard called Dallas.

I hear the siren. In the rearview mirror I see the police car, red light flashing, as it bears down on us.

CHAPTER 16

NOVEMBER 23, 1963 . . . 11:04 A.M.

THE POLICE CAR ROARS PAST US, SCRE-
eches to a skidding stop at the corner,
and the two officers jump out and race
into the office building. Whoever they are after
is a person who can always depend on me to put
in a kind word for him.

There is no doubt that if we remain in this car
for any length of time, those police sirens will
soon be sounding for us. This Rolls-Royce can
serve only as a temporary sanctuary. It got us
out of the hotel, but it will surely take us from
dilemma to disaster if we stay with it. Only my
stealing a fire engine would have made us more
visible.

"Not the freeway, David," Laura says in a

surprisingly controlled voice. I throw a quick, concerned glance at her. It is disquieting to have someone speak that calmly in such a terrifying situation. And, indeed, her entire demeanor *has* changed. A strange sort of beatific tranquility has taken hold of her. She sits there serene, composed. It is the sort of imperturbability, the kind of stoicism, that overtakes soldiers moments before they charge the enemy lines. Resigned to an unavoidable task, they finally face it with resigned fortitude. I have seen women overcome with such self-controlled disregard for danger when coming to the aid of a stricken child. Laura has been pushed to the edge. If she has to be swept over that edge, she will go with style, grace, and dignity. Whatever the outcome, she lives in peaceful coexistence with all possibilities. I wish I had the ability to psych myself out like that. Self-deception is often self-preservation. I am comforted by her presence, but also fearful for her, for she is now partnered with me in what I must attempt to do—a partnership where the risks are as high as the rewards.

"Not that way," she says. She points in another direction. "That way." She is giving me instructions as though we were out on a casual weekend trip to pick up groceries and dry cleaning.

Of course she is right. In the event of a car chase, freeways have only off ramps. Surface streets have side streets, alleys, underground garages, buildings to hide in, other cars to commandeer. She is thinking in terms of immediate survival. I have been thinking in long-term survival tactics, like what I will be doing tomorrow. We must find a place to spend the night, another place for Dr. Koopman to contact us.

"We've got to get another car," I tell her.

"Not a stolen one this time, David."

"Good idea. I'll ask the owner's permission first." Any kind of sarcasm feels good at a moment like this. "And remind me to tell the hotel how to reach us. We owe them for the room and food."

She doesn't even bother to respond to that. "How much did you get for the doubloon?"

"Seventeen hundred dollars."

"It was worth three thousand," she admonishes me, as though the extra dollars make all the difference in the world. Maybe they would have in the world we were once in, but in the one we're in now, the money I have can easily buy us the needed wheels. "There's a used-car dealer around here somewhere."

"Goss on Ross," she says. "I bought my Corvette there."

Of course—Goss on Ross. Goss, the used-car dealer on Ross Avenue. What is it they used to call themselves—"Goss on Ross, the Trading Hoss?" In all their ads they proudly let you know they've been at the same location since

World War II. It's less than two miles from here. Thank God for businessmen who know how to stay put.

☆

The Ross Avenue Baptist Church is just two blocks from the used-car lot. "Wait in there," I tell Laura as I stop in front of it. "Give me a half hour, then meet me out front."

The parking lot adjacent to the church is filled. Kennedy's death is more than a parochial tragedy. On this weekend Catholic, Protestant, Jewish, and even atheist prayers will intermingle on their way skyward. Even those who hated him will cease their public denouncements and go back into their closets, where they can curse in private. For many years afterward, Dallas, in shame and guilt, would wear the scarlet letter "A" as the assassin city. That historical burden was lifted when Robert Kennedy was murdered in Los Angeles. A strange sense of gratitude developed. You very rarely hear Dallas people speak ill of the City of the Angels.

The bulletin board in front of the church tells the passerby that Pastor Robert H. Taylor will be conducting special memorial services that morning. As Laura goes in I cannot help wondering what the congregation would do if they knew where she had come from. They accept the concept of eternity. Would they accept twenty years hence? What if Christ got off the cross and said, "Hello, everybody"—would they run screaming from the church, throwing away their Bibles as they did so? Does the survival of all religions really depend on God never appearing?

☆   *11:24 A.M.*

I drive into an underground public garage. The attendant is a slick-haired, leather-jacketed, gum-popping clone of the Fonz from *Happy Days*. A small radio on the counter next to him, turned up to a deafening volume, blares out some rock music. His eyes stare vacantly into space as he nods his head from side to side with the beat. The song ends and a fast-talking disc jockey cries out, "Rock on, soul mates, that was 'Fingertips, Part Two,' with Stevie Wonder. And now, fifteen weeks on the Hot One Hundred, and now number one, *numero uno*—'Sugar Shack,' with Jerry Gilmer and the Fireballs. Go, Jerry, baby." And the Fireballs blast away.

If word had gone out to look for a Rolls-Royce, this is not a radio station that would cut into the Fireballs to pass the news along. As the clone disinterestedly hands me a parking stub, he blows a huge bubble, which bursts and sticks to his mouth and nose. Assassinations don't bother a fellow like this. World wars pass by him almost unnoticed. He is living proof that he is descended from the ape—and nothing we can do for him can ever bring him back up to the ape level.

As I park I remove the owner's registration slip, which is attached to the shaft of the steering wheel. I may need it for identification. The owner is a Gordon Stallings of Austin, Texas.

☆   *11:33* A.M.

"Yes, sir, Mr. Stallings," the car salesman says as he points to the 1957 Cadillac. "This here is a right smart car." Pointing to its rear end, he says, "College kids love those big tail fins." I've told him I'm buying it for my nephew who is attending SMU.

"Two hundred seventy-five seems a bit steep."

"Yes, sir, it seems so, but it's really not, sir." I like this salesman. In his late twenties, with horn-rimmed glasses, he says "Yes, sir" and "No, sir." I had almost forgotten that there was once a day when car salesmen were friendly, courteous, and honest. That honesty compels him to confide, "I admit this here car has been around the block a few times—but then there's no substitute for experience, is there, sir?"

I like the way this pleasant man is selling mc.

"Yes, sir," he emphasizes, "your nephew and his buddies can knock around in it, and it'll keep going. An old Cadillac and young college students were meant for each other."

He has just made a sale.

In his office, as he fills out the transfer of ownership papers, my attention is drawn to a photograph on his desk—of a teenage Marine standing guard in front of a building. He is young, bright-eyed, proud, secure in his ability to protect that building.

"That's my brother, Ted," the salesman says. "And that's our embassy in Saigon ... that's in Vietnam ... in the Far East."

A place unknown to most Americans in 1963, he has had to, step by step, pinpoint its location in a part of the world that will soon become the flash point of conflict, confusion, crime, Communist belligerence, and capitalist intransigence.

I can see the affection in his eyes as he speaks of a brother he obviously feels a deep love for. "He's a great kid. Has a real flair for painting. You ought to see the watercolors he does."

This salesman and I share a common bond— brothers we love—both still alive in 1963—but if both are to survive, I must get away and be free to go about my desperate business.

When he asks for some identification so he can complete the ownership transfer, I open my wallet, bulging with cash, look through it, then mutter, "Damn, I must have left my stuff back at the hotel." Then, taking out the registration slip, I say, "How about this—the registration slip to my other car?"

There is no doubt he is impressed. A man who is the registered owner of a Rolls-Royce, and the obvious owner of a wallet filled with cash, is a man who can be trusted. "This'll do just fine, Mr. Stallings."

As he Scotch tapes the temporary registration slip onto the rear window of the car, he says, "You should receive your license plates in three to four weeks."

In addition to the car, I have also bought time—not much, but some. Eventually word will be out about the stolen Rolls—it will sooner or later be found at the garage—Mr. Stallings' name will probably be mentioned—this car sales-man might very well put it all together and call the police—and Laura and I and the Cadillac will become the flash point of the search. But even if all I get out of it is an extra day or so, it will be all I need.

It is imperative that I find a new way to com-municate with Dr. Koopman. I can no longer use the classified columns, for what I will re-quest of him cannot be printed in a daily newspaper. My only chance to contact Dr. Koop-man in 1985 depends solely on my ability to contact Dr. Koopman in 1963.

CHAPTER 17

NOVEMBER 23, 1963 . . . 12:25 P.M.

THE CAR RADIO DELIVERS A GOOD NEWS/ bad news bulletin. The bad news is the report that the assassination team is still in Dallas— that they spent the night at the Adolphus Hotel, then escaped in a stolen car. The good news is that no mention is made of the car. Is it because the police feel that a gray Rolls-Royce is easy to track down—or are they afraid irate citizens might overturn and torch every gray Rolls they see?

I have told Laura about my fate as a ten-yearold. She realizes her fortune as a seven-year-old has therefore been no better. She has sat quietly for a few moments, analyzing the situation, trying to sort out and give some order to its implications and its consequences. "Eventually we're going to get back to 1985, right, David?"

"That's the plan," I reply guardedly.

"When we do, will we still fit into 1985 the same way we did before we left?"

"I don't know." Honesty is still the best policy when you are lying between your teeth. *My* chances of ever returning are almost nonexistent.

"But if we died," she says, "did we grow up, go to school, meet each other?"

"We're here together, aren't we?" I say, trying to work my way through that mystery. Oddly enough, I seem to be making sense to myself. "We *did* grow up. We *did* go to school. We *did* meet. We *did* come here from 1985. I mean, we're here, aren't we? We've come from another time zone, another dimension. We're strangers here, *but we exist*. We don't belong here, but we're here. It's like we've come to another planet, but we still belong to the home planet we came from. I don't know how to explain it, but I know I'm here *trying* to explain it. We're the life force that survived. I don't know what else to tell you. We're here."

Somehow, trying to respond, trying to fit some pieces of the puzzle together, has had a calming effect on both of us. It gives us confidence that there *is* an answer. "When we get back, Dr. Koopman will know," she says. There is truth in that statement. Let men like Dr. Koopman explain. Only men who have insight into nature's forces can possibly force an answer from it.

I am again aware of the radio announcer's

voice. ". . . World leaders will soon be arriving in the United States. From Dallas, hospital authorities say that Lee Harvey Oswald, the man who tried to save the President, may be well enough to travel to Washington for Monday's funeral." I angrily turn off the radio. As I do, Laura, adding national insult to personal injury, says, "They're going to name a park after him."

Neither of us discuss that obscene happening any further. I remember watching Baron Guy de Rothschild on a segment of *60 Minutes* when he refused to discuss the Jewish Holocaust with Ed Bradley. He simply said, "It is beyond words."

In death Kennedy has become larger than life, but it is only living, life-sized figures who can help now. When the issue is drawn, a giant in his grave cannot stand up to be counted. Kennedy, may his soul rest in peace, can no longer help. The soul of a nation is now in the hands of a new leader—a man I must reach—the only one who now has the power to stop the Vietnam catastrophe—Lyndon Johnson.

☆   *12:40* P.M.

On Lemmon Avenue I turn off into the Prince of Burgers Drive-in. It is like driving onto the movie set of some nostalgic film Laura and I used to

173

enjoy watching on late-night television. It is encircled by dozens of cars, none of them foreign-made, half of them convertibles, and all of them filled with teenagers. Pretty car hops, in short shorts and tight sweaters, move between the cars carrying trays loaded down with the mother's milk of youth—burgers, fries, and Cokes. I expect to see Elvis Presley jump out of a car with his guitar and start singing "G.I. Blues."

It isn't that these youngsters are callous about the passing of a President. They are simply reacting to the herd instinct. Parents are for passing judgment, peers for passing time. The drive-in is to the sixties what the coffee house will be to the seventies and the disco to the eighties. Too young to have power, too old to pretend, they gather together in a fast-food frenzy. Here they are somebody.

After ordering I go to the public phone booth and wait while a teenager with a Beatles button on her sweater talks to some unseen friend about the Saturday night dance that has been postponed—about going with her folks that morning to a special memorial service for Kennedy—about what a real neat-looking man he had been. It is all simple, teenage talk, but her sentences are not interspersed with words and phrases like "you know," "really," or "for sure." She has communicated full thoughts without once raping the English language. And even when she tells her friend how her brother is getting ready to go back to college the following week, she does not resort to that most vulgar and obscene phrase—"getting his shit together."

Oh, Christopher, I never understood your world the first time I was in it. I'm glad I have had a second chance to see it again, as an adult this time. I like these young people. I like their clothes, I like their cars, I like most of their music, most of their heroes and heroines. I have left Laura alone in the car, but I have no fear that she will be confronted by some punk, some pimp, or some pusher. My rage is directed only against a war that was the beginning of our youth turning against themselves.

How many of the boys here will soon make that transition from hamburgers and hot dogs in Dallas to heroism and heroin in Da Nang— from collegiate to paraplegic—from draft registration to graves registration? How many of them will have God's allotment of three score and ten years reduced to a score of less than one?

It is still within my power to return to them those stolen years. It will depend on how persuasive I am in convincing Dr. Koopman in 1963 that I am living proof that the future exists— and that he is alive and well in 1985.

☆

"Dr. Koopman here."

What a joy to hear that familiar, friendly voice again. It is an emotional oasis to me, replenishing me with life-sustaining confidence. "My name is David Russell. I would like to make an appointment with you to discuss some scientific matters."

"David Russell? Do I know you?"

I must strike quickly, bait the hook with phrases that he will grab on to. "Not yet, sir, but I'm extremely anxious to go over some of your time travel theories, particularly your thoughts about canonical variables and super-luminal velocities."

There is a momentary silence at the other end. He is still only in the formative stages of this experiment. My mentioning it must be as unsettling as someone reading your innermost thoughts before you have finished thinking them.

His voice cannot hide his astonishment. "How did you know about it?"

I have him on the hook and must reel him in as quickly as possible. "Once you break the energy patterns into scaler wave patterns, the trick is how to condense them into matter again. I want to talk to you about that, Dr. Koopman."

This time there is an even longer silence, and then a very cautious, "Who are you?"

"I will meet you at your laboratory at two

o'clock sharp, Dr. Koopman," I reply as force-fully and mysteriously as I can, and then hang up.

☆   1:30 P.M.

"How did he make a mistake in the room?" she asks as we drive to the laboratory.

"I don't know—but we won't have to take out any more ads."

"Then how do we communicate with him?"

"We don't. He communicates with himself," I reply, quite satisfied with my inventiveness. To Laura's puzzled look, I say, "Didn't you tell me that while you and Dr. Koopman were in the laboratory—while all the machinery was in operation—you had no memory of past events?"

"Yes."

"And wasn't that something which Dr. Koopman said might happen—a sort of cocoonlike effect?"

"So?"

"But once you left the confines of the laboratory, went outside its walls, you suddenly recalled everything from the past—my being caught, jailed, everything, right?"

I don't give her a chance to do more than nod her head as I continue. "Who is alive, now, in 1963 who is also alive in 1985?"

"Dr. Koopman," she responds, her tone telling me that she has grasped the concept.

177

"When he leaves the laboratory he, too, will remember what happened in the past, just like you did. If we go to see him, whatever we talk about, whatever we ask him to do—"

"He'll remember in 1985," Laura says, finishing the thought for me.

It is indeed an instantaneous way to communicate our needs to him. Of course there is one last little hurdle that has to be cleared—convincing Dr. Koopman in 1963 that we are indeed from the year 1985, then getting him to go along with us. One way or another, I must persuade him to cooperate. He is now the key figure, the main man, the only chance, the last hope. I am counting on the Dr. Koopman I know in 1985. If he is half that man in 1963, I might still pull it off.

I turn the car radio on, catching the last news flash: ". . . the stolen Rolls-Royce was found abandoned in a Ross Avenue garage by a police officer who had gone there to pick up his car. Authorities are now questioning all neighborhood residents. . . ."

Soon they will be talking to the car salesman. This old Cadillac may be traveling its last few trouble-free miles.

Time is not on our side. We are in no danger from its years, for we have picked them in bunches, like harmless flowers. It is the hours and the minutes that threaten us. They grow out of the days like huge thorns, surrounding us, piercing us as we pass by, drawing blood, attacking us as though we are alien invaders.

The Tom Thumb Market is a block up ahead. It is a five-minute or so walk from there to the laboratory. Assuming that the Cadillac will soon be a collector's item, I cannot leave it parked in front of the laboratory, nor can I simply leave it on the street where passing police might spot it. The odds are fairly high that a police car will not pull off the street and circle around in the market's parking lot. The odds are even higher that grim-faced shoppers, hurrying in and out of the store, will not be aware of any car but their own.

It is then that I have what I at first think is a minor traffic accident.

CHAPTER 18

AS I TURN TO ENTER THE MARKET'S parking lot, a beat-up Model-T Ford tries to exit in the entrance lane. Traveling slowly, we both stop, but not before we bump fenders, which causes one of the Ford's headlights to fall off. I get out and bend over to pick it up. That car was built in a day when replacing a headlamp was simply a matter of taking it off and putting it on—not having to pay for a complete front-end job.

The ancient behind the wheel sits there, staring straight ahead. He is in his eighties, or possibly nineties; his face is wrinkled, the joints of his hands swollen by arthritis. His eyes, once probably as sharp as an eagle's, are now wa-

181

tered, as the tide of his years slowly rolls in on him. He wears a pre-Depression black suit, with a white shirt that has one of those starched, Herbert Hoover-type collars, and a tie that ends in the tiniest of knots. Short in stature, he is lean and mean—a hardworking, God-fearing survivor. Men like him helped build this country. They are its backbone—but like all backbones, stiff and unbending.

As I come up to him I run into the stone wall of a judgmental, unblinking stare. "Where'd you learn to drive, mister?"

Reaching back to my roots, I say, "Linnett, New Mexico."

"Damn foreigner," he mutters. Then, enunciating each word as though he is making me privy to a well-kept secret, he snaps, "Name's Melvin Hartnett." Reaching into a weathered wallet, he says, "Here's my license and insurance. Where's yours, mister?"

Trying to avoid a potential problem, I say, "You were trying to exit in the entrance lane, Mr. Hartnett."

That has no effect on him. Once a person like this grabs on to a familiar thought or ritual, he hangs on to it with all the ferocity of a lion biting down on a piece of meat. "Where's your license, mister," he repeats, not as a question this time, but as a threat.

Appealing to his patriotism, I say, "It's been a terrible weekend, sir. It's not worth getting into an argument over who's right or wrong." Taking some bills out of my pocket, I hold them out. "What can a new headlight cost—fifty, a hundred dollars? I'll be glad to pay for it."

He stares at the money for a moment through misted corneas—but at his age, pride goeth before a buy-out. "Ain't you got a license, mister?"

"Of course I have one. It's just that I left it at the hotel."

"What hotel you stayin' at?"

The Cadillac is trapped between his car and the line of cars behind it, which now extends six deep into the street.

"Would you mind moving your car so I can get out of everyone's way?"

"I ain't movin' till I see your license, mister." In the crowded recesses of his memory, that rule of law guides him like a shining light.

"David!" I hear Laura cry out in alarm. I turn to see the police officer get out of his car and start toward me. My God, I'm only minutes away from the laboratory. Will I be stopped when I am this close? Has this ancient mariner become my albatross?

As the officer comes up I make a desperate effort to appear calm. "We had a slight accident, Officer. No one's hurt. We'll get out of everyone's way and settle it. No need for you to bother."

"He has no driver's license," the old man barks out, a pronounced whistle starting to escape from between his teeth.

I quickly defend myself. "Of course I have a driver's license, Officer. I left it at the hotel."

"Ask him what hotel he's stayin' at," the old man cries out accusingly.

As the officer looks at me I hesitate. I can't say the Adolphus. By now every police officer has heard that's where Kennedy's killers spent the night. I can't risk even planting that association in his mind. "I'm staying at the Sheraton. I'm sure Mr. Hartnett and I can settle this amicably." Turning to the old man, I say, "Isn't that right, my friend?"

"I'm not your friend," he snarls, cutting short that brief relationship. Then, looking at the officer, he points to the Cadillac. "Bet he stole that car."

"That's not true," I protest. Reaching into my back pocket, I take out the papers and show them to the officer. "I just bought this car. Here— see—the ownership papers and the sales slip."

"Check it out," the old man urges the officer. "Bet they're all phony."

The officer holds his hand up to silence this vengeful graybeard. "I'll handlle this, sir. Back up your car and park it somewhere so we can clear the lane."

As the old man starts the motor and begins to back up, he reminds the officer, "Check him out. I got a funny feeling about him."

The officer, glancing at the papers I have given him, says, "Do you remember your driver's license number, Mr. Stallings?"

"No, sir."

He indicates the Cadillac, then points toward an empty parking space. "Put it over there." Then, as he starts toward his patrol car, he says, "I'll be right back."

No matter who he checks with, I'm in trouble. There is no Gordon Stallings registered at the Sheraton. If they call the used-car dealer, he'll connect a Mr. Stallings from Austin with the Rolls-Royce. And if they check the Rolls-Royce out, it will be the one that was stolen at the Adolphus Hotel by the twosome who killed Kennedy.

One quick glance across the parking lot, where I see another exit on the far side. Then a glance back at the patrol car in the street. The entrance to the lot is blocked by the line of waiting cars— the exit by outgoing traffic. There is no way the policeman can maneuver through all that. He'll have to go completely around a long block to get to the exit I will leave from. By that time I should have a damn long lead. I will have the choice of many corners to turn, many directions to take. He can only guess which ones I have taken. It will be a blind chase for him, unless he is lucky enough to choose the right corner to turn on—something which I am betting my life he will fail to do. Eventually he'll radio for help, but that will all take precious moments—moments which, for the first time, have become *our* allies.

185

Laura has slid behind the wheel and started the engine. As I get in on the passenger side I point and say, "Out that way." Without asking why, she starts driving. She has quickly learned the secret of being a good getaway driver—flee first, ask questions later. Down the driveway, between rows of parked cars, around the U-turn at the far end of the lot. The old man has found a parking space there. As we pass him I give him the finger. He starts to angrily blow his horn, which has that funny "ah-ooga" sound— and then, wanting to give chase, backs out and into an oncoming station wagon, causing the Ford's rear bumper to fall off.

As we near the far exit I look across the lot. The officer is standing by the open door of the patrol car talking into the two-way radio. He looks in our direction. The last I see of him, he is jumping into his car and slamming the door shut.

As Laura exits onto the street I tell her, "Turn left at the next corner—and left on the one after that."

"That'll take us back to the market," she reminds me.

"And when you get to it, park there." I am counting on surprise, on doing the totally unexpected, returning to the parking lot we have just left. It should be the very last place they will think of looking for us.

We pull into a space next to a camper. At the

far end of the lot, the old man, holding the bumper, is yelling at the driver of the station wagon. Suddenly he drops the bumper and takes a swing at the man, misses, and only a by-stander catching him keeps him from falling on his face. He is a tough old bird whose run of bad luck seems to be rivaling ours.

Separately we go into the market, then come out, each of us carrying grocery bags. Laura starts walking toward the laboratory. I follow a few dozen yards behind her. To any eye we must surely pass for two still-dazed Dallas citizens hurrying home with a supply of food that will see us through the funeral. On Monday a widowed First Lady will orchestrate a funeral worthy of a mighty chieftain—of a great nation. Only the determination of a Jacqueline Kennedy could bring kings, princes, premiers, prime ministers, sheiks, and presidents together on a day's notice. Only a grand lady can arrange all that.

Without shelter, without wheels, without a way to communicate, we are, without doubt, down to our last move in what has so far been a losing game. Our last hope is to convince a stranger in 1963 that we will be friends in 1985.

CHAPTER 19

WE ARE FIVE MINUTES LATE, BUT considering where we originally started from, we can be considered fashionably late. The laboratory building is the same as it was in 1985—its halls as empty of people on this Saturday as they were on the Saturday I went to see him twenty-two years in the future. And, like the first time, Dr. Koopman is in his office. The moment we enter, the weight of those twenty-two years is lifted from our shoulders.

This is the way Alice must have felt emerging from Wonderland, where she had to deal with a talking March Hare, Mad Hatter, Mock Turtle, Cheshire Cat, and a cardboard Queen of Hearts. Laura and I have come in from our Wonderland,

189

where Oswald is a hero, where *we* are villains, where we have already seen each new movie on late-night television, where we have forgotten the songs that will yet be written, where tomorrow's car is an antique.

In this office we find the reality we came from—the cluttered desk, the books, the photograph on the wall of him and Kennedy, even the 1890 bottle of Rothschild's champagne. Dr. Koopman is a bit younger, a shade less gray, but he still has the same chubby, cherubic, lovable uncle image. Even when he is serious, as he is now, he cannot hide the goodwill he feels for all people. He cannot conceal the aura he casts of holiday good cheer, of far-off sleigh bells, and chestnuts roasting in a fireplace.

There are tears in Laura's eyes. I know she is struggling to keep from throwing herself into his arms. If things go well, she may have that opportunity.

Even though two strangers carrying grocery bags have burst into his office, I know he does not feel threatened. If I were suddenly to brandish a weapon, I can imagine him saying, "My dear young man, why would you want to hurt someone when there is so much good you can do in the world?"

"Tell me, young man," is what he does say, "how did you know I am working on things to do with time travel?"

With a knowing smile, I say, "You started working on it in the late nineteen fifties."

"But how do you know?" Dr. Koopman asks in wide-eyed amazement. "I've told no one about it."

I'm not quite ready to reveal exactly who it was who did tell me. As I repeat the theories he spoke to me about twenty years afterward, he just stares at me, open-mouthed, awe-struck, absorbed in what is really his genius. Then, more to convince himself than me, he doggedly repeats, "I told no one. No one."

"It's been a major stumbling block, breaking the atoms down into smaller components."

"Yes, that's it." He quickly confirms the problem, no longer bothering to ask how I found out about it.

"It's just that the other sciences have to catch up to you, Dr. Koopman. They have to build the machines to help you do that."

"But they will," Laura assures him. "Tell him about the atom smashers and the accelerators, David."

He stares at Laura for a moment in rapt fascination, then turns to me with an innocent, childish look of expectation, as though I am about to show him a magical trick.

"New atom smashers will be able to break atoms down into even smaller pieces of matter—into leptons, T-top quarks, and z-zero subatomic particles."

He cannot repress a look of deliverance as he imagines these desperately needed subatomic bits of matter.

"You will find that there are eleven dimensions, not four, and they can be reached through your hyperspatial theories."

"I have been thinking about that," he confesses, "but I am not sure of it yet."

"You will be." I forecast that fait accompli to this now spell-bound scientist. "Then it's how to find a point of return into the past and program all the complex instructions."

"There is no way to program them. The computers cannot handle it."

"Not the transistorized computers—but you will no longer be limited to them."

"But what else is there?" he asks, confused, his thinking limited to the transistor, the current state of the art in 1963.

"Originally there was the vacuum tube—and it has been followed by the transistor—but that is only the second step, Dr. Koopman. There are other steps to follow."

He rivets his eyes onto mine, not looking for deceit, but for discovery. He is quite ready to climb those steps with me. I will lead him up them as carefully as I can.

"The third step is the integrated circuit." That was accomplished in 1966, but I do not yet reveal years to him. "The fourth step is the miracle chip."

"Miracle chip?" he asks in bewildered fascination.

"It's made of tiny slivers of silicon no larger

than your fingernail." Again I do not tell him the year of that miracle was 1976, although I think he is ready for such revelations. "The fifth and final step is microelectronics, which will create the microchip." Into his intense stare I then say, "Each chip can hold tens of millions of bits of information, of instructions. Think of that, Dr. Koopman, tiny chips holding all that knowledge, all that power."

His straight-ahead, wide-eyed stare tells me he *is* thinking of that.

"Then, beyond silicon chips, comes the answer that makes time travel possible, Dr. Koopman. Gallium-arsenide crystal chips. They will hold *hundreds of millions* of bits of information. They will increase a computer's capabilities by a thousand times. They are the keys that open the doors to time travel."

"A door you will open, Dr. Koopman," Laura assures him.

"You will rewrite the laws of nature," I prophesy.

"It will be your crowning achievement," she declares.

Overwhelmed, he sits there, looking first at Laura and then at me. He asks the only question that makes any sense at a time like this. "Who are you?"

He is in a state of excitement that borders on religious anticipation. I think if we were to tell him that God sent us, there is a fifty-fifty chance he would accept it. Laura, however, leads him along gently toward our promised land. "We've met before, Dr. Koopman," she says, softly, soothingly. There is a tenderness that a mother might use to a child as he gets ready to go to sleep. It is intended to calm, to reassure. It is a voice filled with love and affection—a voice that comforts and consoles—a voice that can be trusted.

He trusts the voice, but he doesn't trust a memory that can't seem to place what he is being told. "I'm sorry," he apologizes, "but I don't seem to remember."

With a warm smile, speaking in carefully measured phrases that have an almost hypnotic effect on him, she says, "This is our second meeting, Dr. Koopman. You and David and I met for the first time many years in the future . . . the year that we have come here from . . . the year that you have sent us back from . . . the year nineteen hundred and eighty-five."

A slight tremor passes through his body. Is it fear or anticipation, panic or exultation? He is engrossed in the tale, completely caught up in what Laura is revealing, of the size of his victory, the scope of our defeat.

"There will be a war . . . in Vietnam . . . it will last for more than ten years . . . a war that might never have happened if President Kennedy had lived. You sent David and me back here to try to save him. . . . We failed. . . . The man who shot him has gotten away. . . . David and I are being blamed. . . . We must contact you in 1985, Dr. Koopman. . . . You are the only one who can help us do that."

He does not even blink his eyes at that, which is a good sign. But then why did I ever doubt the end result? Have I been under so much pressure that I have not seen the forest for the trees, the truth for the truisms? And what is the truth? Two people have come in off the street and told him things that only *he* knew about—and things that neither he nor any other scientist knew about. We have revealed technological triumphs he can barely imagine—verified as fact what are still only flights of fancy to him. Would a couple who had just murdered a President walk in and ask him to help them get in touch with someone twenty years in the future? Our story is too bizarre not to be true, our knowledge of him too accurate to be guesswork. Dazzled at the wonder of it all, he says, "I sent you here."

"From this very laboratory," Laura confides.

I point to the dusty bottle of champagne on the nearby shelf. "We drank that 1890 Rothschild before we left. Remember what the baron said to you—'On the day you feel you have reached the apogee of your skills, then drink the best the Rothschilds have to offer.' "

All he can say is, "Incredible."

"Show him the photograph, David," Laura reminds me.

I have put it in one of the grocery bags. I

remove it and hand it to him. "This was taken of you in 1979, with Jimmy Carter. He was our President then. You had just been given the Medal of Freedom."

He studies the photograph, momentarily lost in thought and time as he sees his future self, the senior citizen he will become. His silence speaks louder than any shouted cry of conversion to the faith. We are indeed who we say we are. We are indeed where we say we're from. We are home.

Home again, in a place we left twenty-two years in the future. Together again, with one of us having grown twenty-two years younger. Old friends reunited, with one of us seeing the other two for the first time. But it is a moment not to be forgotten—and more important a moment that *must not* be forgotten by Dr. Koopman in 1985, for whatever request I make of him here, I am depending on him to remember it in 1985.

Dr. Koopman is on our team. We have cleared the first hurdle in this race through time and against time. It is like a relay, where the baton must be passed to the next runner. I am attempting to hand that baton to a man twenty-two years ahead of me.

CHAPTER 20

OCTOBER 16, 1985

D R. KOOPMAN TRIES TO CONTROL THE fear building within him. This is the second person who has been mistakenly returned. And where is the photograph he sent back? Why wasn't it returned with the stranger? Is it due to malfunctions here in the laboratory or misfortunes there in Dallas? Was 317 the wrong room? Should he now try to reach them in 311? That's where they must be.

There are now millisecond breaks in the surges of energy that reverberate throughout the laboratory. Where once they were deep, full, powerful sounds, the pitch is now quite high, piercing, swelling then ebbing again. Dr. Koopman has to strain, to force himself even to think.

Even simple machinery cannot be used over and over again without checkups, servicing, repairs, replacements. This equipment, far more complex, may at any time fail to function.

He resets the coordinates so that the next object sent back will appear in the center of that room. He knows what he will send back—something that will leave no doubt in their minds that it is from 1985—the license plate from his car.

Opening a drawer, he takes out a screwdriver, then leaves the laboratory. As he steps out into the hall he is again flooded with memories, deluged with remembrances, caught in a mnemonic spillway where he is immersed as a torrent of past events sweeps over him. He is aware of prior happenings which a moment before he had no recollections of.

He remembers David and Laura coming into his office in 1963—literally staggering him with their knowledge of the work he was beginning to do in time travel—overwhelming him with scientific facts he was still unaware of, telling him he would one day perfect time travel, and finally informing him that they were the product of his success—that they had come from the future. He remembers how they knew what the Baron Guy de Rothschild had told him—how they showed him the photograph that had been taken with a future President, Jimmy Carter. He remembers David telling him how he had come back to save President Kennedy and failed—and then Laura telling him about her aborted effort—and how they were both being sought as the killers. Desperately trying to flee within an ever-tightening net, frantically trying to find another point of contact, they had found their way to his office. He remembers David saying that everything they told him in 1963 he would remember in 1985.

It is all Dr. Koopman can do to keep from shouting his pleasure to the heavens. *He has remembered.* It was a brilliant stroke of David's, a most inventive way to establish a new way, a sure way, to contact him. There is still a chance to save them.

But there is also something else he *must* remember. David said it was most important. There was something David wanted sent to him—something that might help avert the coming Vietnam War. Dr. Koopman puts his hands to his forehead. Just what was it David wanted? He must remember.

It was about a reel of film David wanted sent to him from 1985. He remembers David writing out the instructions on a piece of paper so he wouldn't forget—then putting the piece of paper into an envelope. He remembers David taking an old photograph down from the wall—the one of his graduating class at Leiden University in

Holland. He remembers David taping the envelope to the back of the photograph, then hanging it back on the wall again. He remembers David telling him, "Don't forget the envelope taped to the back of the picture."

Dr. Koopman returns to his office. Trembling with expectation, he takes the photograph down, turns it, and sees the sealed envelope.

The briefness of the enclosed note attests to the urgency of the request.

Dear Uncle Hendrik,

As you know, Laura and I have encountered serious problems. It is imperative, absolutely vital, that you secure a certain film for us.

Go to television station KFAA. It is located in the Communication Center in Dallas. They recently showed a documentary film called *The Vietnam Years—A Study of the Violent Sixties*. Ask them where you can obtain a 16-mm copy of it.

I will wait for it in your office. Send it to me on November 23, 1963, at 5 P.M. I think the top of your desk will be a suitable place to return it.

Love,
David and Laura

P.S. Dr. Koopman sends his warmest regards.

Dr. Koopman smiles as he remembers David

writing that postscript. They all thought it was quite humorous at the time. But why can't he remember what happened after that? Why has he suddenly come to the edge of a dark chasm that he can't see across? Why doesn't he remember David receiving that film? But then how can he remember something that he hasn't done yet? Of course. That's the answer. At this moment David, Laura, and he, as a younger man, are waiting for him to send the film. Both their worlds, 1963 and 1985, are coexisting at the same time but in different dimensions. Only when he sends the film, only when it gets to them, only then will he remember them receiving it.

☆

The production coordinator at WFAA smiles as Dr. Koopman comes into her office. He looks like a huggable, befuddled, overgrown koala bear who will probably ask her how he can find Qantas Airways. There is an instinctive feeling to help him, to do kind things, for he reminds her of the good things that have happened in her life.

"Excuse me," he says, "they told me you can tell me where I can go to get a film you showed on your station."

"Which film is it?" she asks, trying to recall

some of the old films they have recently shown. It's obviously a toss-up between *Mary Poppins*, *Pinocchio,* and *Bambi.*

He takes a crumpled piece of paper out of his pocket, meticulously smoothes it out, then says, *"The Vietnam Years—A Study of the Violent Sixties.* I need a 16-mm copy of it."

It takes her a moment to respond as she tries to find a connection between this dear old man and that violent decade. "Are you sure that's the film you want, sir?"

"Yes, the war film," he replies eagerly. "The one all about the war."

The woman studies him for a moment. Are looks that deceiving? Is it possible that this sweet grandfather type was once a rock-throwing radical college professor in the sixties?

She scans the record sheet. "It's down in Transportation. They're shipping it back."

"But I want to buy it," he protests in alarm, his face becoming flushed. "It's very important that my friend get a copy of it."

"We're not allowed to sell it, sir. Your friend might try calling the distributor. They may have a print to sell."

Impatiently, he waves that suggestion aside. "No, where my friend is, the distributor won't have it yet."

"Where is your friend?"

"Far away," he answers, not revealing where

far away is. He stands there for a moment, uncertain, confused. "My friend must have it," he says in mounting concern.

"I'm sorry, sir." Then, somehow wanting to ease the old man's discomfort, she says, "Is watching the war again that important to your friend?"

"It is important to all of us," he says as he starts toward the door. "Who knows, maybe he can make it turn out different."

"Turn out different, sir?" she calls after him, but he is gone.

☆

The shipping clerk in Transportation, searching through the shipping orders, pulls the pink slip out. *"The Vietnam Years*—to Sheffield Distributors in Chicago. It just went out."

"Went out?" Dr. Koopman groans in dismay.

The clerk points toward the Federal Express truck parked in the loading area. "Federal Express just picked it up." Then, as he lifts a large package onto a small cart and starts to wheel it toward the freight elevator, he casually says, "My uncle died in that war." An uncle and a war become nothing more than a passing comment.

Dr. Koopman stands there, flustered, disconcerted. Unsure of what to do next, for lack of a better plan he walks up to the truck. Not seeing the driver, he looks into the back of the truck through the open door. There among the assorted packages is a can of film. His heart begins to pound a burglar's beat. For the first time in his life he feels the thief's thrill, the rush, the high when one is about to get something for nothing. Swiftly adopting the transgressor's ways, a cunning smile crosses his face. It cannot completely conceal his basic lamblike innocence, but it is cunning nevertheless. He furtively looks both ways, then enters the truck.

Crouched over, he steps into the rear compartment, picks up the precious can of film, then drops to his knees as he hears approaching footsteps.

The driver, having answered nature's call, gets into the truck, slides the panel door shut, and drives off.

Minutes later the truck stops in front of the Atlantic-Richfield Building. A moment after the driver enters the building, Dr. Koopman gets out of the truck and hurriedly starts down the street, anxiously looking back every few yards. Three blocks away, he enters the Kirby Building, steps into a public telephone booth, takes the reel of film out of the can, and smiles. He has begun a life of crime on a triumphant note. It *is* the film of *The Vietnam Years*, and it *is* a

16-mm print. David wanted the Vietnam War, he's got it. What he will do with that war is strictly up to David.

☆ *NOVEMBER 23, 1963 . . . 5:12 P.M.*
It is twelve minutes late—twelve agonizing minutes in which I have imagined every possible human and nonhuman calamity. Has Dr. Koopman, in 1985, not remembered the instructions I gave him in 1963? Has he been unable to find the film? Is he prevented from sending it because of equipment failure? Everything must go right to succeed. Only one thing need go wrong to fail.

Suddenly a can of film is on the desk.

"Daar is het. Hier is het," Dr. Koopman jubilantly cries out in Dutch, reverting to the language of the past to praise his feat in the future.

Elated, Laura throws her arms around him. "You did it."

"No, not me." He starts to modestly decline the honor, then stops and sheepishly smiles as he realizes that homage *is* being paid to the right man.

"You did it," Laura insists, not allowing him to avoid the acclaim due him.

"I did it," he echoes her words in a state of humble euphoria.

It is a spiritually intoxicating moment, rivaling a religious experience. Only when we all go up in the rapture will a moment be more uplifting.

Almost reverently, I lift the can and hold it up, a sacrificial offering from the future to the past. I have in my hands a film documenting things to come—a film of a war that has not yet occurred—of all the violence and hate and destruction and death that happened but that can still be avoided.

CHAPTER 21

THE WHITE HOUSE, SUBDUED IN LIFE, is filled with life's noises in death. Brothers and sisters and in-laws form the inner circle. Behind them, personal aides, political advisers, protocol chiefs, and pastoral counselors make up the outer circle. All of their energies are focused inward, toward the young widow in the center.

The staff functions because trauma, tears, shock, and rage have acted as cushions, temporarily protecting them from the ultimate pain they will face in the months and years to come— the sense of loss.

In another part of the house, Caroline and

John, surrounded by cousins and friends, ride tricycles down the corridors and have their fill of games and ice cream as they celebrate Caroline's birthday. Under the watchful eye of Dave Powers and Marine officers in their dress blues, they are unaware of the chaos in the adult world. Isolated from those who keep the death watch, they are immune to the ravages of grief. They watch cartoons on television, where the dead rise again in a following scene. Caroline and John do not know that their daddy spent the night on a catafalque in the East Room.

On a floor below, Ken O'Donnell stops and looks past the open door that leads to that prestigious, most powerful, most sought-after piece of square footage—the Oval Office. All that remains there of a man he loved are the objects the man loved. In a day or so they, too, will be gone.

Tears welling in his eyes, O'Donnell walks toward his office. Walter Jenkins, Johnson's man, has asked him to stay on temporarily as appointments secretary. Eventually Jenkins will have that job, but that's the way it should be. At least it will be an orderly transition. Nothing is more embarrassing to a President than schedule goof-ups, like having the Iraqi and Israeli ambassadors arriving for lunch at the same time.

Lyndon Johnson, like all Presidents, will want to leave his own mark. It's amazing how little a President really knows about his Vice President, outside of the fact the man can help him get votes. Though just a heartbeat separates their powers, the two are often worlds apart in personal and political beliefs.

And what about Vietnam? What will Johnson do about that?

An aide holds the phone out to O'Donnell. "It's a Dr. Hendrik Koopman calling from Dallas. He says he met you at Hyannis Port, and then at the dinner for Prince Bernhard."

Even in this gravest of moments, the slightest of smiles crosses O'Donnell's face as he recalls the delightful little scientist with the Dutch accent. Kennedy had been quite taken with him.

"This is Dr. Hendrik Koopman. Do you remember me?"

"Yes, of course."

The accent is still the same, but the humor is gone. Awkwardly phrased sentences, which once brought forth a smile, are now spoken with such solemnity, such intensity, that the listener is forced to strain to make sure he is not missing a single critical meaning.

"This is not a good time to call you, but no time is good when bad things happen. . . . I am calling because I am in possession of something so important, a discovery so unbelievable, not many people would bother to believe it. . . . If President Kennedy were still alive, he would be the first to ask me to come to Washington to show it to him."

"Can you tell me what it is, Dr. Koopman?"

"I mean no disrespect—not that you are not important—but I cannot tell you. There is almost no one I can tell. That is how important it is."

O'Donnell, a man who made ten thousand appointments during Kennedy's one thousand days, has always prided himself on ferreting out the salient calls, those of substance, from the insignificant and the trivial. He learned to weigh the caller's character against the caller's need. There were those who wished to see the President to deliver worthwhile messages—and those who simply wanted to receive ego massages that they had spoken with Kennedy. Instinct tells him that this Nobel winner is not a man who makes frivolous calls.

He tries to guess at the reason for the call. He remembers the urgent calls during the Bay of Pigs and those during the missile crisis. Then there had been the ones that started to come in at odd hours as odd things began to happen in a land nine thousand miles away. But, instinctively, he knows this call deals with affairs that have far deeper consequences—that it has to do with things beyond his knowledge—that he is standing in ignorance before an unfolding momentous event.

Almost deferentially he says, "How can I help you, Dr. Koopman?"

"My two friends and I must meet with President Johnson. We must meet with him today."

Not being argumentative but practical, O'Donnell says, "Is it something you can possibly speak to someone else about?"

"No, no," comes the immediate, distressed reply. "It must be with President Johnson. No one else."

"Let me call Walter Jenkins. He's his personal assistant. Maybe he can arrange it."

"Maybe is not good enough," comes the out-of-character, sharp response from this mild man. *He must.* There are things I must tell President Johnson." There is a momentary pause followed by words spoken with such surety they can almost be mistaken for prophecy. "There is something I must show him that can change everything he is going to do. . . . I promise you, it will be a change for the better."

CHAPTER 22

NOVEMBER 24, 1963 . . . NOON

FOR THE FIRST TIME I AM AWARE OF the respect in which a scientist is held. A call from a Nobel Prize winner who declares he has highly sensitive information has been enough to start bureaucratic wheels turning—and although they often move slowly at the beginning and not always in a straight line, once they pick up speed, once the juggernaut is hurtling through the pipeline, it is a marvel, if not of efficiency, certainly of single-minded purpose. Less than two hours after Dr. Koopman has spoken to Ken O'Donnell, he receives a call from Walter Jenkins. Yes, it's possible to arrange a meeting with President Johnson.

Laura has had the presence of mind to buy

camouflage for us at the market. A bottle of hair coloring soon turns her into a brunette, and a can of hair spray leaves streaks of gray at my temples. Our real protection, though, will come from the minds of rational people who simply will not give credence to the possibility that the two people who killed one President will now be accompanying a world-famed scientist to Washington to meet the new President.

At three o'clock a pale green government sedan arrives. It is driven by Special Agent Hiddell. His face is expressionless, his clothes commonplace, his manner bland. He is neither friendly nor hostile. He is simply there.

This trip, cleared by the President's personal aide, opens up a new world of travel—that of the privileged wayfarer. We pass by the passenger terminal at Love Field and enter through the east gate, off Lemmon Avenue. Having been anointed with celebrity status, we will not be subjected to noncelebrity irritants like purchasing tickets, selecting seats, and securing boarding passes. In fact, we will also be spared the burden of having to fly with our fellow citizens. Driving straight onto the field itself, we head toward an isolated area far removed from the common, competing, commercial airliners. Our very own 707 awaits us.

Gently, expertly, we are transferred from car to plane. It is a pleasant feeling to be safely tucked away under the government's protective wing—but it also causes a slight uneasiness, as we are, in a way, also under its protective custody. We are now no longer in control of our own movements. But that is a temporary psychological inconvenience, for we are in control of something far more important—the information we carry on that reel of film. This is exactly where I want to be, on a plane that is taking me to see the only man who can help us—and in so doing also save himself from the embarrassment of a humiliating defeat and a shameful legacy.

We are delivered into the hands of a Colonel Whittaker. Of average height, he has a lean body that makes him look taller than he is. A face sharply defined by the prominent bones beneath his weathered skin makes him seem older than he is. Receding gray-black hairs that lie flat on his head produce a high forehead, which makes him seem wiser than he may be. A New Englander by birth, close-mouthed by nature, courteous by training, he speaks sparingly, concisely—but compared to Special Agent Hiddell, he comes across as the friendliest of fellows.

"Should be in a little after eight, Washington time," is a long speech for him, but it does say it all. He follows that with, "We have hard drinks and soft drinks, hot food and cold sandwiches." He almost looks as if he is ready to apologize for running off at the mouth.

The 707 is a chartered plane, and we are its only passengers. We take off with over one hundred empty seats—a classic case of the misuse of tax-payers' money. I remember the thrill of riding the swift, sleek, luxurious 707 as a boy—but it no longer looks or feels that, not after a 747. Its narrow, cigar-shaped body produces a confined, almost claustrophobic feeling. It has become a lumbering, vibrating, flying fossil. Old airplanes, like old lovers, are better remembered, not revisited.

Dr. Koopman, like an exhausted mother hen whose two chicks are safe and cannot get away, falls asleep.

I sit there holding the can of film on my lap—film that is irrelevant up here, for there is no time up here. The stars have been there forever, the earth is ancient. I hover between forever and ancient. In flight we belong to no age, we belong to all ages. It is the same when sailing alone on a vast ocean. Only human contact starts the clock again.

Laura is that human contact, expressing more timely concerns, more earthly problems. "What do you think will happen, David?"

"What will happen when?"

"When he sees it."

"He has to believe it," I assure her, firmly convinced he has no other choice. Dr. Koopman will legitimize the concept of time travel—the film will document that claim. Johnson may go into shock or cardiac arrest—he may be struck dumb or become hysterical—he may go through an intense religious upheaval or some kind of psychological

Armageddon—but he has to believe it. I am betting more than our lives on it. I am also betting Johnson's life on it, for there has never been any doubt that watching America lose a war for the first time broke his heart, and being driven into political exile finished him off.

He will be given what no other leader in world's history has ever been given—a second chance to correct a grievous mistake, to avoid a brutal historical judgment. Believe it, he will. Act on it, he must.

"What does he do with us, David?"

"Keeps us to himself," I reply almost flippantly. "No politician is going to share anyone who can see into the future."

"But we won't be able to do that."

"Won't be able to do what?"

"See into the future," she forecasts. "I mean, if there's no war in Vietnam, it means there're no antiwar protests here at home, no marches, no riots. Johnson runs for reelection in 1968, which means there's no Nixon, no Watergate, no recession, no Gerald Ford, none of those things. Robert Kennedy wouldn't have run for President that year—he wouldn't have gone to Los Angeles—he wouldn't have been shot. It all changes, David. If there's no Vietnam, the future changes to something we know nothing about."

Of course. Why didn't I see that? Laura's right. Sure, we can tell Johnson there'll be faster cars and planes, men in space, medical breakthroughs, progress in civil rights, continued problems with Communist aggression, more exotic weapon systems, things like that—but those are things he probably visualizes anyhow. What he doesn't see is a war that will be lost, a political career that will be ruined, a presidency that he will have to abandon. Once we open his eyes to that, everything will change—and with that change, a different future—and, as Laura says, one which we also know nothing about.

Resting her hand on mine, she speaks with the surety and confidence born out of logic and hope. "There'd be no reason for him not to allow Dr. Koopman to return us to 1985."

That, too, makes sense. Johnson is a rational, realistic man. Hasn't he, many times, said, "Come, let us reason together"? Wouldn't the reasonable thing be to take our information, use it to his political and personal advantage, and then be quite pleased to see us go back to where we came from? One of his first acts as President cannot be to point to us and say, "These folks are here from 1985, and they've talked me out of getting involved in a war we're going to lose." There's no doubt that our usefulness is in our private information, not in our continued presence.

It all comes down to this one man in power, and his one all-powerful vote. He once cast it for war. He can now cast it for peace. He is the last hurdle we must clear in this desperate race through time. I swear one silent vow—that I will also let them know about Oswald. I cannot allow that murderous little bastard to live free, much less honorably.

☆   *8:10 P.M.*

Less than thirty seconds after we roll to a stop at Andrews Field, a black limousine with tinted windows comes onto the runway and alongside the plane.

Colonel Whittaker, standing at the open cabin door, economizing on words, simply says, "Sir," as I go past him.

We have been passed up the ladder from Special Agent Hiddell to Colonel Whittaker and now to Walter Jenkins. The next step up the ladder should lead to the Man Himself. The closer one gets to the real seat of power, the more unreal the settings of power become. There is something about the limousine's tinted windows that is ominous to those looking in, yet omniscient to those looking out. It breeds a reverse fishbowl effect, where those within the confined area view the outside world as being in the fishbowl. Even a few minutes of riding under those conditions gives one a feeling of indestructability, a feeling of disdain for those on the other side of that glass wall.

We were spared the waiting lines at the airline terminal, the bother of fellow passengers on the flight. The sky was rendered more comfortable, and now the streets more passable, for as we leave Andrews Field a second car pulls in front of us to clear the way. Its flashing red light outranks the red lights on the street corners. Its siren causes foot patrolmen to run out into the middle of the street and hold up traffic until we pass.

These evening sorties have not yet caused Walter Jenkins to lose his patience or find an excuse to avoid the assignment. Bright eyes peer out from behind horn-rimmed glasses that sit astride a pudgy face. A Stetson does not completely hide a receding hairline. A neatly knotted tie on a freshly laundered shirt shows beneath an unwrinkled topcoat. He holds a shiny leather attaché case that does not yet show signs of presidential wear. And he possesses the main trait a good presidential aide needs—the ability to make the visitor feel expected and respected.

He has greeted Dr. Koopman warmly, as befits a man with Dr. Koopman's impeccable credentials. Laura and I have been welcomed cordially. If he knew *our* credentials, I'm sure he would have reacted with more enthusiasm—but that bit of information, like the film, is for Johnson's eyes and ears only.

As we turn onto Constitution Avenue I can see the white-domed Capitol and the thousands of silent Americans waiting in line to file into the rotunda and past the flag-covered casket. In the distance Lincoln fixes sad, marble eyes on the proceedings.

The streams of light from the White House reach out and merge with the harsher rays of light coming from the adjacent Executive Office Building, where a new President, using his old office and the mystique of night, is trying quickly to establish his sovereignty. He is wetting his feet in the first of many treacherous, incoming tides from all over the world—the most harmless-looking one arriving as a trickle from Vietnam. He does not see the vortex beneath those innocuous drops. He is already making the first of his major Asian mistakes by surrounding himself with men who cut him off from the reasonable men he professes to be looking for.

As we park, silent shadows move alongside us, and one of them opens the car door. Secret Service, having just lost one President, does not want to find themselves bearing the brunt of another oversight. Only after they recognize Walter Jenkins do they blend back in with the plant and mineral shadows.

There are more of them in the corridors and by the stairwells. Two of them wear PT-109 clips. They had been with Kennedy in Dallas. Do they wear those tie clips out of loyalty or in a mea culpa gesture—in self-flagellating penance—baring themselves to the world that they were the ones who failed?

The Pentagon is already camped on the doorstep. As we enter the outer office a general and an admiral sit there patiently waiting. Each wears what seems to be a dozen rows of multicolored ribbons. How can anyone win that many decorations and still be alive?

They are ordinary-looking men—yet, clothed with extraordinary influence and spoiling for a fight, they sent men like Christopher to do their fighting—and dying—for them.

Presidents make decisions based not on advice handed down by God on stone tablets but on memos, bulletins, research papers, secret reports, and not-so-secret opinion polls. Presidents want to be right, they want to be loved, they want to be remembered. We can show Johnson how to accomplish that. Our message is not written on stone, or typed on paper, but shot on film.

Walter Jenkins, who has gone in to see the President, reappears and beckons us to enter.

CHAPTER 23

NOVEMBER 24,1963 . . . 8:50 P.M.

AT FIFTY-FIVE, LYNDON JOHNSON HAS worked hard and waited long for this moment—and though the prize arrived in a bloody package, his name is on it and he will accept it.

He is possibly the most adept politician in Washington. He knows whom to stroke and whom to strike—which arms can be twisted and which backbones tested. He knows whom to convince and whom to coerce—whose ox not to gore and whose ox is expendable. He knows where all the bodies are buried, having laid a few of them to rest himself.

At six foot four and two hundred and thirty pounds, he is a bear of a man—and, like all

223

bears, unpredictable. At this moment, as he comes around his desk, he is affable, inquisitive. He envelops Dr. Koopman's hand in his. "I consider this an honor, Dr. Koopman—a great honor."

"It is my pleasure, Mr. President," Dr. Koopman responds. Each man has downplayed his importance, but I get a feeling only one of them has been sincere about it.

Pointing to us, Dr. Koopman then says, "These are my two dear friends, David Russell and Laura Watkins."

As we each say, "Mr. President," he presses Laura's hand in his, then mine. It gives me a brief instant to look into his face. One is not captured by any outstanding facial feature. He has thinning hair, dark eyebrows, brown eyes that look out at you but screen off any effort by you to look beyond them. His nose is a shade too long, the loose skin on his jaws and neck beginning to hang in small folds. It is a face that searches for answers, not questions—for compliance, not criticism. It is a face you remember only because it belongs to the President.

The formalities over, we now have to earn the handshakes he has given us. "Walter tells me you have some very important information." Only a President can come to the point that quickly without the guest feeling he's being rushed. And only a scientist of Dr. Koopman's stature can then say, "More than important. It is momentous, unparalleled, astounding," without the President feeling he is being hustled. "What we are about to tell you and show you, sir, will change the world as you know it."

There is a momentary flash of surprise as Johnson reacts to this immodestly declared claim—but that flash has also kindled a fire of immense curiosity. With a smile of anticipation, he says, "Change it for the better I hope, Dr. Koopman."

"For the better, sir," Dr. Koopman assures him.

"We have the projector and the screen as you requested," Walter Jenkins says, pointing toward a corner of the office.

"Good. Thank you." Dr. Koopman then turns to me. "Would you please put the film on and set up the screen, David?" Then, apologizing to Walter Jenkins, he says, "I am sorry, but this is only for the President to see."

To Walter Jenkins' credit, he does not react with hostility or even annoyance. He simply glances toward his boss, who nods, and with that nod Jenkins is gone—and with his going, our time has come, or rather our time in 1963 has come again, and with it a second chance for this President to avoid a blunder that will send him back to the Pedernales—a sitting President not even invited to sit in at the 1968 convention—a man forgotten in his prime.

My hands tremble as I thread the reel, so intense is the sense of expectancy that surges through me. We have reached the end of a journey that started so many years in the future. We have overcome the odds and, oddly enough, even the failures. We did not save Kennedy, but we may still save the dream he had.

"Ask not what your country can do for you ..." he had said. We already know what this country was willing to do for Johnson. We are now going to ask Johnson what he is willing to do for his country to prevent that tragedy.

It all now rests with this one man. He may look like a 7-Eleven store manager, and sound like a country-fair pitchman, but he is a shrewd, wily, pragmatic politician. I am counting on his sense of survival, on his sense of his place in the history books.

Dr. Koopman, a seasoned lecturer, begins with a statement designed to capture the listener's attention. "Mr. President, sir, what I am about to tell you may sound implausible, even impossible— but I assure you, it is all true, it all happened."

He pauses to make sure Johnson is properly intrigued. It is an unnecessary pause, as Johnson's eyes are riveted to Dr. Koopman like a bolt to a steel girder.

"One of the great men of science, Wolfgang Pauli, once said to me, 'There are shallow truths and deep truths, Dr. Koopman. A shallow truth is where the opposite is false. A deep truth is where the opposite has value.' "

He again pauses—this time only to let the thought take hold.

"One of the deepest truths was written in a book called *The Rubaiyat*."

"Yes, of course," Johnson volunteers. "Confucius."

Dr. Koopman, bless his kindly, crafty soul, doesn't correct him and tell him it was Omar Khayyam. Authorship is not what he wants to convince him of. "He said, 'The moving finger writes; and, having writ, moves on: nor all thy piety nor wit shall lure it back to cancel half a line, nor all your tears wash out a word of it."

"How true, how true," Johnson sighs.

"But, sir," Dr. Koopman suggests, "what if the opposite of that was also true?"

Puzzled, Johnson stares at him. "But the opposite would mean you *can* go back and change things after they have happened."

Dr. Koopman presses the thought. "What if a man *could* have it to do all over again—to correct terrible mistakes—wouldn't he do it—wouldn't *you* do it?"

"Why yes—naturally—who wouldn't?" he replies.

"What a remarkable opportunity, Mr. President—to see the errors one has made and be able to undo them."

Johnson nods his head in philosophical agreement. "If only we *could* see into the future, Dr. Koopman."

Dr. Koopman rests his hands on the desk and leans forward so that he seems to be confiding a secret thought. "Or have someone *come back from the future*—to point out our errors."

"Come back from the future?" Johnson cautiously asks. Will Secret Service men momentarily rush in and drag us out? But Johnson, staring at Dr. Koopman, makes no move to press any hidden alarm buttons.

"Suppose, sir, that the future exists," Dr. Koopman suggests, "and this present moment we live in is already part of someone else's past." Johnson says nothing. He only adjusts his glasses. I do not know its implication. Dr. Koopman takes the next bold step into Johnson's belief system. "And suppose, sir, that a scientist in that future, wandering through an almost impenetrable forest of universal mysteries, stumbles upon the answer to one of them—that past, present, and future are constructed of indestructible building blocks, which can be bridged. And suppose this scientist was able to send us back proof of this on a reel of film."

Johnson's eyes seem to glaze over, as though he is trying to keep his thoughts contained behind them. "Send back proof from the future?" he says quietly, almost too patiently. We may be on the verge of losing him.

Dr. Koopman ignores the implied disbelief. Pointing to the film, he says, "It is all there. To see it is to believe. To see it is to have the world of tomorrow in your hands."

Johnson's eyes dart to the reel on the projector. Whatever his doubts, the enticement is too great. There is no way we could leave that office without showing him what is on that film.

Pointing to the bright overhead light, Dr. Koopman says, "Laura, would you please turn the light out?" A standing lamp near Johnson's desk will keep the room from total darkness. "And, David, will you please start the film?"

Flickering beams of light, traveling at 186,000 miles per second, deliver the film's images onto a screen less than ten feet away. For a brief moment *The Vietnam Years—A Study of the Violent Sixties* seems to be a mild, nonviolent, pre-1963 mixed bag of old newsreel clips. There are the familiar shots of Eisenhower's military advisers showing peasants how to fire a semi-automatic rifle, additional personnel arriving, Diem's overthrow, the Dallas assassination.

In the eerie shadows cast by the standing lamp, President Johnson seems to be restless, impatiently tapping his fingers on his desk. He has seen all this before. Suddenly he stops in mid-tap, his mouth drops open, and he rises a full foot from his chair, supporting himself by leaning on his desk. He is seeing something that no one has seen before—Kennedy's funeral—an event that will not take place until the next day.

There on the screen, moving across the Memorial Bridge on its way to Arlington, is the mighty procession—the military escort, the colors, the caisson carrying Kennedy, the caparisoned horse, the Kennedy family, and, in the limousine behind them, the new President. Johnson gasps as he views himself. Then the foreign dignitaries, former Presidents, the Supreme Court, Cabinet, Senate members, congressmen, governors, and close friends.

Fifty Air Force and Navy jets fly over the gravesite, followed by Air Force One. The Marine Band plays the national anthem; the Air Force Pipers slow-march past the casket playing "Mist-covered Mountain"; the Irish Guards file by in their silent drill; the twenty-one-gun salute; the benediction; three volleys from the infantry firing party; the bugler sounding taps; Mrs. Kennedy handed the folded flag by the body bearers; then her lighting the eternal flame.

Speechless, frozen into immobility, he watches the burial of one President and the slow self-crucifixion of the one who followed. In response to an attack on a military compound in Vietnam, President Johnson orders air raids in North Vietnam, sends in U.S. troops, and the war begins. As a half million soldiers fight in the fields of Vietnam, millions of antiwar demonstrators fight in the streets of America.

Benumbed, stupefied at what he is seeing, Johnson sinks back into his chair as he watches American soldiers sink into the quicksand of an Asian war. B-52s bomb Hanoi and Haiphong—C-135s carry Americans home in wooden boxes.

Naked, napalmed children hysterically run down country roads there—inflamed students race through city streets here.

He sits there motionless, rocklike, as he sees villages burning there and draft cards burning here. There are antiwar marches and civil rights marches: police dogs here, the dogs of war there. Martin Luther King is assassinated in Memphis, Robert Kennedy in Los Angeles, and Lyndon Johnson is being destroyed in Vietnam.

I see him grip the arms of his chair and wince as he sees himself go on television in 1968 and announce he will not seek reelection. He gives up the presidency, the job he spent his adult life working for. Nixon becomes President. I see Johnson clench his teeth.

The Vietnam War, started by Johnson during that terrible decade of the violent sixties, will not end until the mid-seventies. The film runs out, the screen becomes a glaring white, and there is the tat-tat-tat-tat sound of the last few frames of film as it spins on the reel. As I switch off the projector Laura turns on the overhead light. Johnson continues to stare at the now blank screen. He has just experienced future shock. How he will come out of it, only the future will tell.

He his indeed seen things that were momentous, unparalleled, astounding, just as Dr. Koopman promised. The only outward sign of his inner emotions—of the turbulence that must be raging within him—is the slight trembling of the fingers on his right hand. It is a good sign. He has witnessed what has not yet happened, and he has not panicked, run, or shouted for help. He has not broken out into religious hysteria, fallen into a deep coma, or curled up in fetal fear. A few quivering fingers is an acceptable safety valve.

His first words are most encouraging. "I'll be damned," he says. Shocked, he has not been stampeded. Stunned, he has not been stricken. He has faced an enormous personal crisis with great personal self-control. He has behaved presidentially.

He stands, walks over to the projector, takes the reel of film off, then sits down on a nearby chair. Holding the reel on his lap, he studies it thoughtfully, then again says, "I'll be damned." It is indeed a healthy sign. He is in control of his emotions. He can be talked to. We will be able to reason with him. He then looks up at Dr. Koopman, expecting answers without asking questions.

"I completed my work on time travel in 1985," Dr. Koopman says.

"In 1985?" Johnson repeats, in awe, but also in acceptance. The man has resiliency. He has guts. He is as tough as the mesquite that grows in his home state.

"That is where I met David and Laura."

Johnson gives Laura and me a long, penetrating look. "You're from 1985?" he asks, fascinated, not frightened. It is more of a declaration than a question. He is handling himself well, which bodes well for us.

"Yes, sir."

Again he utters the phrase that makes me most comfortable. "I'll be damned."

It's time for me to reveal why we are here. I decide not to tell him how we came back to save John Kennedy, for Kennedy can no longer help us and, in fact, may hurt us, for the record shows that Johnson was jealous of him, that he had even ripped the PT-109 tie clip off of a Secret Service man who was wearing one. While Kennedy lived, Johnson, a country boy with country ways and a country vocabulary, had been totally overshadowed. And in death Kennedy's shadow, left behind, still eclipsed him.

"It was a terrible war, sir." I affirm what he has just seen. "I lost my brother in it. I knew that if we could come back and show you what happened, you would do things differently."

Laura quickly picks up on my having bypassed Kennedy. "We lost fifty-eight thousand men there, Mr. President," she says, informing him of things he could never know. "There were hundreds of thousands wounded, tens of thousands psychologically damaged."

We have to hit him with everything we have. There must be no doubt in his mind as to what he must do. "All your programs, sir," I say, "in civil rights, Medicare, education—they all suffered. All you are remembered for is a war we lost."

That gets to him. "A war we lost," he says sadly.

"It's not too late, Mr. President," Laura urges him. "The war hasn't started yet. We just have a few men there. Bring them home, sir."

Johnson looks up at her, reflecting on this hope she has offered of saving a lost presidency. "Bring them home," he muses, speculating on the suggestion.

Encouraging that possibility, Dr. Koopman points to the reel of film on his lap. "It will change everything you saw."

Johnson picks the reel up and balances it in his hands, as though weighing what it contains against what Dr. Koopman has promised. Then, indicating the film, and with what seems to be an apologetic smile, he says, "It seems I made a lot of mistakes."

We are making headway. I press the advantage. "But no mistake that can't be corrected, sir."

"No mistake that can't be corrected," he repeats wistfully. Rising from the chair, he walks over to the drapery-covered window. On one side of the window is a standing American flag, on the other side the presidential flag. He draws the drapery and looks out past the darkness that separates him from the White House. Lost in

234

thought for a moment, he finds himself able to reveal that thought to us. "No man wants to leave that building less honored, less respected than when he went in."

I hold my hand up, cautioning Laura and Dr. Koopman not to say anything. Johnson is making our case for us. With his back to us, still staring toward his inheritance, he quietly asks, "What sort of a President did Nixon make?"

"Not too good, sir," I say. "He covered up the illegal activities of some of his men and was forced to resign."

Johnson turns and almost absentmindedly touches the presidential flag as he says, "I'll never know what Eisenhower saw in him." Then, as he places the reel on the desk and sits down, he makes an inquiry any man in his particular line of work would ask. "Who came after Nixon?"

"Gerald Ford."

"Congressman Ford?"

"Yes, sir."

"They elected him?" he asks in surprise.

"No, sir. He was appointed after Nixon resigned."

He nods at that. It makes sense then.

"Jimmy Carter was elected in 1976."

"Jimmy who?"

I have to smile, as that was what people were asking in 1976. "He had been governor of Georgia," I explain, as if that somehow justified his election. Bringing Johnson up to date, I then say, "Ronald Reagan is President now."

His eyes narrowing even more, he stares at me suspiciously. "Ronald Reagan?"

"Yes, sir."

"The actor?"

"Yes, sir."

He seems to want to make a comment about that, but can't find the words. I can understand his feelings. It must be obvious to him by now that things haven't gone well since the Vietnam War.

He stares at the reel of film, then, almost in a whisper, in distress, he says, "It's the first war we ever lost."

"It should never have been fought, sir."

"What happened to Vietnam after we left?"

"It went Communist."

He flinches at that. "And Cambodia?"

"Communist."

He removes his glasses, puts his hand to his eyes, and, as he rubs them, lets out a sigh of despair. Then casually, in an offhand manner, as he takes a handkerchief out of his pocket and carefully begins to wipe the lenses of his glasses, he asks, "Am I still alive in 1985?"

I hesitate for a moment. "No, sir. You died in 1973."

He holds his glasses up to the light to see if the lenses are clear. "And my legacy is a war we lost?"

Although my silence by itself would be a cruel enough affirmation, I have not come back to be concerned about his feelings but to make sure he sees the tragic results of his original ways. "Yes, sir, a war that we lost."

"Everything else I tried to do . . . forgotten?"

"Not forgotten, sir, but overshadowed."

"But that *doesn't have to be your legacy,* sir," Laura consoles him. "It's within your power to change all of it."

He puts his glasses back on, sits back in his chair, and takes a deep breath, as he seems to take hope from Laura's words. "It's within my power to change all of it."

"None of it need happen the way it did," she encourages him.

His face has taken on a ruddy coloration, his eyes a bright glow. "Yes, ma'am. None of it need happen that way."

We have convinced him. We are home. I am ready to cry with relief.

He opens a desk drawer and takes out a book that has a battered, worn black cover. "This here Bible was given to me by my mother. She said, 'Son, there ain't nothing that'll ever happen to you that ain't already been told in this book.' "

Standing up, his face now flushed, he holds the Bible in front of him. "She said, 'There's no question you can ask that ain't already been answered in this book.' "

He opens the book and begins to turn its pages, searching for one of its many answers. "She said, 'The Lord's ways are mysterious only to those who refuse to follow His ways.' "

Finding the passage he is looking for, he walks over to Laura, pointing to the page. "Here—right here in Deuteronomy—the Lord said he would send forth prophets from among our countrymen—and that they would deliver His message, which we were commanded to obey."

I am feeling more secure with every sentence he speaks. He is convinced of who we are—but to validate that belief he must also convince himself that God has ordained our coming here. Heaven-sent legitimizes any inexplicable happening. If he wants to believe God's hand guided Dr. Koopman's hand, so much the better. If he wants to believe we have revealed prophetic warnings, that also is to the good, as long as it will give him the wisdom to stop that dreadful war.

His eyes can only partially reveal the fervor within him, the excitement that is now gripping him. His body no longer has that slightly stooped look that comes with age, weight, and worry. He stands erect, shoulders back, chin thrust out. There is no feeling in the world that can equal the one of knowing God has touched you.

"I thank you," he says to the three of us. "I thank you from the bottom of my heart. You *have* given me a second chance—a chance to do things right this time."

I am totally unprepared for what happens after that.

CHAPTER 24

A ND TO DO THINGS RIGHT," HE DE-
clares in a voice filled with the passion
of a call to duty in a redemptive cause,
"you cannot go halfway, halfhearted with half
measures. Wars must not be fought to produce stalemates. Wars must be fought to be
won."

I catch my breath at this unexpected, terrifying possibility. At the same time that I say,
"But, sir, you can't ..." I also hear Laura and
Dr. Koopman begin to protest, but he cuts us
off with a demanding "Hear me out." There is
no way to challenge a President who insists on
speaking.

Leaning for moral support on the Bible he
holds in his hand, he vows, "As God is my witness, never again will I send American boys to

fight a war we're not trying to win. We've been given a second chance, and this time we'll do it right."

Laura, unable to contain her dismay, cries out, "You can't. You mustn't." She points to the reel on his desk. "You saw what happened. The American people were against that war."

Almost contemptuously, Johnson dismisses that argument. "People are only against a war they're not winning—against a war that drags on. It took us four years to defeat Germany *and* Japan. Why ten years with Vietnam? You can't fool the people. They know when you're not trying."

The harsh voice now becomes a persuasive voice. He will do what he thinks a President must, but the politician in him, wanting to be loved by everyone, wants to convince us his decision is the proper one, the only one. "Is the world a better place to live in in nineteen hundred and eighty-five? Are there fewer people under Communist domination than there are now?"

He gives us the briefest of seconds to respond, and since the answer is not to our benefit, we say nothing.

"That's because we didn't stop them in Vietnam," he lectures. "And Vietnam is the result of not stopping them in Cuba, in Eastern Europe—not stopping them after World War Two. A burglar in the house won't be satisfied with robbing just one room."

"But, Mr. President—" Laura begins, and is again quickly silenced. A raised hand overrules the protest, silences the protestor. He is once again the sole arbiter, the one who governs. The need to be persuasive applies only when those you want to persuade are cooperative.

We can only stand there, silent, appalled at his vision of a new future. "If half a million men weren't enough, I'll send a million. And if that's not enough, we have other weapons." Then, deliberately, grimly, he makes a solemn pledge. "I will not be the first American President to lose a war."

Laura, desperate, attempting to change the mind of a man who is now consumed by this second chance to clear his name and his country's record, in her desperation resorts to a phrase of the seventies: "Give peace a chance, Mr. President."

His reply rules out debate. "We did and it didn't work." He then skewers us on a point our film has fashioned. "We gave up the fight in the seventies and got out. Did we get out with a treaty?"

"Yes, sir," I tell him. "It was signed in Paris."

"And did that keep them from taking over South Vietnam?"

"No, sir, but there was a reason for—"

"Damn it, mister"—he cuts me off as though I were an incoming freshman in a political science class—"show me a treaty they've signed

241

and honored, and I'll show you a treaty that ain't been written yet." He points a finger at us and vows, "If I have to die in '73, I ain't gonna face God havin' lost a war to that Ho Chi Minh fella—with everything else I've done down the tubes. I ain't gonna be put out to pasture like some broken-down horse that's not needed anymore."

As his energy level has risen, his grammatical skills have lessened. He has retrogressed to the speech patterns of his youth.

He takes a deep, politically inspired breath and says, "I will not be responsible for Richard Nixon becoming President." And then the promise: "I'm gonna do what's right for these United States, and what's right for all those people who's had their ass kicked by those Vietnamese." Gazing at Laura and me, he requisitions our assistance. "And you two are gonna help me."

I have looked into the eyes and hearts of many a man, but never have I seen a man more determined, more a master of an unshakable resolve as he vows, "I will not be driven from office."

CHAPTER 25

A S DR. KOOPMAN LEAVES THE LAB- oratory he is almost overcome by the surge of returning memories. He leans forward as he walks down the street, as though he is forcing his way through a storm. He trembles in a spasm of regret as past events stagger the sensibilities. He remembers Johnson telling David and Laura that they would be kept in protective custody until the war was over—that he would call on them for advice in formulating future government guidelines—that eventually they would be given their freedom and a generous government allowance so that they could live out their remaining years in comfort. He remembers Secret Service men quietly but firmly taking them away.

He remembers objecting vehemently, and Johnson trying to calm him, assuring him, "They will be well treated, Doctor. You have my word for it," but refusing to reveal, in the name of national security, where they were being taken.

Johnson had then told him that he was free to go back to Dallas, for he was too well known to suddenly disappear—but that there would be no record of David and Laura, for there was no record of their being there to begin with. And, as for their trying to convince anyone where they had come from, Johnson held up the reel and said, "Without this film, who would believe them?"

He remembers Johnson then cautioning him about his saying anything to anyone. "It wouldn't do for the government to be called on to produce two people from the future." That was followed with an ominous threat. "And I can assure you, Doctor, the government would never come up with them." He again gave his solemn word that David and Laura would be released at the proper time— but the proper time never came.

He remembers writing to the President, and going to see him, and always receiving the same assurance that David and Laura were well—but he never saw them again. When any government decides to hide someone, whether it be on some remote army post, isolated island, or distant gulag, they do their job well. And when any government decides to stonewall a question and play dumb, no one can play dumb more effectively.

The last time he went back to see President Johnson was in 1967, right after the United States had won the Vietnam War.

☆

In 1965, after the Vietcong attacked a military compound, President Johnson responded with force and with purpose. The American and South Vietnamese armies headed north. It took a million American soldiers, and a hundred thousand dead, but they took North Vietnam. Historians would later say that Johnson showed an overall leadership that at times was uncanny. He seemed to have a sixth sense, an instinct about what to do. Above all was his tenacity, his resolve, right from the beginning, to win that war.

Hanoi in ruins, Haiphong Harbor totally destroyed, all supply lines interdicted—Ho Chi Minh knew the war was lost and went into honorable exile in Moscow. Nguyen Van Thieu was set up as President of the newly unified country and Nguyen Cao Ky became its Premier. American soldiers were permanently stationed there to secure and protect this new democracy.

China, a centuries-old foe of Vietnam, would

rather see that hated neighbor controlled by Americans than by another enemy, the Soviets.

Brezhnev was preoccupied with trying to catch up in weapons systems, with poor economic conditions at home and in his major satellites, East Germany, Poland, and Cuba. He was also readying the Warsaw Pact invasion of Czechoslovakia. In a superpower game of Global Monopoly, America put up hotels in Vietnam; Russia put theirs up in Czechoslovakia.

Victory in Vietnam was the linchpin that assured the status quo of that area. Southeast Asia remained poverty-stricken but, fortunately, it remained stable.

Dr. Koopman stops and squints up at the street sign, making sure he is on the street that leads to the gun store.

President Johnson was right. No war is unpopular if you win it. Antiwar marchers were simply out of step with the times. They were quickly roughed up by angry citizens shouting "U.S.A. all the way." Great victories produce even greater patriots, particularly those who remain at home during the fighting. Johnson had the best of all worlds—guns *and* butter. Despite his best intentions, he had set in motion nationalistic feelings that could not easily be kept in check.

Dr. Koopman can only guess at the despair David and Laura must have felt as they became aware of the events. Wherever they were being held, they surely would have heard. Having failed to save Kennedy, they had then, with the noblest of motives, tried to stop a war—with this undreamed of, unthinkable result.

From the safety of the time they lived in, they had looked back, seen the sorrow of those former days, and returned to ease the pain. They had looked back, seen the violence, and returned to bring peace. They had looked back, seen the death, and returned to breathe new life into the victims. They deserved better. They had earned better. He had grown to love them. Desperately he had tried to see a President who was no longer available to him.

Lost in these thoughts, caught up in recollections of the past, he crosses against the streetlight, narrowly being missed by a passing car. He does not notice the bumper sticker on the car, which reads, "God Bless President Westmoreland."

Dr. Koopman remembers how Johnson carried all fifty states in the 1968 election. A hard line continued to serve him well the next four years. Vietnam had made that old saying "Don't Tread On Me" fashionable again. Johnson's Great Society became a society that was not afraid to protect its self-interests around the world. It prevented a Colonel Qaddafi from coming to power in Libya, and it made sure Salvador Allende Gossens lost a presidential election in Chile. Some critics said it was the CIA who rigged the elections, but they didn't say it too loud or too often. It was America's vote that kept Taiwan in—and Communist China out of—the United Nations. In a memorable moment that forever preserved the image Johnson wanted to leave of himself, he went before the General Assembly at the United Nations and said, "Gentlemen, it's up to you. It's either Communist China that's out of the United Nations, or it's the United Nations that's out of the United States. Take your pick."

Dr. Koopman steps aside and stands up against an office-building wall to allow a group of perhaps ten or twelve young, laughing soldiers to pass by. They instinctively act as if they have the right of way.

Another Texan, John Connally, was elected President in 1972. His running mate was the military hero of Vietnam, General William C. Westmoreland. In a graduation speech at West Point, Westmoreland endeared himself to the cadets when he said, "I hate war—but if there's anything I hate more than war, it's cowards who won't fight in one." He received a standing ovation.

The military draft was made permanent. In Nicaragua, American Marines went in to help Anastasio Somoza reestablish order after an aborted coup. From Nicaragua they sailed on troop ships and anchored outside of the Panama Canal to discourage Torrijos from attempting to take it over. Fidel Castro remained uncharacteristically silent as a U.S. invasion force was assembled in Key West. Castro knew that in case of an invasion, the Soviets could not bail him out, no more than the United States could stop the Soviet tanks from entering Budapest.

Central America was in the hands of men we could trust. The countries of South America were in the hands of men who didn't trust each other, which gave both superpowers a sense of well-being.

Dr. Koopman remembers making desperate calls to President Connally, trying to find out about David and Laura—and how, when he finally did get Connally on the phone, he was told, "Lyndon told me you would be calling, Doctor. I haven't the slightest idea what you're talking about."

The gun store is at the next corner. Dr. Koopman watches a military convoy go by. In the back of one of the army trucks are a half dozen young men with shaved heads and wearing white robes. They are probably the remnants of some cult on their way to a deprogramming camp in Arizona. Passersby jeer them.

Dr. Koopman enters the gun store, walking into a world where sudden death is the ultimate object of each customer. A dozen or so men and women examine revolvers, pistols, rifles, shotguns, and semiautomatics. Others look at bullets, shells, and cartridges of varying sizes and shapes. Some look through night scopes and telescopic sights. There is an air of camaraderie among them as they are held together by the herd instinct, of being partnered in their common survival.

Dr. Koopman remembers Westmoreland becoming President in 1980 and being reelected in 1984. He showed his mettle in 1981 when our embassy in Pakistan was stormed by a rampaging mob and ten of our citizens taken hostage. In a speech that ended with the words "Touch our embassies, lose your investments. Harm our citizens, lose your lives," he immediately confiscated all Pakistani holdings in the United States, seized their embassy in Washington, and held their entire diplomatic corps hostage. In the event of an American hostage being killed, he promised to surgically bomb a key Pakistan industrial and transportation center. Within seventy-two hours the ten Americans were released, and President Westmoreland had achieved a mythical hero's status with an increasingly xenophobic public.

In Iran we kept a dying Shah in power, and after his death helped his son succeed him. The CIA vigorously denied having had anything to do with the assassination in Paris of a religious leader called Khomeini.

In response, the Soviets initiated the invasion and annexation of Afghanistan. They tightened all security measures in their satellites—in the process arresting, sentencing, and deporting to a distant gulag a Polish agitator by the name of Lech Walesa. All Jewish emigration from the U.S.S.R. ended when the request for emigration was termed slander against the state punishable by ten years in prison.

America and Russia were locked in nonnegotiable, ideological battle—with no insult going unanswered, no injury unavenged. One crisis pyramided atop the other in ever-increasing ferocity, in ever-decreasing concern for where they would lead.

The salesman walks up and studies Dr. Koopman with an amused smile, trying to relate this funny-looking old man to a weapon. "Can I help you, sir?"

"I would like to buy a gun. Can you recommend one?"

"Depends what you want to do with it, sir."

"I want to shoot something."

The salesman knows he is talking to a novitiate. "Is this your first gun?"

"Yes, it's my first one. I would like one that is easy to work."

"Is it for self-defense, for hunting, for target practice?"

Dr. Koopman is evasive. "Self-defense," he says, knowing it is a safe answer.

"Perhaps a Smith & Wesson .38. Would you like to see one?"

"Is it a good gun?"

"They've been making it for over fifty years."

Dr. Koopman, rationalizing that men like Mr. Smith and Mr. Wesson wouldn't be making a gun for over fifty years if it wasn't good, says, "Yes, please, I'd like to see one."

As the salesman turns to take a gun out of a glass-enclosed case, Dr. Koopman remembers how in 1982 the Israeli Mossad uncovered a Soviet-Syrian plot in time to save Anwar Sadat from assassination—and how Sadat, afterward, realizing a moderate Muslim was a marked Muslim, threw his country's lot in with the West. In return for its protection, America set up nuclear missile sites throughout Egypt.

A frustrated Assad then invited the Soviets to set up their nuclear missile pads in Syria. A future Armaggedon was no longer the exclusive property of the Judeo-Christian religions. It was an age when even Allah needed SS-20s to feel secure.

In 1983, when Greek Communists blew up a TWA plane at the Athens airport, President Westmoreland was true to his word to seek retribution. Three days later, Americans, watching on TV, cheered as the Athens airport became one big bomb crater.

Minor wars, revolutions, and counterrevolutions were so commonplace that most of them were ignored on the evening news. Only major events like the killing of Pope John Paul by a suspected Communist in 1984 was deemed worthy of headlining the seven o'clock news.

Ambassadors were brought home, flags were unfurled, nationalist fever rose. The war virus had taken over the body politic.

The salesman turns and lays the revolver down on the counter. "Here you are, sir. You'll be well protected with this."

"Are you sure it's easy to work?"

With a patronizing look, the salesman replies, "Working it is easy. It's hitting what you're aiming at that can be the problem."

"Yes, that's it." Dr. Koopman concedes the problem. "I want to be sure to hit what I'm aiming at. How do I learn to aim?"

"Well, you can go to a firing range and take lessons."

"No, no." He waves the suggestion off. "I have no time for lessons."

The salesman, becoming amused with this seemingly confused old man, says, "Then I'd suggest you get real close to the target so that you can't miss."

"Real close to the target," Dr. Koopman repeats. "Yes, that is a good idea." Pointing to the revolver, he asks, "Is this a good gun to get real close with?"

"Yes, sir, it's perfect for close-range firing, and it has a kick like a mule. You just open the chamber like this—put the bullets in—close the chamber like this—aim, and fire."

"Yes, that's good. I'll take it. And make sure you give me enough bullets."

"Enough bullets for what?"

"In case I should miss," Dr. Koopman responds, revealing the need for the bullets, not the use of them.

"Be right back," the salesman says as he goes to get what he thinks will be enough bullets.

As Dr. Koopman holds the revolver in his hand, he remembers how, in January of 1985, the President had persuaded Congress to pass National Emergency Bill 2599, which modified and suspended certain basic rights. The perils of the time they lived in demanded it. From the right of free speech, Bill 2599 eliminated the right to speak out against the government. From the right to peacefully assemble, it limited those assembled to seven persons. Anything more than that was considered contentious. From the right to redress grievances, it made a list of acceptable grievances. From freedom of religion, it removed choice. America was declared a religious nation. Until the emergency was over it was unlawful to advocate atheism. In keeping with religious beliefs, homosexuality was prohibited. In planning for the possible need of future soldiers, abortion was also a criminal offense. In concern for national security, illegal aliens were to be deported.

Dr. Koopman stands there, tears in his eyes.

This was not what David and Laura had sacrificed themselves for.

The salesman returns, setting two boxes of cartridges down on the counter. "This ought to do it."

"Yes, yes, that ought to do it," Dr. Koopman agrees. Then, noticing a small, cylindrical metal object lying nearby, he asks, "What is that?"

"You put it on the barrel of the gun—like this—and when you fire the gun no one can hear it."

"No one can hear it. Yes, that too is good. I'll take it."

CHAPTER 26

OCTOBER 16, 1985

D R. KOOPMAN BOLTS THE DOOR THAT leads to his laboratory. He must not be needlessly disturbed or possibly deterred. It is no easy choice, no simple matter, to do what must be done—to destroy a life's work, to forever leave a surrounding he has naturally aged into—but it is no longer an environment that is tolerable to him. Just as high mountain drops of clear water can become a rampaging river, an innocent spark turn into a raging fire, or an ultradense, ultrasmall clump of matter explode in a big bang into the universe, so has a President's desire not to lose a war created this distortion of a democracy.

Dr. Koopman will do what has to be done, not

257

really for his own sake, not even for the country's sake, but for David and Laura. This is not what they had sacrificed themselves for—David out of love for his brother, Laura out of love for David. He, Dr. Koopman, will take this final step out of love for both David and Laura.

Setting coordinates, adjusting dials, pressing buttons, flipping switches, pulling levers, setting codes in computers, checking control panels and their readout screens, he then crosses cables and wiring systems that ought never to be cross-connected. It will ensure that after he is gone no one who comes around will be able to experiment with his invention. The ability to travel in time is also the ability to cause profound and untold grief. The motives to change things may be idealistic, but the results are often less than ideal. Man's need to know is not always matched by man's actions after he knows. He remembers Robert Oppenheimer's thoughts after the first atomic explosion: "We scientists have learned sin."

Emptying his pockets of all identification, he takes one last look at his life's work, sets the machinery on an automatic countdown, and enters the adjoining chamber. He, who has played such a major role in all of this, must now play one final role.

He stations himself below the overhead tubing and waits. For a moment there are the sizzling malfunctions of overworked machinery, overheated parts, overextended systems, under-energized components, and other elements that are simply worn out. And then, in one final, cohesive gasp, it all comes together. The over-head tubing, crackling with flashing, lightning-bolt brilliance, lowers and encloses him, and he is gone. Seconds afterward the entire laboratory implodes upon itself, collapsing into its center, crushing itself into a superdense mass of fused, smoking chunks of useless matter.

☆*THURSDAY, NOVEMBER 21, 1963 . . . 10:00 A.M.* Dr. Koopman appears outside the carport, looks around, momentarily confused. He knows *where* he is, but he is not sure he has returned at the moment he wished, for everything looks exactly as it did in 1985—the house, the Buick, the un-attended foliage. Only when he sees the 1963 license plate on the car does he breathe a sigh of relief.

As he makes his way to the front door three mourning doves in the branches of an old pecan tree look down at him, a bit puzzled. This is the man who leaves bread crumbs for them at the foot of the tree every day, but the color of his hair has changed, and he walks a bit bent over.

259

A gray squirrel sitting on a small, white rock is also mystified. It recognizes the friendly smell of this man who goes by, and yet there is something different about him, something its squirrel mind cannot quite figure out.

Dr. Koopman takes out his house key, which opens a lock that has never changed. Once inside, he heads for the living room. He has no time to waste, for in less than an hour Laura will appear outside the carport—and he must see to it that she is not hit by the car.

The living room is a disorganized assemblage of furniture from around the world. There is country English and country French, and pieces that no country would confess to having produced. Books, magazines, and scientific journals lie strewn about, casually but lovingly left on the first available open space.

He finds his address book under a copy of *Catch-22*—then finds the phone number of the Gregson Brothers Garage under the letter "F" and the words "Fix Car." He dials the number, and while he waits he gives the room a quick glance. If there is any feeling of nostalgia, it is for the future, when he will have added a red divan and a green wing-back chair he has been lucky enough to stumble upon during a seminar in Buenos Aires.

"Hello—Gregson Brothers Garage? This is Dr. Hendrik Koopman. I just called to tell you not

to come by to pick up my car this morning. . . .
Yes, I'm home. I came back a few days early."

His next call is to the Fairmont Hotel in San
Francisco. He must learn the effect his return
has had.

"May I speak to Dr. Hendrik Koopman, please?
He is in Room 922."

There is a pause, and a man's voice says, "Resident manager. May I help you?"

"Yes, I'm waiting to speak to Dr. Koopman,
in Room 922."

"I'm sorry, but there seems to have been an
accident, sir."

"What kind of accident? Is he all right?"

"Are you a friend of his, sir?"

"Yes, of course. What happened?"

"We're trying to find a relative, some family
member to call. Perhaps you can help us."

Without answering, he hangs up, knowing he
has just heard of his own demise. Since he has
no relatives, there is no one to mourn him except himself—and even that must be fleeting,
for soon word will be out that he has unexpectedly died in San Francisco, and someone at
the garage will remember they just spoke to a
man who claimed to be Dr. Koopman. That will
bring the police—followed by his lawyer, who
will secure the house for probate. It would not
do for them to be greeted at the door by an
older version of himself.

Step by self-inflected step, he is being cut off from everything familiar. Cast back from 1985, cast away into 1963, he has returned to his young years as an old man. He cannot contact friends and colleagues who have grown old with him. Once he leaves this house, he will never be able to return. He will no longer even be able to use his own name, for that name will soon be buried with him.

But it is not *his* fate he came back to change. He tried to play God for a young man who grieved for a lost brother. If he really had been God, could he have made things turn out different—or is man's free will stronger than God's perfect will? Is God in control or does He look down on a world out of control? Is being God a humbling experience?

Should he and David and Laura have been as wise as the lowest animal, and just lived the seasons as they came?

Reaching into a Chinese porcelain vase, he removes a bulging envelope. Then, from a drawer of the Dutch cabinet, he takes out a second envelope. As he stuffs them into his pants pockets he silently thanks his old country parents who taught him that a prudent man keeps some of his money in a bank and some of it in a safer place. If he should succeed, they will need money to start over. If he fails, it won't matter that he robbed his own house.

He cannot risk contacting the authorities, for the more associates one has, the greater chance for error. He realizes this very last opportunity must not be left in any hands but his own. He touches his jacket pocket to make sure the gun is still there—then the other pocket to be certain it contains the ammunition and the silencer. When the time comes he must remember what the salesman told him—to load, get close, aim, and fire.

☆   *NOVEMBER 21, 1963 . . . 11:15 A.M.*
The first thing Laura hears upon rematerializing outside the carport is a familiar voice saying, "It's me. Don't be afraid." She turns and sees Dr. Koopman standing in the doorway, waving and smiling.

She is powerless to move, rooted to the ground in growing bewilderment—unable to put what she sees into any kind of acceptable framework. She is looking not at the Dr. Koopman who exists in 1963 but at the one who just sent her here from 1985.

She forces the words out, weakly, hesitantly, hopefully, "Dr. Koopman?"

"Yes, yes, it's me. It's all right. I came back ahead of you. I will explain later."

IRVING, TEXAS ... FRIDAY,
NOVEMBER 22, 1963 ... 7:45 A.M.

Having spent the night with his estranged wife in a futile attempt at reconciliation, Lee Harvey Oswald leaves for a more promising future.

Putting $175 on a dresser top, and his wedding ring in an old Russian teacup, he goes to seek a destiny that has always eluded him. He needs no breakfast, for he is feeding on the bitter feelings he holds toward that Irishman, and the sweet thoughts he has about the ultimate solution he has planned.

Tense, almost fevered by the malice within him, he enters the garage where he has hidden the rifle. Disassembled, it lies concealed in brown wrapping paper. Picking it up, he feels its hardness beneath its paper sheath. Soon it will bring him the sense of self-worth he has so desperately sought all his life.

As he leaves the garage he wipes some damp hairs away from his forehead. Ignored, overlooked, he is a stranger in a land he once deserted. He has returned, having been equally unheeded and unneeded in the country of second choice, a nonperson in two societies. That humiliation will soon end.

Crossing the lawn, he stops at the curb, waiting to be picked up by a co-worker for a ride to the Book Depository Building. The passion within him builds. Only one of the mighty falling can elevate him. Soon the man he has pinpointed as the fountainhead of his misfortunes will serve as the source of his satisfaction.

He does not pay attention to the green Buick as it comes around the corner or to the woman behind the wheel and the gray-haired, bearded old man who sits next to her.

☆   *7:58 A.M.*

As Laura drives down the street she sees Oswald standing by the curb, the concealed rifle in his hand. In a few hours this wretched, floundering, unfulfilled wanderer, a man who has nothing, will take the life of a man who has it all—and, in so doing, plunge a nation onto a path of war, toward dark deeds and even darker days. It seems almost inconceivable that such a scrubby, pitiful person could have authored such a tragic ending for a President and such a beleaguered beginning for those left behind.

Dr. Koopman, a man who spares the lives of houseflies and avoids stepping on ants, sits there quietly, the gun on his lap, the bullets in its chamber, and the silencer on its barrel.

Laura stops the car alongside Oswald. They have reached back through time and cornered the beast.

Startled at first, stiffening in surprise, Oswald then glowers in irritation at these two people who stare at him. "Yeah—what d'ya want?" he asks pugnaciously.

"We want justice, Mr. Oswald," Dr. Koopman replies as he remembers the advice to aim and then fire.

The Buick starts down the street, leaving Oswald lying on the curb, one arm reaching into the gutter, trying to retrieve the dropped rifle.

He knows he will die on that curb, unnoticed, unknown. He is filled with outrage at this last cruel turn of a star-crossed life. He curses a fate that always stopped him just when he was about to make a move that would have given that life meaning. He dies wondering why anyone would have wanted to kill him.

8:20 A.M.

Sergeant Okrand is told to go investigate a random, drive-by shooting in Irving. Someone named Lee Harvey Oswald, an employee at the Texas School Book Depository Building, was the victim. Sergeant Okrand mutters under his breath as he stalks to his car. He knew this would be one of those days. His son's playing in the big football game tonight, and here he might be stuck looking into an absolutely meaningless homicide.

☆   *12:15 P.M.*

I run to the roof door pull on it, but it won't open. It is not locked, but stuck, either swollen shut or warped by rain. Panicked, I pull on it, wrench it, tug on it, bang on it with desperate fists, trying to work it free. "Open up, you son of a bitch," I both plead and curse. I am hyperventilating, wet with sudden perspiration, terror-stricken at this unspeakable catastrophe—to have come this far and be stopped by a balky door.

In the distance I hear the police sirens of the presidential motorcade. The wedged door suddenly gives way and opens.

I vault down the stairs, taking three and four steps at a time. The sirens are almost upon me. I can hear the crowd beginning to cheer. I leap the final seven steps to the sixth-floor landing, fall, roll over, and as I get up to race toward the window I am frozen in mid-stride, for standing by that window is not Lee Harvey Oswald but Laura and Dr. Koopman.

She turns, waves to me, and calls out, "Quick, David, President Kennedy is coming."

Even that name cannot cause my legs to move or my mouth to close.

Dr. Koopman shouts the words that create sanity and movement. "We came back ahead of you. Do not worry about Oswald."

"Hurry, David," Laura pleads, pointing out the window. "He's almost here."

I run to the window, and as Laura takes my hand in hers we look out onto the street below, where the President's limousine is passing by. John Kennedy waves to the crowd—and then, in a moment I will never forget, as the limousine reaches the spot where he was once shot—what instinct possessed him to do it I will never know—he turns, looks up toward us standing in the open window, smiles, and waves to us. . . . The three of us, starting to cry, wave back.

CHAPTER 27

I AM CELEBRATING MY THIRTY-FIFTH birthday today. Laura and I were married in 1963. Dr. Koopman was best man. We honeymooned at the Adolphus Hotel, where the desk clerk never knew why I came up to him and handed him a generous gratuity.

Our daughter, Jennifer, who was created in 1985, was born in 1964. I will never attempt to explain it to her one day, for math is not one of my stronger subjects.

John Fitzgerald Kennedy was reelected in 1964, decisively defeating Senator Barry Goldwater, whose major campaign theme was his criticism of Kennedy's removal of the American military presence in South Vietnam.

It was, as Kennedy had said, not our fight—and a short fight it was—a civil war that was over by early '66. While Ho Chi Minh won, we did not lose. We did not lose 58,000 men. We did not lose faith in ourselves.

"Ask not what your country can do for you, but what you can do for your country," he told us. I am content, knowing what Laura and Dr. Koopman and I have done.

Year by year, John Kennedy grows in stature—the literate, photogenic leader of the free world.

The other night, in a televised fund-raising party in Dallas, he spoke nostalgically about another enjoyable visit he had had to Dallas in November of 1963. I just sat and watched and felt an inner peace and sense of self-worth.

For Laura and me and Dr. Koopman these have been good years, happy years. With the money from the gold doubloon, and the cash Dr. Koopman had in the two envelopes, I made some propitious investments in the stock market—and with the profits, I made even larger profits. Onlookers are amazed at the sixth sense I seem to have about the future.

Once we had all the money we could ever possibly use, I bought a ranch on the outskirts of Houston. Laura has gotten involved in social work on a voluntary basis. To Laura, volunteering means six days a week and being available on the seventh. I have no doubt that someday she will be known as the Mother Teresa of Texas.

I have a wife I love, a daughter I adore, and the three of us have a treasure we cherish in Dr. Koopman. We have built a small laboratory for him near the main house—and there he spends his hours puttering, calculating, and formulating theories that are light-years ahead of the scientific world. He is as ageless as the universe he now contemplates and once conquered. He is never without a smile or a kind word. I have saved the best for last—my brother, Christopher.

Not having to answer a call to arms, he responded to the letter of acceptance from Rice University. A straight "A" student in the classroom, an All-American quarterback on the field, he was, he is, he always will be, the stuff that heroes are made of.

He was the reason I bought the ranch outside of Houston, for it was just a few miles away from the university. There wasn't a football game Rice played that year that I did not attend. Sitting in the stands, I would watch him, not being lowered into a grave but raised onto the shoulders of his teammates—and as others cheered, I wept.

I agonized about how I would go about meeting him again. Laura solved it by simply inviting the Rice football team to a barbecue at the ranch.

I know I did not sleep the night before he

271

arrived—and when the bus bringing the team drove up to the ranch, and he stepped out, and came up to shake my hand, I could barely answer him. It was all I could do to keep my composure, to keep from throwing my arms around him and crying out, "It's me, Chris. It's me, David, your kid brother. I love you."

From the moment our hands touched, we became the best of friends. He cannot get over the coincidence that my name is David Russell, the same as his younger brother, who had died suddenly in 1963. When he talks about it a great sadness comes over him, and his thoughts are far away as he says, "There were things I had promised to teach him . . . and never did. Things that were so important to him. How to throw a curve ball . . . how to fix a car engine . . . how to track a deer." He stops, unable to go on. I reach out and rest my hand on his, saying nothing myself—afraid of what I might say if I tried.

He visits us at the ranch almost every weekend. Jennifer is wild about him—and, as he once lifted me high into the air and swung me over his head, he now does that with Jennifer. She calls him "Unca Christopha." Little does she know how accurate that is.

When he heard that we had no family to visit on Christmas, he invited the four of us to spend the holidays with him and his parents in New Mexico.

Our car followed the gentle snow that fell in

front of us, forming a soft white carpet that led to our parents' home.

They waited at the door to greet us, not knowing that both their sons had returned. They greeted one with a parent's love—the other with warm Christian friendship.

I sat on my bed in the room I had known as a boy—a room that had remained unchanged, every childhood possession exactly in the place I last remembered it. I had not been forgotten.

I helped Christopher string lights on the Christmas tree; I helped my father chop wood for the fireplace; I stood in the kitchen and watched my mother prepare the holiday meal. I, at last, knew the meaning of the words "My cup runneth over."

We sat at the dinner table, a family again. My father, wineglass in hand, stood to offer the toast. A man who speaks at length is a man who has measured and mastered his emotions and speaks from the mind. A man who speaks from the heart has found his deepest feelings and often cannot find the words. My father, whose life has been to sow and reap and sow again, looked at us, the harvest of his life, and said it all the only way he knew how. "I love you—all of you sitting here." Then, not forgetting a lost son, he said, "And David too."

Christopher softly repeated, "And David too."

Laura reached over and held my hand in hers.

273

☆

We go back to visit them as often as possible—and Laura has talked them into occasionally leaving the farm to fend for itself for a few days while they're our guests at the ranch.

Christopher will be graduating next year. We have already discussed going into business together. He relies a great deal on my advice. The other day he paid me the ultimate compliment. Putting his arm around my shoulders, he said, "David, I look upon you as an older brother."

Each morning, as I face the new day, I look past the rolling hills, where bluebonnets grow and white-tailed deer roam, and I say to Laura, "This is the best of all possible worlds."

It is indeed a time to remember.

ABOUT THE AUTHOR

STANLEY SHAPIRO has received many major writing awards, including the Writers Guild of America Award, the Academy Award, the Golden Globe Award and the Laurel Award. He resides in California with his daughter, Saskia, who is a college student.